Kirkwall, Orkney
May 2000

Clinging to the Edge

CLINGING TO THE EDGE

Journals from an Orkney Island

JIM HEWITSON

MAINSTREAM
PUBLISHING
EDINBURGH AND LONDON

Historical photographs courtesy of the islanders of Papa Westray
Contemporary photographs courtesy of Angela Catlin, Douglas Hourston, Morag Hewitson and Alex Davidson

First published in Great Britain in 1996 by
MAINSTREAM PUBLISHING COMPANY (EDINBURGH) LTD
7 Albany Street
Edinburgh EH1 3UG

ISBN 1 85158 821 3

A catalogue record for this book is available from the British Library

Typeset in 11/13pt Sabon
Printed and bound in Great Britain by Butler and Tanner Ltd, Frome

To the people of Papa Westray
past, present . . . and future

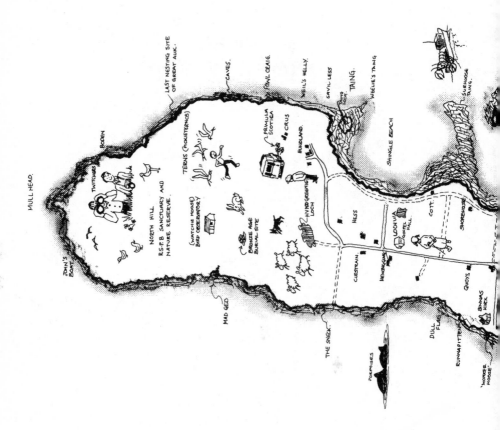

PAPAY

MULL HEAD

JOHN'S BOAT

BODEN

TWITCHERS

NORTH HILL
R.S.P.B. SANCTUARY AND
NATURE RESERVE.

LAST NESTING SITE
OF GREAT AUK.

CAVES.

TERNS (PICKIETERNOS)

(WATCHIE HOUSE)
BIRD OBSERVATORY

FOWL CRAIG.

PRIMULA
SCOTICA

CRUS

NEIL'S HELLY.

SAVIL-LESS

TAING.

WEELIE'S TAING

SURHOOSE
TAING.

BRONZE AGE
BURIAL SITE

RUADLAND

LIVND (GREENING)
LOCH

NESS

SHINGLE BEACH

MAD GEO

THE SNECK.

PORPOISES

CLESTRAN.

NEWBIGGIN

LOCH VA
HOSTEL
HALL

COTT.

SHOREHOOSE

QUOYS.

RUNNA PITTEN

DULL
FLAG

BINNAS
KIRK.

HONKER
HOOSE

Contents

Acknowledgements

Thanks are due to *The Herald* for making available Angela Catlin's marvellous island portraits and for faithfully carrying my despatches over the years; to all the members of the Papay Camera Club for a selection of modern and archival photographs which would have filled half a dozen books; to Harald Nicolson for 'capturing' life on Papay so neatly in pen and ink; to Johnny Rendall and Willie Gray, two islanders who helped make the book possible and have died since it was written and last but certainly not least to Avril Gray and Janene Reid at Mainstream for their constant encouragement and professional guidance.

Foreword

I readily recall my visit to Papa Westray during the 1987 election campaign. It was no ordinary election visit as it coincided with the day chosen for the start of a children's pilgrimage from the island of Egilsay, where St Magnus was martyred, to commemorate the 850th anniversary of the founding of the Cathedral in Kirkwall which bears the saint's name. Each Orkney island was marking the occasion with a bonfire and appropriate celebration, and I quickly discovered that the majority of islanders on Papay were picnicking in the sunshine on the North Hill.

Discussion of tax, freight subsidies or the common agricultural policy would have been wholly out of place, so I simply joined in the party and enjoyed a welcome break from the hustings. But, by the time for my election meeting in the guest-house arrived, the turn-out of islanders was such that, if a similar proportion of the electorate had turned up at a meeting in a compact inner-city constituency, they would have numbered several thousand.

For me, that day summed up much of what island life is about. On the one hand there were bonds of community life, the consciousness of local history and the natural world, and the relaxed atmosphere where time was certainly not of the essence. Yet, later in the day, I was engaged in public debate, not only on matters of immediate relevance to Papay and Orkney but on wider issues of national and international topicality. My constituents are islanders but let no one presume that they are insular in their attitudes.

In this book Jim Hewitson vividly brings alive these different and contrasting aspects of life on Papay. Start reading and it will not be long before you become aware of sea, sky, birds and the ever-changing elements, as the author so clearly is himself. You will readily come to appreciate that Papay is one of those places where people can still truly be described as characters and where values can be measured in something other than pounds and pence.

The author never makes the mistake of portraying Papa Westray as a North Atlantic paradise, ring-fenced from the problems, threats and challenges of the last years of the century. We are constantly reminded of the hard toil required to make a living from the harvest of the land or the sea. We are reminded that the oil tanker, *Braer,* went on the rocks only 50 miles to the north; we are exposed to the dilemma faced by many island communities over whether too many tourists is a good or a bad thing; and we sense something of the understandable obsession which many island residents have with the cost and availability of transport. Above all there is a basic challenge of keeping the island viable, after decades of depopulation.

These are all issues which are familiar to me as a constituency MP and *Clinging to the Edge* aptly describes that challenge. But progress can bring opportunity as well as threat. The well-established air ambulance service, for example, provides a reassurance denied to previous generations, whilst the revolution in telecommunications can overcome some of the disadvantages of remoteness.

Living in Orkney and not least in Papay also allows a sense of historic perspective when looking at these matters. After all, the Knap of Howar is evidence of settlements on Papay stretching back beyond the third millennium BC. People might be forgiven for thinking that, placed against such a backdrop of history, individuals could easily become insignificant. Nothing could be further from the truth. For if there is one feature of Papay which shines through more than any other in Jim's book it is the basic worth of each individual and the importance of helping each other. The author's account of an island funeral simply but movingly sums this up.

Possibly there is an element of mutual self-interest in this clinging together but I believe there is also a strong determination to cleave to those values which have held the community in good stead in the past. Living on Papa Westray or even just visiting you know that there is so much more to life than can be found in the accountant's bottom line. With this book Jim Hewitson allows us to travel with him to Papay and to share in a literally sensual experience.

Jim Wallace MP (Orkney and Shetland)
March 1996

Chapter One

The Wave Now Arriving

BENDING THE ARROW OF TIME

As the twin-engined *Islander* banked sharply in preparation for landing, the entire length of Papa Westray rushed into view beyond the cow-shit-spattered windows. Below us lay the curve of the Bay of Moclett with its golden strand and beyond the steely grey waters of St Tredwell's Loch. Soon the cluster of houses around the kirk, the war memorial and the single-track road leading to the barren North Hill passed beneath the wing.

Continuing in a straight line from here the next landfall would be found beyond the pack ice and the North Pole on the Arctic coast of Siberia. But the familiar drystane dyke, painted red-and-white candy stripes in stretches by the boys of Whitehowe to guide the pilots down to the grass airstrip, rushed up to greet us. Soon we were bumping, revving and rattling across the Holland pasture towards the one-room terminal below its orange windsock. By the gate bearing the weathered 'Passengers Only Beyond This Point' sign, Morag and the children were waiting among a crowd of friendly, and by now familiar, Orcadian faces. It was the spring of 1988 and a new chapter in the saga of the wandering Hewitsons was beginning.

For a few years, while I worked in the increasingly crazy world of national newspapers, our house at School Place had been merely a holiday home; a refuge and a summer sanctuary. Then one afternoon we decided (over a beer, as it happens) to take the plunge; to take our chance, sell up and settle in a little community clinging precariously both to the stormy Atlantic edge and, in a quite real sense, to its very existence.

During three decades I'd searched Europe for a location where the pace of life made more sense, where traditional values such as feeling for place and family still mattered but most importantly where you got full value from each precious, unhurried moment. Strange that I was to find it here, almost on my own doorstep, in the jade necklace of islands that is Orkney.

Scientists tell us that time, stealthy companion of life's affairs, doesn't necessarily flow forward but can be bent and twisted in ways which defy our commonsense notions. This all seemed a bit far-fetched – until we reached Papa Westray. Now I'm a believer. Time here has indeed a very special pliable quality. This rolling and fertile landscape of prehistoric villages and tombs, mist-covered lochs and endless horizons has done something quite magical to the fourth dimension. Although there are still officially 24 hours in the day, seven days in the week, these units often seem stretched, elongated in an almost mystical way.

Just occasionally moments can be compacted, events racing past in a dizzy blur but, generally speaking, time here is still a reflection of the changing seasons, the pulse of creation, the beat of the waves and our circuits of the sun, rather than the ticking of the clock. It is not spent recklessly but slowly and methodically, wringing eternity for all its worth. Confused? Me, too! Having tried and failed many times to explain this puzzle to visitors I usually resort to a neat limerick (with apologies to Professor Buller):

> There wis a young wifie cawed Bright,
> Whose speed wis far faster than light,
> She went creeling one day,
> Fae Papa Westray,
> And cam' back the previous night!

This island, perched on the fringe of the Orkney group off Scotland's rugged north coast, some 30 miles from the largest town in the archipelago, Kirkwall, lies on the same latitude as Alaska. In summer there is no real night, in winter little daylight to speak of. Almost everyone on the island seems to be related in some way to their neighbours; second cousins and school-age aunties and uncles can be found. There's a wealth of legend and tradition on Papay (the local name for the island) and its unique history lives to such an eerie extent that events of a century ago are spoken of as if they happened yesterday.

For the past eight years in this kingdom of elastic time, I've

coalfish

plugged away at my writing, fished from time to time for lobster, partans and cuithes and cared for our motley menagerie of goats, sheep, cats and horses – usually as apprentice to my womenfolk. Morag has cooked for the children in the school and for visitors in the guest-house, and produced beautiful paintings on silk; landscapes of our adopted home. Our kids, Lindsey, David and Katy, have now gone away under their own steam, but here they got a start in life which was overflowing with unimagined freedom and adventure – voyaging, for example, every day in the school boat across the unpredictable Papay Sound to the secondary school on Westray, our neighbouring isle.

DOUBLE JEOPARDY

By any geographical standard our island is a small place – just four and a wee bit miles by one at its widest – and its land mass, believe it or not, could fit comfortably 1,000 times into Jamaica. And it's getting smaller, almost before our eyes. I've heard it said by visiting geologist Dr John Brown that the islands of Orkney are slowly sinking beneath the waves. The sandstone slabs of Papay were laid down almost 400 million years ago on the bed of a vast, freshwater lagoon, at a time when Orkney was located 15 degrees south of the equator!

Now the surging sea with its destructive backsook chews away at the crags around Mull Head and bites into the soft, sandy bays along the east shore. Old tracks, sometimes entire pastures, have, within living memory, disappeared under the relentless pressure of the ocean. Will people in the not too distant future talk of the mysterious isle of Papa Westray, part of the lost earldom of Orkney, as the new Atlantis? I wonder.

However, it took the loss of my collection of sea-worn crockery a year or two ago to alert me to the fact that we had settled on the fragile rim of the Atlantic and that the apparent permanence of this far-flung spot may be a mere illusion. Gathered from rocky pools and sea-washed beds of shell, the display had lain undisturbed in a dark crevice on the shore at Skate Geo, just below the derelict farm of Nouster. Every so often I would add a new discovery until there must have been upwards of 50 exhibits on show.

Betraying the last faded image of a mauve petal, a willow pattern or a simple blue edging, the shards may have come from the discarded stock of kitchenware from Holland (the big house on the hill) or from the cargo of some ill-fated vessel dashed to pieces on one of the taings, the saw-toothed reefs which guard the sheltered anchorage on Papa Westray's east shore. Their origins mattered little – my idea was that they would serve as a mute timepiece, safe, or so I thought, from the surging tide on one hand and the blades of the plough to landward.

Some vague notion – no doubt after a night of stargazing and home brew – that these shards might still be there among the sandstone shelves a couple of centuries hence, a tiny landmark from the late twentieth century, prompted this seemingly pointless exercise. Through the storms of winter and the long, clear days of summer I passed by twice daily on my tideline walks with the dog. Most days I merely registered their presence, on others I might add a new find and check to see if time and tide had moved my exhibits, even a fraction. The collection, however, seemed to have become a fixture; it had assumed an air of durability.

Then it was gone, carried away in one night, probably by one powerful breaker, during a ferocious storm when waves broke way up the field and lifted a raft of tangles and boulders on to the pasture; a storm which not only changed the shape of our island, sending massive sandstone pillars tumbling and flipping over 20-ton flagstones as if they were playing cards, but also swept away any romantic, starry-eyed notions I had about the unchanging character of this place.

Hereabouts we've listened to all the talk of global warming, of holes in the ozone layer and shrinking icecaps, but with goats to be milked, boats to be met and vegetables to be tended, we've little time for contemplation of such threats. Yet, not so gradually, changes which cannot be ignored are becoming apparent. The older folk can't remember the like. Autumn and spring seem somehow compressed; it's becoming windier, wetter and warmer; to me low tides appear lower, high tides higher. And maybe it's no longer sufficient to describe these conditions as freakish.

In the summer of 1993 I reported, in a despatch to *The Washington Post*, some worrying figures in relation to these changes:

> New statistics show that the sea is much warmer compared with the early years of this century. More tellingly for Orkney, a recent study indicated that the average Atlantic waves in our vicinity are 50 per cent higher than they were in the 1960s, while storm waves are 10 per cent higher. Deep

depressions brought into existence by increasing differences in sea temperature have been crashing in from the Atlantic.

We must prepare for more such storms and sea surges in the future. We'll be battening down the hatches, I fear, for the next century or two at least. Already there are strange, unsettling spells of rain when more of the island seems under water than above it.

ON THE CRUMBLING ATLANTIC EDGE

Indeed, it was easy, not so many years ago, to look at the stacks – great, natural rock towers by the shore – and the stone villages, brochs and burial places and feel a sense of primeval resilience. Now it does seem that our islands are, quite visibly, crumbling, being eaten away by the hunger of the wild seas and their constant companion, the angry wind. Even the Old Man of Hoy is suffering from brittle bone disease.

If anything, social changes – most notably depopulation – which have overtaken the island since the turn of the century, have been even more dramatic than the battering we endure each winter from the ocean. They are certainly of much more immediate concern.

Strange, for instance, to pass the Dykeside road end these days, to see the gate closed over, the weeds pushing through the track and to watch the postie, Jim o' Backaskaill, cruise past the croft which was formerly one of his daily halts. If you've ever peeked through the curtains to watch your neighbours at the end of the street excitedly helping to pack the furniture van, preparing to move on to pastures new, then you probably reckon that the departure of the Symonds family was an unremarkable event.

Certainly in towns and cities, especially when the property market starts to pick up again, the chances are that you'll have new neighbours before the afternoon is out. New folk to greet, new friendships to make. Out here in the isles life is never so straightforward. Maggie, Paul and Joel left for new beginnings in the south but their decampment was worrying for a small island community such as ours, not only in terms of the loss of their purchasing power but probably, more importantly, because of the shrinkage in the number of people who call Papa Westray their home. Although there are a few new faces on the isle this haemorrhage continues.

At the moment, allowing for the comings and goings of our students and the boys at the fishing, our population is holding shakily at around the 70 mark. This equates to roughly 25 households, able to cling together like limpets when the world threatens but just as capable of squabbling like a pack of hungry gulls. Only last century the islanders were counted in hundreds rather than tens. The 1851 census reported 371 people on Papay with 43 different occupations and a working population ranging from ten-year-olds to an old boy aged 78. Soon figures began to show the effect of the drift away to the wilds of Canada with the Hudson's Bay Company or the goldfields of Australia, but generally the census figures of a century ago still provides a picture of a bustling island.

In 1881, up at the farm o' Cuppin', overlooking the loch, George and Ann Miller and their four children were in residence (present status: a roofless shell); along the east shore Hookin' was home to the nine-strong Cursiter family (present status: menaced by the sea); at the little steading of Edgeriggs, with its spectacular views across to Westray, we would have found three generations of Robertsons (present status: part ruinous, part cattle shelter). The list of abandoned, derelict or semi-derelict properties today goes on and on. As many empty now as occupied, I fear.

AN ISLAND WITH A FUTURE?

Let's not, however, paint a picture of unremitting gloom. Recently, Douglas and Inga have transformed the old steading at Whitelooms into a beautiful new home in the lee of the North Hill; OAP Kitty Harcus moved into a two-bedroom kit house at the other end of the island, built with assistance from Scottish Homes and Orkney Islands Council; a new North Rendall has risen beside the squat, ramshackle croft of that name; and Geirbolls has been modernised and now has tenants. The old bothy at Holland has become a little heritage centre for the island and roofs are being restored on the outbuildings, including the smiddy.

However, the pull away from the island remains strong. The huge families of yesteryear, when 13 or 14 would crowd into a but and ben, are no more and for decades younger people have been demanding more from life than the often austere existence to be found on Papay. To Kirkwall, Stromness and the cities of the south they've drifted off the land in search of more lucrative employment,

an extended education and entertainment. In total, a broader experience of what life has to offer. Similarly some older folk seeking comfort and security in their twilight years have gravitated to the 'toon'.

Even 20 years ago the island still had 110 residents but now Papa Westray's population level hovers perilously close to the make-or-break zone identified by experts as necessary for a viable small island economy. Our shop in particular is under threat in this situation. With this steady loss of people has come further, insidious social erosion. The island has no resident doctor or minister these days and with only a handful of youngsters in the school the future provision of education on the island is always carefully watched. To our dismay, we discovered in 1996 that our primary school is on a hit list for closure as education spending is cut drastically throughout Orkney. The first skirmish has been won but retaining the school has now become a top island priority. Fewer numbers also means less clout in arguing our case in the corridors of power. Although paradoxically it seems to give us a head start in grant applications for all sorts of projects; the mystique of far-flung, half-empty isles, I suppose.

To say we are in crisis would be an exaggeration; to say there is no problem would be foolhardy.

This is how I updated the depopulation issue in my columns during the winter of 1993–94:

> Other remote islands, notably Fetlar and Papa Stour in Shetland, have actively lobbied for settlers in recent years and there seems to be no shortage of folk willing to give the hard life a go. Here on Papa Westray there is no such campaign – yet. What we do have are complications, not least the ownership of land and property which is indeed a tangled web. When visitors, entranced by this place, inquire about the availability of the decaying homesteads they find, for a variety of reasons, that they are often swimming in marshmallow.

So, what's the difficulty? Many of the buildings are ruinous, well beyond repair, but others are being retained for a variety of reasons I can only begin to guess at – for unspecified future family use; in the hope, perhaps, of making a quick buck; to prevent an influx of second-home owners and/or settlers; or simply to keep things as they are. But surely people who are prepared to take a chance must be encouraged. And indeed a few houses have become available for rental recently. Fair enough, we may attract the occasional heid-banger but time, tide and the strange magic of this place will achieve a balance – sort the wheat from the chaff.

How has the island faced up to the dilemma of dwindling population in the past 20 years? Such challenges have to be met head-on and there can be no criticism of the islanders of Papa Westray on this count. The great watershed came when they were faced with the closure of the island's only shop in the early 1980s. The community, led by formidable figures like Bill o' the Links, Jim the postie, Maggie o' Midhoose, Marion Cooper, teacher to trade, and John Rendall from the big farm of Holland, along with the family groups of Fletts, Davidsons, Cursiters, Millers, Rendalls,

Grays, Hourstons and Groats, came up with the idea of converting the New Houses, a row of derelict farm-workers' cottages looking east to the Holm of Papay, into a shop/guest-house/hostel complex.

TOURISM — THE DOUBLE-EDGED SWORD

Tapping into the growing tourist potential of the isle and providing much needed part-time work for a sizeable percentage of the island's population (serving in the shop, cleaning, cooking and ferrying guests around the island) the enterprise got the backing of the former Highlands and Islands Development Board. The pioneering Papa Westray Community Co-operative was born.

Run by a management committee, the Co-op, despite regular personality clashes and seemingly terminal crises, has survived and performed small miracles which have unquestionably helped to stem the drift away from the island. It still soldiers on but the lines of internal communication are in need of repair and fresh direction is being sought. This became necessary because, rather than a rallying point which has, over the years, earned the admiration of folk from five continents, it had by the mid-1990s become too often a forum for feuding. Inevitable, you might say, in such a close-knit community, but infighting is a luxury we can no longer afford.

Links to the speedy roll-on-roll-off service operated by Orkney Ferries to Westray and economy air flights have opened up our island in the past few years to a new breed of day-trippers and the bed-and-breakfast brigade. A whole new set of challenges have been presented to Papa Westray and its Co-op. The future role of the guest-house, upgraded to hotel status a couple of years ago, and the successful hostel, is the subject of animated daily discussion among the populace. Great concern is felt about the shop and the best way to operate it economically and efficiently and yet still provide a spread of employment among the islanders. Worryingly, the shop's turnover was down 9.2% in 1995.

Diversification into areas like market gardening and crafts is regularly spoken of as a way ahead for the Co-op but, unlike one observer of the international island scene, I can't agree that all we're needing is a 'kick up the backside' to get us moving. As they say, the jury is out on the future of the Co-op but without the shop the already challenging century ahead will be more threatening.

On the plus side we learn that social strife on other islands can be much more ferocious and unlike other parts of the Scottish margin, the people of Papa Westray are very much in control of their own destiny. There is no distant landlord upon whose whim the future of the community turns (although Papay has its legacy of despotism in centuries past), a higher percentage of the land is used productively compared with other small isles and in the Co-op the island should have a perfect forum for debate and development.

Success – or failure – rests with the islanders themselves and a confidently stated and carefully structured plan to take us into the next century will let the world see we're serious about survival.

Farming, principally beef cattle and sheep, and to a lesser extent shellfishing, still underpin our mini-economy but the growing importance of the hospitality trade has been inescapable. In 1990, writing in Mainstream's *Book of Scotland,* I recalled what I consider to be a smashing anecdote to introduce an essay examining, among other things, the effect of tourism on far-flung island communities such as our own:

> It's late on a luminous northern evening. Down by the pier where the basin is being deepened three old men lean on the railing and gaze, misty-eyed, across the bay. Yet another soul-stirring Orkney sunset burnishes the horizon in a coloursplash of gold, crimson and orange. 'Boys, boys, wid ye look at that,' says the first veteran in awe. 'Magnificent,' says the second. 'Aye,' says the third, 'finest bit o' dredging equipment we've had here in 20 years.'

The English journalist who harvested this anecdote, I know, retold it with relish. It seems that media fascination with our Scottish islands and their curious inhabitants is insatiable. Although he doesn't know it, our newsman's tale, apocryphal or otherwise, operates at more than one level.

As well as being a couthy yarn it illustrates the startling metamorphosis overtaking these northern isles, perhaps the single biggest change since the Crofters Commission sailed through the islands in the 1880s and helped bring the ordinary folk out of centuries of agricultural servitude. The natural splendours of Orkney, taken for granted since Magnus Barelegs was a boy, now hold a key to the area's future prosperity.

Tourism is catching up with farming and fishing as a principal money earner but only recently have folk come to appreciate that golden sunsets can be translated into hard cash. Small islands with

their unusual appeal are now big business. Each year we've seen a steady increase in the number of visitors venturing across the Pentland Firth.

Over the years I've been in two minds about this money-spinner. On one hand tourism could be the saving of Papay but there is also the possibility that, if handled clumsily, it could prove the island's ruination. Let me elaborate a little. When, in July 1964, consideration was first given to the establishment of a tourist association for Orkney these pioneers could scarcely have imagined the explosion in the leisure industry during the past decade. Unrestricted growth in holiday business, despite the changes it brings in its wake, is seen by most as totally justified. For too long, it is argued with some validity, Orkney missed out on the spoils while others profited. Geographically at the end of the line Papa Westray has, nevertheless, already seen modifications in our lifestyle brought about by tourism.

When that tourist association took its first tentative steps over

30 years ago Papay was still on the edge of the known universe. Only a few brave adventurers found their way out here to be rowed ashore at Moclett into a genuine world apart. It was, and is, perfectly reasonable that islanders should reap the benefits of guest-house and shop work, bed and breakfast, transport provision, etc., which have accrued. But, in leaving the door wide open, are the very features which people travel vast distances to experience, endangered?

It's maybe a bit invidious of an incomer like myself (a ferrylouper as the Orcadians quaintly style us) to poke my nose into this situation. We came north to live a more basic lifestyle. That was our choice. In making these observations I could easily be accused of trying to keep my little corner of paradise untouched. Not so. Papa Westray cannot be frozen in time, it cannot remain unchanging, simply ticking over. With a little care a genuine community can be retained, benefiting from tourism but not shaped 100 per cent by the needs of the visitor. Some changes in our lifestyles are now inevitable. The pace will have to change to suit the needs of others. Such is the nature of tourism . . . and survival.

However, let's ca' canny. The generally held belief in Orkney is that these islands, with one of the best-run tourist economies in Scotland, can handle everyone the trade steers in our direction. I can't speak for the other islands of Orkney but I don't believe this to be the case on Papa Westray. In the past few summers I've spoken to people who were surprised and even slightly dismayed at the unexpectedly large numbers of folk sharing the sands of the North Wick; I've seen visitors who fail to understand that the shop queue is a social happening and that shoving your way to the till is unacceptable; I've listened with amazement to the tale of the thieving hiker who dug up a rare orchid and I've been disappointed to find campers leaving crisp packets and soft-drink cans outside their tents.

Isolated, insignificant happenings in the greater scheme of things, I hear you cry . . . perhaps. It has to be admitted that scores of people come here, act responsibly and leave enraptured by the beauty and mystery of the isle. But we must learn to read the signs. Such changes have overtaken communities not so far from here almost before they knew what was happening. I find it increasingly difficult to describe the island as remote despite the fact that it is clearly so. Likewise its uniqueness may be in jeopardy. Yet these are the reasons why folk, in increasing numbers, want to come here – a perplexing paradox.

Trying to make sense of this enigma, I wrote in the winter of 1989:

> The truth is that on our six square miles we can only happily absorb a finite number of visitors. Even though the climate and the short season will always act as a restricting factor an effort should be made to determine this magic number before something special is lost.
>
> Surely sensibly controlled development where tourism is used to create a more broadly based economy, allowing an agricultural/fishing/crafts co-operative to flow from the existing tourism based enterprise, perhaps allowing for old skills such as boatbuilding to be resurrected, is the way ahead. It would be so easy, but awfy shortsighted to put all our eggs in one lucrative basket.

An open-door policy on tourism, full steam ahead at the expense of everything else, may have its attractions, but surprisingly quickly, I fear, visitors would search in vain for the special qualities of community and environment which drew them here in the first place. Then where do we turn?

Before the community co-operative was established 15 years ago there were genuine fears that Papa Westray might become a desert island. The situation remains delicately balanced. However, Orkney Islands Council and Orkney Enterprise – well aware of the importance of the Co-operative to the future of our island – are looking at ways to assist. A gentle application of the tourist brake and planning ahead with diversification in mind may ensure an unexpectedly bright and open-ended future for generations of youngsters who may now be persuaded to remain on the island. If not, everyone could be a loser – locals, visitors and ferryloupers alike.

AN OBSESSION WITH ISLANDS

Although the far-flung northern isles of Orkney are now my base of operation, I feel drawn from time to time back to my roots beside the Clyde; my anchor drags as it has done in Edinburgh, Athens and Umbria on a restless tide, ebbing and flowing between novelty and nostalgia. Private pilgrimages can take many contrasting forms. Venturing south I always pay my respects at my childhood home – one of the few Clydebank tenements to survive the hammer

of the demolisher who sent the great, grey buildings tumbling in a way which surpassed even the *Luftwaffe*.

The second stage on this spiritual journey draws me inevitably to an unremarkable side-room in the National Museum of Antiquities in Edinburgh, which is packed with Pictish symbol stones and incised sandstone from Scotland's Dark Ages. Here I can view the cross-slab from the Kirk of St Boniface on Papay. This part of the pilgrimage usually comes towards the end of my sojourn in the south when, in the midst of the scurry of the city, I need a durable lifeline to a place where events progress at a more sensible pace. When you're queuing for a ticket amidst the throng in Queen Street Station in Glasgow or fighting to order a round in one of the howffs down Fleshmarket Close in Edinburgh, our isle can seem about as real as the fantastic, fogbound Orcadian kingdom of Hether Blether.

My first visit to that sanctuary of venerable stones in Edinburgh, to strengthen my new northern connections, gave much food for thought. I found our Papay cross-slab nicely displayed among its cold, expressionless companions, but to my confusion discovered that the large wall chart of Scotland not only failed to pinpoint the St Boniface site but also appeared to have allowed Papa Westray, perhaps prophetically, to slip beneath the waves.

I suspect that Scotland's scatter of islands have been as much trouble to the map-makers over the years as they have been to the long line of Scottish kings who have tried to keep these distant, independently minded territories under their sway. Cartographers always seemed to have it in for Orkney and Shetland in particular, dropping them into waterproof boxes, usually somewhere off the Moray Firth; mysterious floating archipelagos existing on the boundaries of reality. In a sense I think this is often how the United Kingdom looks on our island fringe: romantic, scenically attractive yet somehow unconnected with the greater life of Scotland – the soft, outer edge.

Of course, nothing could be further from the truth. Lack of population does not equate with lack of enterprise. Some of the most exciting initiatives of the past decade have come from these peripheral areas, such as co-operative ventures, educational innovation, fish-farming, arts and music festivals and many imaginative tourist projects.

After a year or two on Papay I began to try and analyse my island obsession:

> But how did this strange island fever, or what Lawrence Durrell called Islomania, overtake a level-headed lad from the sandstone canyons of Clydebank where the nearest we had to sceptred isles were the upturned supermarket trolleys in the canal?

The fact is that summer holidays spent in the 1950s at North Berwick were the root of the passion. A little way along the coast towards Gullane is Fidra; a lump of rock, I was told later, which had provided the inspiration for Robert Louis Stevenson's *Treasure Island*. Building sandcastles at Yellowcraig, I would look out over the surf towards this volcanic stump; the haunt of seabirds and holy men, so close to shore yet so tantalisingly far away. It was like looking at another world through a half-open door.

For me Stevenson's book conjures up images of palm-shrouded tropical isles with sweeping sandy bays and dark jungle glades where one-eyed pirates lurk behind every tree-trunk – as different as could be from the windy outcrop with its lighthouse in the Forth. Yet Fidra remained mysterious and compelling. I did eventually visit and there was no sense of let-down. It was a kingdom waiting to be ruled; a private paradise.

It may have commenced as a childish fancy but the truth is that I was hooked. As the years moved on I developed similar attachments to the beautiful islands of Loch Lomond, to the Bass Rock and to Inchmahome on the Lake of Menteith where lawns reach for lapping waters in the shadow of tumbled priory walls. This location provides the best illustration I know of islands in aspic, places frozen in time like St Kilda and Fidra. They are attractive, certainly, perhaps spiritually uplifting, but they lack people, the society no matter how small needed to breathe life into their empty acres.

On the other hand we find Papa Westray and islands like Foula, Fair Isle, Colonsay, Eigg and Coll. They may also be small but they have genuine communities, societies in microcosm with all the consequent joys and kindnesses, petty jealousies, occasional scrapping and bloody-mindedness. They are not perfect – paradise they are not – but in their struggles they are vibrant, decidedly alive.

THE WHISTLESTOP TOUR

There are said to be as many islands around Scotland as there are *a mirad of vanished islands* days in the year (<u>Hether Blether</u> appears in leap years, of course). Although they have many common features, each island has a distinctive personality. I want you to get to know Papa Westray and, as a taster of what's in store, let me take you on a whistlestop tour of the island. Prepare for a sharpening of the senses.

Let's listen to the groan of the steamer's mooring-rope as she strains to be away from the New Pier on her three-hour haul to Kirkwall; the chug of Maggie o' Midhoose's vintage Fordson tractor as it climbs the brae to the shop; the screech of the terns as they divebomb the foolhardy backpacker and the whoosh of the skua as he swoops to declare his territorial rights; the excited playtime shouts of the children in the schoolyard; the throaty roar of the afternoon flight from the town turning on the tarmac apron; the haunting calls of the seals across on the Holm; the bleat of a new-born lamb; or the last shallow breath of an old ewe at Tirlo.

Or gaze into the aquamarine transparency of the South Wick, water so clear you can count the partans crawling across the seabed 20 feet below the keel; kittiwakes and razorbills diving and carousing under the formidable, overhanging cliffs north by; weather fronts fast approaching, great battlements of cloud rolling in from the west; lights twinkling on fishing-boats as they cut north for Fair Isle; the high jinks of the kittens in our cluttered backyard as they chase a Red Admiral; the Co-op bus with its daily cargo of wide-eyed tourists; and the huge winter seas smashing into the geos on the west shore, their Atlantic voyage complete.

And smell the pungent odour of the tangles piled feet high along the shore, torn last month from their watery bed by the fiercest of seas; the distinctive aroma of freshly caught crab or lobster boiling in the pot; the new-mown hay; the sweet scent of the carpet of wildflowers at Moclett; and the breathtaking bouquet of Bill o' the Links' home brew.

Feel the blown hay itching your back midway through a warm afternoon at the baling; the creel rope opening the blisters on your fingers as you haul out beyond Weelie's Taing; the soft, warm down of the wayward snipe chick as you return him to the nest; or the smooth perfection of the stonework at the ancient farmstead of the Knap of Howar – built before the mighty pyramids.

Taste the island delicacy of clapshot and the salty flavour of the Holmie mutton from the seaweed-eating sheep; Mima of Cott's flavoursome duff; the clean, wholesome tang of the whelks gathered below the Old Mill; and the silky, deceptive quality of Peter Miller the builder's rhubarb wine which has graced many a shindig.

And that's just for starters. Hold on to your hats while we explore some more.

Chapter Two

The Leg of Pork Affair

THE SPANISH CONNECTION

History just seems to reach out and grab your attention hereabouts – even in the most unlikely of settings. The Muckle Supper is a sort of rustic, winter muttonfest when the people of Papa Westray range themselves at long tables in the school and devour as much prime lamb as the body can stand. This strange ritual, a fund-raising effort for the youth club/Community Association in recent years, harkens back to the dim, agricultural past when every feature of the season, whether it was lambing, harvesting or going down for the tangles, was marked by a gathering to give thanks, or to politely plead for something better.

Diners cart along their own cutlery and crockery. Seasoned campaigners can be recognised by their enormous bowls which have been taken down from the kitchen press for an annual airing. After the grace, proceedings are launched with endless plates of tattie and mutton soup. This is followed by platters piled high with chunks of cold lamb accompanied by clapshot, baked beans and peas served cold from plastic margarine tubs and gallons of tepid orange juice to help wash down the repast.

The victims of the evening are Holland farm's well-fattened Holmie lambs, caught earlier in the summer on the annual pilgrimage to the Holm of Papay for the clipping (you see, Holmies). Each participating family gets a ewe to fatten up for the freezer as a reward for their day's efforts. For a few hours the Holm, normally a bleak desert isle, is transformed as the great round-up gets under way, whoops and excited hollers echoing out across the still waters of the South Wick. At dusk the little flotilla crosses back to the Old Pier with its cargo of sun-bronzed and knackered frontiers folk.

At my first Muckle Supper, being a bit of a hell-raiser by nature, I decided that the traditional tomato sauce just wasn't good enough for such a grand spread, so I smuggled in a jar of mint sauce under the unsuspecting gaze of the youth club 'heavies', Alistair of Cott and Ian of Charleston. Normally not men to be messed with.

The jar was dramatically produced mid-meal to general astonishment and, I have to say, to the embarrassment of my family. Call it sacrilege if you must but it helped me demolish a third plateful of mutton. As if that was not enough nail-biting tension for one night, the Muckle Supper, unlikely as it seems, was the occasion for an amazing moment of enlightenment. A troublesome enigma was explained.

The tables had been cleared away, the organisers were counting the night's takings in the corner and the floor was being dusted in preparation for the jiggin'. Jim Rendall, our cheery, bearded island postman, announced a 'Dashing White Sergeant' before jogging to the top of the hall where he produced his famous washboard and thimble. Wife Margaret was already giving the squeezebox laldie as the formations charged across the floor and Jim, the original wee Papay rapper, joined in with a nice, tidy scratch.

Let me tell you about Jim. He does not look like an Orcadian, not at all. His sleek, dark hair, dark eyes and complexion point to a Mediterranean background. This has troubled me since the first day I met him in the gloomy little post office down on the west shore at Backaskaill. In Orkney, and especially in the North Isles, you can still see traces of the Norse heritage in fair-skinned folk. But Jim is not from that mould.

In the community he is a man of many roles – docker, postman, JP, lay-preacher, registrar and he has served on both the community council and the community co-operative. A formidable record of service. And in that staggering catalogue of activity lies the key to his heritage. You see, just before the Muckle Supper I'd been reading of the Dons, not the heroes of Pittodrie, but the shipwrecked survivors of the Armada who settled on our neighbouring island of Westray in 1588. Apart from their distinctive swarthy appearance, the learned article confirmed: 'They were in manners fidgety and restless, a true Don being rarely able to sit in one position for five minutes.' Watching Jim in feverish action on the washboard and trying to list his jobs on the island,

the mists suddenly began to clear. He perfectly fitted the description both in terms of appearance and manner. He is a descendant of the Dons, a living link to the Armada.

Now, I wanted desperately to speak to him about this flash of insight but how do you approach someone with a long Orcadian family tradition and suggest that one of his antecedents might have been a randy matelot from Malaga? There is no easy way. 'So you reckon there's a bit o' the Spaniard in me, eh? Well, you're no' the first to have remarked on that, Jim. It's got worse since I grew the beard. Actually, I think there's more Chinese in the family than Spanish.'

The 400th anniversary of the defeat of the Armada was marked in 1988 so I suppose it's safe enough now to talk of how Orkney gave succour to the Spaniards. The 'invincible' Armada of 130 ships was sent packing from the English Channel and fled northwards rounding Scotland with the intention of taking the long route home beyond Ireland. However, on 21 September, a hurricane hit the disconsolate fleet, sinking 20 galleons and driving others back into Scottish waters.

Only 60 vessels limped back to Spain. The wreck in Tobermory Bay on Mull is the most famous relic from this dramatic episode, sunk by an explosion after having sought refuge in the bay. In Orkney waters, the *Gran Grifon*, a 380-gun flagship which ran aground and sank on Fair Isle, has been much studied by marine archaeologists. But there could also be a Papa Westray connection as I speculated in an article for newspapers in the Caribbean:

> Oral tradition speaks of other wrecks around the fringes of the north isles. On Papay, only 25 miles from Fair Isle, there is talk, Jim lad, of Spanish treasure. Aye, pieces of eight by the chestful, me hearties. The story goes that survivors of another wreck made landfall near Mull Head, the place of the rushing waters. Having scrambled ashore on to our bleak North Hill, the Spaniards are said to have buried their treasure at a spot from which, so the legend relates, it is impossible to see the ocean. There is indeed a little valley above Bewin' from which the sea is hidden on all sides. Tantalisingly, it is ringed with marker stones and fits the story perfectly.

Subsequently I learned that enterprising islanders had been out over the moor with metal detectors. The fact that no one is obviously living the high life out here or has moved to Mustique, suggests that the treasure still awaits discovery. Just to add a little to the suspense, up at Micklegarth Neil and Jocelyn have a piece of intricately carved wood which looks for all the world as if it might have come from the ornate gunwale of some man-o'-war. Who knows?

Anyway, we move away from speculation and closer to fact. Interestingly, the Spaniards are said to have arrived on Westray rowing in from the direction of Papay and were offered sanctuary. Whether the sixteenth-century equivalent of the Papay heavy mob had sent them packing is not noted in our annals.

They formed a little settlement at a place called North Shore and adopted local names such as Petrie, Reid and Hewison (no connection that I can find with the Ayrshire Hewitsons). Over the years they were noted as daring fishermen and seafarers and were reported to be fine actors and keen practical jokers. They were, according to the scribes, restless and fidgety, except when dead drunk.

From time to time almost hidden Spanish connections break surface. *The Orcadian*, our local paper, announced that the Spanish government wanted to commemorate one of the Armada officers, Captain Patricio Antilinez, who was buried at St Magnus Cathedral after the Fair Isle wreck. Orkney Islands Council was asked by the Spanish Embassy to provide a bench with a suitably inscribed plaque, perhaps to be located near the cathedral.

They might have asked Jim to officially inaugurate the bench, to be the first to plant his posterior thereon. However, the likelihood is that he wouldn't have been able to sit still long enough to see the ceremony through!

Currently, there is a cluster of more than a dozen Rendalls on Papa Westray, the single biggest family name group. In fact, we can be certain they were around this isle long before the Armada hove into view. An article by William P. Thomson, author of the definitive history of Orkney, makes mention of a meeting in Sanday in 1490 to decide on levels of taxation and methods of collection in the isles. Among those in attendance were the 'best men of Papay and Westray', including William Rendall, Brandy Drever, John Drever, Marius Mailson and Henry Rendall. Strangely, in the 1851 census of Papay, although 42 different surnames were recorded, the Rendalls didn't even make the top ten.

Earliest recorded names associated with Papay, apart from the Dark Age dedications to St Boniface, St Tredwell, and a speculative link with St Findan, are to be found in the Orkneyinga Saga, the stories of the Norse settlement of Orkney from the ninth to the thirteenth century.

First is the adventurer Earl Rognvald Brusason. Murdered in a family feud, he was brought to Papa Westray for burial around the year 1046. The most logical location for his burial place is the graveyard at St Boniface on the west shore. Intriguingly, there is a rare hog-backed stone with a scallop carving in imitation of a longhouse roof on the site. Although the red sandstone is badly weathered, it's possible to visualise this monument in all its gilded glory. A cross-slab which may have been associated with the murdered earl was also uncovered in the yard. Brusason is regarded by many experts on the period as the greatest of the Orkney earls.

The other saga character connected with Papay was a landowner called Ragna, a formidable, intelligent lady who ran farms on North Ronaldsay and Papa Westray with her son, Thorstein, and wasn't averse to offering advice to the earls of Orkney when danger threatened.

However, there is a prime candidate for the first recorded resident of the island. While working in the Orkney library, I came across a reference to a Kirkwall Charter dated 1391 which mentions one of the signatories as Simon of Papay – 'knight, dominus, a most discreet and noble person'. Scholars have apparently debated whether this Simon's fief relates to Papa Westray or Papa Stronsay since another signatory for Westray is noted. However, we know that Papa Westray was an important religious centre as far back as the Dark Ages, significant far beyond its geographical size. It seems possible that this Simon was the first 'doondie' on record and it's also worth noting that this charter was signed almost a century before Orkney became part of Scotland, when it was the dowry of Princess Margaret of Norway on her marriage to James III.

[handwritten margin note: ABITANT PAPAY OR D FISH]

LAST CALL FOR KING CANUTE

Every summer, just as flocks of migrating birds alight on their traditional nesting sites, teams of eager, slightly eccentric archaeologists descend on the Orkney Islands to explore our past. Much of their effort is directed to what is called in the trade 'rescue archaeology' – the excavation of Orkney's many coastal sites which are being steadily eroded by the relentless appetite of the sea.

There is never enough money for this important work, the cash somehow becoming more scarce the further away you are from the decision-making centres of Edinburgh and London. So many locations cry out for attention in Orkney and the competition for what little is available remains fierce. We knew we'd struck it lucky when, thanks to the persuasive powers of the Orkney Islands' official archaeologist, Dr Raymond Lamb, a team was sent north to probe the mysterious secrets of the St Boniface settlement site here on Papay. When details of the dig were published, the full importance of the site became apparent.

The old kirk dates from the twelfth century and is an important monument in its own right, but it is surrounded by an even more significant area of buried settlement along the shore, dating back some 2,000 years, back through the medieval period and the Viking era to the time of Christ, perhaps beyond.

Often when graves are being dug in the kirkyard, passageways and upright stones are discovered but the only real work done on the shore site in the past 200 years took place in the 1850s when parents, anxious about a stone-lined corridor which had been exposed, filled it in with rubble in case the island children followed the rabbits into the warren of low tunnels.

As the archaeologists carefully uncovered layer upon layer of habitation, the corridor was found to have run round the exterior of the base of what was once a broch or stone fortress-tower, now almost totally washed away by the sea. If those adventurous nineteenth-century kiddies could have followed the tunnel it would have led them to the heart of the structure.

Over the years Papa Westray has become well enough tuned to the activities of the diggers. The island abounds with sites of historic interest. Elsewhere in Orkney there have been murmurings about archaeologists who remain aloof from the local community, somehow unwilling to share their secrets with the islanders. Such criticism cannot be laid at the door of Dr Chris Lowe and his St Boniface team – local people even helped out with the menial tasks at the site. Admittedly, it took a wee while before we could treat the team with due deference, especially after they erected the biggest tent ever seen on this windy isle, a garden-party style marquee which sat incongruously on the blustery shore beside the kirk. It housed the amazing machine which washed the samples but fears were expressed by locals that the first modest Atlantic gust might send the whole encampment off in the direction of Scandinavia.

Walking on to the site from the kirkyard, only marker poles and areas sectioned off with string gave any clue to unusual activity. Clambering down on to the rocky shore it was a different story. A remarkable scene unfolded. Cutting deep into the bank, a complex jumble of passageways, walls and flagstone floors criss-cross each other at a bewildering variety of levels and angles. Here a slabbed drain; across there a paved floor under which a child's grave was found; and a stone footpath runs tantalisingly into the bank. An enclosure resembling the traditional Orkney boat noust was uncovered. Nearby a whalebone weaving-sword was found, probably the oldest known specimen in the British Isles.

Each discovery helps the trained eye assess how this little community developed. Ironically, the major significance of the site – as a possible Dark Ages bishopric – may be contained in the grassy mounds atop the banking. These, alas, will remain unexcavated until more money becomes available.

Even if the professionals are now absent, there is every opportunity for the enthusiastic amateur. A couple of years after the dig was completed, a piece of tile was picked up on the shore just below the eroded settlement site by two regular visitors to Papay from the sooth – Julia and Russel from Suffolk. This turned out to be a sensational find. Experts identified it as part of an end panel from an eighth-century reliquary used to house the remains of a saint and suggests, as island folk always suspected, that Papay may have been an important Dark Ages pilgrimage site as well as the principal missionary station for the far north of Scotland, Orkney and Shetland.

Such discoveries are by no means commonplace but they do happen. On one occasion when our girls were patrolling the east shore near Cott on the lookout for our missing Siamese cat, Asia, Katy picked up a branched piece of antler about nine inches long from the sand. Others have turned up in this general area over the years and, amazingly, have been dated, like Katy's, to the Bronze Age, some 3,000–4,000 years ago. It's thought that red deer were shipped from mainland Scotland then onwards to the outer isles. The quantity of antler does suggest that deer were plentiful in Papay in those distant days.

Noted in my School Place Diaries after this find:

> Certainly at Weelie's Taing there is a huge tidal pond enclosed by what seems, at least from the elevation of the top road, to be a partly artificial reef. Low walls, a paved area and the outline of buildings, most notably one called 'The Castle', can be made out. A deer farm? It's not impossible. Pieces of antler seem to surface from the pond after a spell of storms.

Tankerness House Museum in Kirkwall, who confirmed the antiquity of the antler, wanted to hang on to it but were persuaded to let us have it back on the basis that it might eventually go into some sort of heritage display here on Papay itself. The Viking trumpet (Papay's equivalent of the jungle drum) has it that ambitious plans are being mooted for the dilapidated sheds by the Old Pier.

Apart from St Boniface, the main archaeological target for our visitors is the Knap of Howar, a 5,000-year-old farmstead à la Skara Brae, south of the old kirk. I can be back there time and again and I still find myself marvelling at the craftsmanship which went into the construction of the two oval-shaped buildings, utilising techniques which are in use on Papa Westray to this day, having altered not at all in the intervening millennia. My own favourite piece of Papay wall-building which comes damn near perfection is the south-west facing wall at the abandoned farm of Hookin' on the island's eastern shore. It is the work of one of the Davidson clan.

Also popular are St Tredwell's Chapel on the artificial island in the loch, another Dark Ages religious settlement constructed on top of a Pictish broch and the eerie chambered tomb on the Holm. This tomb seems to attract a remarkable cross-section of travellers to Orkney, from the cerebral rock star Julian Cope, who apparently talked incessantly to his pocket recorder as he explored the tomb, to Harry Flynn, the famous twentieth-century mayor of the ancient East Yorks town of Beverley. And it was here, of course, that Scots celebrity Jimmie Macgregor sustained a crack on the nut when the iron door leading down into the cairn fell on his head.

Despite that incident, no curse that we know of attaches itself to the tomb, but no one can properly explain the strange pattern of shallow trenches around the site. Irrigation has been mentioned but Papay legend contains no reference to anyone ever having lived on this lonely isle and there are no indications of farming.

With so much history crammed into such a small place, mysteries do abound elsewhere on Papa Westray. We have the supposed curse of St Tredwell. A cross-slab, a great sandstone monolith, has been seen in six or seven feet of normally opaque water near the chapel. Two separate attempts to raise it from the loch, so the story goes, have resulted in the premature deaths of the principals. Whaur's yer Tutankhamun noo? One summer we took our leaky dinghy out on the loch and, near the legendary spot, didn't our oars strike a slab of some sort on the uniformly silty bottom? We made no attempt to raise it. Why? An uncanny breeze sprang from a still afternoon and evaporated the moment we rowed off. We haven't tried again. Scary, eh?

A final thought about the work of the archaeologists on Papay. Within a few weeks of the St Boniface team leaving the island the winter sea was wreaking havoc along the shore, sending newly exposed walls and corridors tumbling. How much has already been lost to the sea at such sites is as teasing a question as what remains to be explored.

Unfortunately, it appears that it isn't only the physical landscape of Papa Westray which is disintegrating. The late John D. Mackay, a schoolteacher, writer, sage and uncle of Tommy o' Maybo', was unquestionably one of the island's most significant gifts to the twentieth century. He even has a lecture in his honour at the annual Orkney Science Festival. Mackay noted that in the 1920s the older inhabitants of the island could recount a fund of anecdotes, pieces of folklore and superstitions but, by the 1950s, he was concerned to discover that this rich seam of native legend had all but dried up.

John D. Mackay himself is something of a legend. It seems that even in his primary school days he was regarded as an exceptional intellect. He carried around a collection of creepie-crawlies in a matchbox which he gleefully examined and showed at every opportunity to his apprehensive classmates and teachers. Like so many others in the north isles, he also became a very proficient lay-preacher. This talent, as tradition has it, was honed as a child when he went along to the kirk to listen to the sermon before returning to the hennie hoose at Maybo' where, word by word, he preached the self-same sermon to the attentive poultry.

As we approach a new century, there are precious few islanders with more than a passing knowledge of Papa Westray's old traditions. If Rescue Archaeology is seen as a valid exercise then maybe we should have the John D. Mackay Heritage Hotline, or something of that ilk. Preserve the island's history with a cheap-rate phone call!

The auld Orkney dialect is undergoing a bit of a resurgence of late, thanks in no small way to the efforts of Alastair and Anne Cormack of the local heritage magazine, *The Orkney View*, who have encouraged children's writing competitions and offered a forum for short stories and articles in the patois. Here on Papay folk will speak slowly and sympathetically in a one-to-one conversation with a 'soothmoother', but if you're on the fringes of a pierhead debate about the price of cattle or the weather, then you'll soon be submerged beneath a fast-flowing terminological tidal wave.

PAPALOGICAL DELIGHTS

On Papa Westray —ological delights are many and varied. Even after you've dealt with birds, history, weather and the social scene, you can always turn to palaeontology. Fossil hunting is a regular, and compulsive, extra for visitors to School Place.

Scouring the sandstone shelves below the empty farm of Moclett or across the Dull Flag is a fine way to spend a summer afternoon. The most common fossil remains resemble specks of coal in the rock, mostly black but occasionally brightest blue, sometimes betraying their presence by standing proud of the surrounding rock, weathering more slowly.

The books say these are the fins and scales of small creatures which occupied the freshwater lake that was Orkney all those years ago, their remains locked for a little eternity in the sandy bed. Stretches of the shore are peppered with relics of a time unimaginably far off. Other common fossilised finds on Papay include ferns, leaves, shells, sand ripples and checkerboard cracks from the dried-up bed of this ancient Lake Orcadie. Set against such a vast expanse of geological time our island monuments, tombs and neolithic farms seem almost youthful.

As ever, this island has the habit of discreetly guarding her treasures. On one such fossil hunt, west of the New Pier, we stumbled across a complex series of markings in a slab which looked for all the world like a ribbed skate wing. We photographed it but sadly, when we went back the following day, it had been covered by a wash of pebbles.

Littering the window sills at School Place, however, are a hundred other fossil finds; trophies of expeditions to the beginning of time.

Beachcombing apart, it pays to keep your eyes peeled along the shore for all sorts of reasons. Regularly you'll encounter lumps of pink or white, or speckled rock which are clearly far from home on these sandstone shores. The explanation I'd always heard tell was that they are carried here by ice sheets from the Highlands or Scandinavia. An interesting enough story in its own right because there are certainly shelves of boulder clay (indicating the passing of an ice sheet) along the east shore. But it has also been suggested that the rocks might be the discarded ballast from the Viking longships which were hauled up at Skennist or Nouster – remnants of granite from the mountains of Norway perhaps. Either way, these rocks have an interesting pedigree and a number decorate our porch.

BORROWED FROM TOLKIEN

Magical and secret places are plentiful on our small island. Don't let the open, unpromising acres of Papa Westray fool you. Adventure lies at the end of every muddy track, if you only know where to look. Take, for instance, the house of Nouster with its collection of tumbledown outbuildings looking south through dark, ivy-shrouded eyes across the North Sound, towards the sandstone ramparts of Eday.

Old Nannie o' Nouster, who rented the house and its contents, died years ago. She was the last occupant and the stout door, obscured in summer behind the untended bushes, has remained locked fast since the day the boys carried out her coffin. Just occasionally on my solitary walks, when the morning sun illuminates the old house, I have, just for a moment, thought I'd seen a figure, there in the west window. If you ventured down the overgrown track and peered in through the grimy, salt-stained windows the rooms lay untouched . . . the unmade bed, the scatter of magazines and papers, the little ornaments, the crushed cushion in the fireside chair. Everything frozen in a moment. Decidedly eerie.

Further up the road, behind its tall drystane dyke, nestles the walled garden of Holland. This enchanted place beside the big house once provided vegetables for the laird's table but until recently it lay empty and abandoned, truly a secret garden. This was the domain of weeds and wild roses, the paths derelict, the old greenhouse with its twin stone chimneys cold and forgotten.

That was until Jocelyn married Neil, son of the Rendalls of Holland, and they moved into Micklegarth, the former grieve's cottage. Jocelyn has breathed new life into this charming spot and the vegetables march in rows again. The garden has rediscovered its purpose.

Right on the northern tip of the island, in the bird sanctuary, is the Dale o' Caman, a miniature valley a couple of hundred yards long, cutting down to the sea cliffs below Errival, the highest point on the North hill. Here, on a summer's day when the Atlantic wind still beats in over the breakers, you can lie among the grass in this sanctuary and watch the puffy white clouds racing for the Norway shore or listen to the squabbling of birds on the spray-splashed rock ledges below.

Surpassing even these romantic locations is the old kirk of St Boniface, crouching for shelter among the weathered, moss-covered gravestones of the kirkyard. For decades the church stood empty, gradually deteriorating. Battered by winter storms, it was a refuge for wild birds; a place of only memories – the roof falling in, the once impressive box pews and pulpit sadly broken and worm-eaten. But there is a cheering story to be told here.

There had always been muted interest on the island in bringing the old kirk back from the brink, but a programme of vital structural renovation was only possible in the 1990s after legal complications over landownership were untangled and financial backing became available from Orkney Islands Council and Historic Scotland.

During one winter Peter Miller and boys – Alistair, Johnny and Rab – rebuilt the teetering gables and put on a new roof. Meanwhile, a major fund-raising effort aimed at partially restoring the interior gained support from influential figures such as Marjorie Linklater, widow of the novelist Eric Linklater, and Lady Laura Grimond, widow of the statesman Jo Grimond. The splendid pulpit with its sounding board and a few box pews are now back in place, thanks to Peter's carpentry skills, and the kirk has since been used for carol services and concerts. The project, in which the islanders feel justified pride, has received a Civic Trust commendation.

The kirkyard itself is a fascinating place; the original yard being long since filled to overflowing, a new section was opened to the south. Many of the earliest gravestones have been weathered beyond recognition but stones from the early 1700s can still be identified. The family names, Cursiter, Gray, Irving, Rendall and Flett are everywhere. Among the memorials are those to island men killed in the wars, to a boy who fell to his death from the mast of a sailing ship in the Archangel River in Russia last century, and two plain wooden crosses identify the last resting place of sailors swept ashore during the Great War. Evidence is found in the script beneath the lichen of infant mortality, little ones who survived only a few short months, weeks or even days in this austere setting.

The history of the church in recent times (since the Reformation in Papay's crazy chronology) is dominated by its connection with the Traills of Holland, lairds of the island for 300 years until the early part of this century. Relations between the kirk and the Traills, who are said to have exercised the *droit de seigneur*, the right to the bride on her wedding night (hence the presence of Traill middle names in some families), well into last century, were mostly strained.

In the summer of 1718, the laird refused to allow the visiting minister from Westray, his brother-in-law as it happens, to set foot on his land. This dispute arose, as did many others, over fines imposed by the kirk on the Traills for their sexual exploits. For a time the poor minister could only reach St Boniface by clambering over slippery rocks along the shore from the nearest suitable landfall, a spot still called the Minister's Flag to this day.

I wasn't too many months on the island before I was to discover that the Traills and their legacy was still very much a live issue. From the School Place diaries:

John o' Holland cornered me in the shop to say that the leaflet I had penned on the history of the farm and the big house had been a success. However, in the text I had mentioned that for 14 generations the Traills ruled the island and several other Orkney estates with a firm, some would say severe, hand and that this harsh dynasty, even today, is recalled with dismay by some of the older folk. This was all too much for one lady visitor who, according to John, left a day early after reading the leaflet. It will come as no surprise to learn that her name was Traill. You win some, etc.

In her marvellous pocket history of Papay, Jocelyn Rendall refers in some detail to the colourful Traill sagas. Thomas III, 'The Wicked Laird', was thought to have been in league with the devil and regularly profaned the Sabbath by having the week's work ordered from the steps of the kirk, while George, who built the present Holland, didn't marry until middle age but, says Jocelyn, 'lived a cheerful bachelorhood seducing the girls of Papay and sired innumerable Traill progeny, hence his nickname – "The Parish Bull"'.

Certainly it's true that hardly a month goes by without a new legend of the iniquitous Traills resurfacing in casual conversation. Last century the tenants were ushered into interviews with the laird to find him seated with an unsheathed sword in front of him on the writing table. Menacing or what?

The family clearly believed they owned everything – and everybody – on the island. Apparently, this even extended to driftwood collected along the shore. The islanders were in the habit of hiding the wood beneath stones at the loch's edge for use during the coldest months of winter. The Traills, it seems, got word of this 'deceit' and took their horses plootering through the shallows freeing the trapped timber and ordering it gathered up and taken up the hill to Holland.

Even in death the Traills are closely bound to the story of St Boniface. In the kirkyard their burial ground testifies to odd legends connected with these feudal landlords. One of the Traills is said to have been buried alive – after waking up in his coffin from a cataleptic slumber, his desperate pleadings were ignored by the boys who were humphing the box. It's said that the very ground in which they were laid is cursed and no flower will ever grow there.

Strangely, even in midsummer, when the rest of the yard is strewn with buttercups and daisies, the Traill lair lies choked with weeds. I don't give much credence to the local cynic who whispered that the legend is kept alive by one of the old boys who takes his scythe to the blooms on the Traill plot under cover of 'simmer dim' – the few hours in summer that pass for night in these northern latitudes.

For years I've struggled to find someone with a good word to say for the Traills but have to admit failure.

MAGICAL AND SECRET PLACES

The kirk of St Boniface does have a very special place in Papay's catalogue of unusual sites, but there are other spellbinding spots on the island, places across which the casual visitor is never likely to stumble. Let me take you to just two of my own favourite haunts, both hidden away from the main tracks – Gurgly Geo and the Ha's o' Habrahellya. Both sound as if they've been borrowed from Tolkien but they're real enough.

Gurgly Geo, a narrow cleft which undercuts the rock tables, doesn't even rate a mention on maps of the island. It lies on the west shore below the bird sanctuary at a site where the sandstone edges are pounded and pulverised by the huge force of the sea. The cleft opens up in the middle of a grey flagstone shelf as a distinctive open oval bowl, perhaps 15 feet deep, into which the Atlantic breakers surge. Compressed by the tight channel, the water rushes in and explodes skywards as it strikes the back wall of the bowl. However, it is at the lower states of the tide that the sea-smoothed chamber with its crystal-clear water and floor of first-sized, beautifully turned pebbles, earns its onomatopoeic nickname – given, I have to confess, by the Hewitson clan.

The walls in the lower part of the geo have been deeply undercut. Judging by the flow, these low vaults, perhaps no more than a couple of feet in height, run back some distance under the rock table. As each wave rushes to the rear of the geo and cascades down the polished walls, air is pushed into these dark recesses. The retreating waters then allow the air to escape in a wonderful symphony of gurgles and glurgs, slurps and splashes, to the rumbling, rattling, percussive accompaniment of the turning pebbles. Pure magic. I have listened mesmerised for hours to these wonderful melodies, each wave adding a new bar to nature's melody which has been a-building, without an intermission, for a million or more years. Forget Handel's *Water Music*, here's the real thing.

Across the island, right at the bleak northern tip of the sanctuary, are the Ha's, a much more daunting and awe-inspiring location altogether. This place is so well hidden that the casual visitor would wander past without being aware of its presence. Once a vast cave stood here among the flagstones which slope crazily at 45 degrees into the sea. This cathedral-like place was said to have been almost 80 feet in height. One morning in the middle of this century a lobsterman from the house of Dykeside passed by in his skiff *en route* to the creels. He noticed nothing untoward about the familiar, gloomy cavern. However, on the return leg a few hours later he was astonished to find the roof had collapsed, sending hundreds of tons of rock slipping down the rock terrace and into the sea.

Today only the massive side walls and about 30 feet of the rear of the cave remain. But it's still a wondrous place to behold, accessible only on the driest of days and at the lowest of tides, because there is real danger here. One slip on the seagrass-coated incline and recovery is almost impossible. A teenager drowned not far from this spot, unable to haul himself up the slope and out of the churning surf. Like the flagstones which support it, what remains of the cave leans towards the sea. It's unsettling in the extreme to linger below this great mass of rock. It looms over you as you lean backwards to compensate for the strange angles. Too long in this spot and an odd form of vertigo tinged with claustrophobia can overtake you.

WHAT CHANCE A RELIGIOUS REVIVAL?

The choir is at full strength today – Kathleen o' Skennist, Maggie from Midhoose and Jess from Charleston – and that introductory hymn with a nice scattering of grace notes suggests that Margaret from the post office is in good form on the old harmonium. Sunlight slants through the coloured panes of glass in the arched windows of the west gable on to row after row of empty, dark-varnished pews. Dog-eared Sankey hymn-books coorie in the bench corners, mostly untouched since the last funeral a year or two back.

Decline in church-going has affected Papa Westray as much as the more densely populated south. Nevertheless, between the gospel hall meetings of the brethren up at the north end and the kirk services, more than 30 people regularly attend a religious service and on an island of 70 souls that's pretty good going – well above the national average. Interestingly, the wee kirk has the best record of giving of all the parish churches in Orkney.

In 1991 as the process began to select our new minister (Mary Spowart having left for retirement in Fife), we watched with interest and concern as Foula, our neighbour out here on the Atlantic fringe, put their case for a missionary. Here, although we are still, in a society dominated by the number of car miles you can cover in an hour, considered remote, the problem is not so acute. We are linked with our larger neighbour, Westray, and the normal practice is for the minister, resident on Westray, to make the sea crossing each Sunday (weather permitting) to take afternoon service and perhaps also once a week to make house calls and visit the school.

One of the first Papay ministers whose name is recorded was Allan Hutton, who came to take charge in the 1590s. In 1624, shortly before the arrival of the Traill landlords whose harsh regime also brought a mini agricultural revolution to Papay, Mr Hutton had 64 communicants. By 1993 the latest recruit in that long line, a young minister called Iain MacDonald, was in place. The search for a suitable candidate had taken much, much longer than anticipated. Impressively, *The Orcadian* told us, Iain is the cousin of far-famed lead singer of Runrig, Donnie Munro. Lively, up-tempo services have materialised.

Unfortunately there seems no prospect of a sudden growth in church-going on Papa Westray today. The bulk of the worshippers are older folk. Although we can speculate that on an island with such a long Christian tradition there must have been good and bad times before, it's unlikely that we'll experience a religious revival such as swept Orkney in 1861. It was first reported on the island of Sanday and spread like wildfire through the parishes with 'unrivalled scenes of religious enthusiasm'.

On Mainland, Orkney's rather unimaginatively named largest island, the revival had apparently resulted in a marked decrease in vice – hyperbole was surely applied fairly thickly when we're told, 'strong drink is absolutely given up'. The minister of Papay's St Ann's, the Revd John Peddie, began to notice signs of a revival among his own flock just before the Christmas of 1861. Prayer meetings were being held each evening, lasting up to three hours, and in a letter to *The Orkney Herald* Mr Peddie declared: 'Some are engaged in public prayer at our meetings who have never opened their mouths before in public.' Little children on their way home from school were praying together in boats, on the beach or by the dykeside. In March 1862, the revival exhibited its full-blown symptoms with dozens of Papay folk violently declaring the Lord and even suffering physical collapse.

History does indeed show us that there is a time and a season for everything under heaven, whether it's a religious revival or congregational apathy, conflict with the kirk session or ministry bordering on the eccentric. Should you be in need of any confirmation of this theory then let me introduce you to the Revd George Cochrane, Free Church minister, who flourished (in more ways than one, as we'll see) on Papa Westray in the 1880s. This colourful preacher has been immortalised in the island annals because of his liking for a wee dram and his roving eye which alighted on more than one of the island lassies.

His church was, of course, St Ann's, still the most substantial building on Papay, gifted by the Traill family to the first General Assembly of the Free Church in 1843. In 1900 it became United Free, remaining so until 1929 when it became part of the Church of Scotland. An interesting sideline is the background to the St Ann dedication, the origin of which remains a bit of a mystery. Could there be any truth in the legend that part of the precocious deal struck by the Traills on donating the church was that it should be named after the 'saintly' Ann Traill?

Anyway, back to the redoubtable Revd Cochrane. His behaviour on occasion could be quite outrageous. As that great chronicler of island affairs, John D. Mackay, noted: 'Though a married man, Mr Cochrane was not blind to the charms of the island girls and did not hesitate to use intoxicants not wisely, but too well, especially on festive occasions.' Little wonder that he was soon at loggerheads with the kirk session who were eventually forced to hold alternative services in the adjacent building which at that time served as a church hall but which had been the island school up until 1877. Nowadays this is the Hewitson homestead – School Place.

The minister, quite naturally, was locked out of these breakaway services at School Place but, undaunted, he made his presence felt by shouting abuse through the keyhole and thumping the door during prayers.

Amused by his exploits, I tracked down George's greatest adventure in the now defunct local paper and reported it in our local heritage magazine, *The Orkney View*.

> Perhaps the biggest sensation of his tenure is related to *The Orkney Herald* of May 1889. It's said that Cochrane spread a rumour that one of his deacons, David Cursiter of

Geirbolls, had stolen a leg of pork from the manse. Now, Davie was not about to take this lying down and in a sensational development, which had the island talking for weeks, he sued the Revd Cochrane for £50. The newspaper reported that at this time the Free Church was the only church represented on the isle. Cursiter's case was that the alleged theft was a 'slanderous accusation which had caused much comment and had seriously injured the pursuer in his character, feelings and reputation and in the estimation of his friends and the general public'.

After serious deliberation the sheriff at Kirkwall awarded £10 damages and £3 expenses to Mr Cursiter. Stirring times and no mistake! The minister was advised to apologise to the complainant. Whether he did so, we do not learn.

Eventually, the congregation dwindled to three or four and Mr Cochrane was forced to resign his charge. However, he departed in another characteristic burst of eccentricity, eloping with a Papay girl (a Hewison from Shorehouse, so I'm told) and left his wife behind where she had to be cared for in her dilemma by the kind-hearted islanders.

Small in the greater religious scheme of things we may be these days but we are certainly not forgotten. Far-travelled missionaries regularly visit the gospel hall and a wee piece of history was made in the summer of 1992 when the Moderator of the General Assembly of the Church of Scotland, the Rt Revd Hugh Wyllie, in his full ruff and regalia, arrived on Papay – the first moderatorial visit to the island since the Reformation, as far as we know. During his brief stopover, Margaret of Backaskaill, church organist for the past 36 years, was presented with a long-service award. Said the Moderator: 'Very often people like organists are forgotten for the important part they play in churches.' A few weeks earlier, along the road at Bilbo', I spotted Stuart Gray, one of the island's brethren congregation, busy with his paint brush touching up his yellow 'Prepare to Meet Thy God' slogan on the flagstone roof of his outhouse.

This inspiring motto, prepared for the summer visitors as well as celebrities, we assume, always has the cameras clicking. Stuart has left his three score years and ten well behind, so the precarious repainting at the top of the ladder is likely to bring him closer to his God, long before the fresh-faced backpackers.

SAND-DANCING AND A MINIBROCH

'Come north and see my broch,' Donald White suggested to two visiting French girls. A nice opening line in any circumstance, I think you'll agree. But the Glasgow-born artist, operating in 1991 out of Edinburgh's Stockbridge, who had just completed the first stone fortress to be built on Papa Westray since Christ was a boy, was about to make a startling discovery.

Let Donald tell the tale himself: 'We walked along the shore and out there in the open the conversation, quite naturally, was a bit restrained. But once we got into the central chamber of the broch, the atmosphere relaxed immediately. In no time we were swapping stories and telling risque jokes. There's a tremendous feeling of security in there.' So, it's a fair assumption that our broch-dwelling forebears also enjoyed a bit of a laugh behind those gaunt, sandstone walls. It's somehow comforting to learn that life in those far-off days wasn't all blood and thunder and war sails on the horizon.

This historic insight wasn't the only important revelation resulting from this island's month-long brush with the world of art. When a multi-disciplinary group of artists selected Papay for their project it was because of our remoteness and lack of previous contact with organised art. Whether the artists did indeed grow spiritually from their encounters on the island or whether the islanders ever really got to grips with what they were about, only time will tell. But for a month Morven House, just up the track from School Place, was the cultural capital of Orkney.

Some of the artists, I think, brought fixed ideas, preconceived notions about the nature of the community they were entering, its isolation, lack of sophistication, innocence even. They left, I believe, appreciating that our island is a much more complex organism than they ever imagined and scarcely the 'blank slate' upon which they had hoped to inscribe their signatures. As John David of Sooth-house told the young playwright after a supposedly shocking one-man show staged in the grain loft at Holland, 'I've seen worse than that on the telly.' Disappointment or seal of approval? We're not quite sure.

Their project, which drew support from the Scottish Arts Council and Highlands and Islands Enterprise, was to conduct community-based artistic experiments at Skerray in Sutherland and on Papay. The theme was 'Margins' and a high level of community involvement was reported right enough in Skerray. The real test came, as the artists themselves admitted, on Papa Westray. Here the umbilical cord to artistic endeavour in the sophisticated south was cut. They were on the frontier. For four weeks the island was immersed in what, in the 1960s, we would have called a series of 'happenings'.

Take a typical afternoon. On the sloping beach of the South Wick, Lindsay John, dancer/performer, lies on his back inscribing flowing patterns in the still-wet sand with his arms and legs. In these loops, spirals and arcs, Lindsay sees the common heritage of many races, Celt to Aztec, Maori to Native American. An acre of beach is transformed. Balanced on top of a metal stepladder, award-winning playwright Angus Reid is getting it all down on

video. Loganair over-fly the site and perplexed passengers are reported disembarking from Kirkwall.

A mile north at Neil's Helly the last few stones are being placed within the encircling arms of Donald's minibroch. He is offering a link with our past, but wandering Willie Gray o' Hundland asked the $64,000 question: 'Do folk pay ye tae do this?' In fact, funding from the HIE and SAC offered only what Donald described as 'bed and breakfast money'. The artists may have left spiritually enriched but their pockets won't be bulging.

At the water margin Orkney photographic artist Richard Welsby dives in and out of the surf experimenting with what are poetically described as 'spumeographs', photographs without a camera. Don't ask me to explain this mystery.

Yorkshire artist Miles Richmond was the loner of the party. Bill o' the Links first encountered him early one morning, 'I looked over to the Knowe o' Burland and thought at first one o' the beasts had its legs in the air. But it was Miles humphing his easel up the hill. By the time I'd walked over there he'd painted four yellow lines and spent a lot o' time looking at them. Ah couldna' make it out at all.' At the show of paintings on the final weekend in the grain loft 'gallery', Miles was politely but firmly asked what the hell he was trying to portray.

Folk, frankly, were baffled by his abstract style. He confessed: 'I can be really stupid sometimes. I forget people don't see things the way I do.' Right on, Miles! But the artist was convinced that there's something very special about Papay. 'It has a certain magic, a place where natural forces are concentrated, like Lindisfarne.'

Angus Reid's two plays were originally staged to positive reviews and awards at Edinburgh Festival Fringe. 'Yes, yes,' admitted Angus testily, 'the titles have been a drawback.' 'How to Kill' and 'Trouble with the Dead' were not guaranteed to have the islanders queuing up to be introduced to live professional theatre. The only time the entertainment gets heavy up here is when the visiting country singer launches into 'Old Shep'. Nevertheless, about a dozen people turned out each night.

'The Dead', Angus's shorthand for his second show, was particularly powerful stuff. At one point he dragged a funeral cloth weighed down by dozens of plaster death masks the length of the loft. Papay had never seen the like. Afterwards someone whispered in my ear, 'Ye couldna' take yer eyes off it for a moment . . . but whit was the story?'

So what's the verdict? The artists, I think, set themselves some high, perhaps unrealistically high, targets. It's arguable whether community involvement was, or ever could be, at any sort of worthwhile level, and it remains to be seen whether the visit was a thing of 'lasting value opening the possibility for continuous development of artistic activity' as the organisers hoped.

Have the islanders an increased sense of their past or of their place in the wider scheme of things – both project targets? Unlikely, I think. In the usual way this community operates, everyone wanted to know what the artists were up to but few would confess any real interest in their work. The fact that the team arrived virtually unannounced may help to explain this but I think it may be more fundamental. Our introduction to the arts, avant-garde or otherwise, will be a very gradual one.

The truth is that the artists were on a hiding to nothing as I concluded in a review of the visit:

> You see, we're spoiled up here. The forces of sea and sky combine daily with the ever-engrossing island feuds to provide us with drama and spectacle on an almost Wagnerian scale which our guests could never hope to match. However, what these gentlemen did bring to this little island was a vision of a world beyond the pierhead where ideas and images can be juggled and caressed into the most unlikely forms. As magicians, they are welcome back whenever.

D-DAY REHEARSALS

More than 50 years on, the story of another of the island's dramas can finally be told. The first fatality of the Normandy landings in June 1944, which changed the course of world history, was Mrs Hewison's cow at Shorehouse, Papa Westray. The island's unique role in the preparations for the biggest amphibious landing in military annals reached out across the years to us when Willie Groat unearthed the coastguard log for the period January 1943 to October 1944 from the byre at Kimbland.

For over a year thousands of tons of high-calibre shells whistled in from the horizon to shake our North Hill to its foundations in a little-known dress rehearsal for D-Day. Fighter aircraft came and went, strafing mock targets on the hill.

First indications of an extra-special role for Papay came in a cryptic phone call to the coastguard in April 1943, asking about ownership of the North Hill. The inquirer was told that it was common property, held by all the islanders. Up until then the coastguard work had been fairly routine, even for wartime. The log kept by the six-strong lookout team – Thomas Groat (Quoys), William Groat (Ness), Andrew Groat (Kimbland), Thomas Hourston (Whitelooms), Thomas Drever (Skennist) and Donald Mackay (Mayback) – reported windspeeds, visibility, sea conditions, the activities of passing fishing boats, occasional aircraft sightings and unexploded mines washed ashore.

But by early May it was clear something extraordinary was afoot. Military planners decided that they had a reasonable likeness of the Normandy coastline around Papay's North Hill – completely uninhabited except for the seabirds. On 25 May the old coastguard shed, more a garden hut than a communications centre, was moved south from the highest point on the hill to Hyndgreenie. A Walrus seaplane splashed down in the South Wick and two officers came ashore with a notice-board warning of the shelling and bearing a red alarm flag. In the coming months Papay youngsters were to see this flag as a challenge. Who would be last off the hill before the shells started falling? Their folk would have tanned their hides if they'd known of this mischief.

The day after the flag arrived the exercises began, a destroyer appeared round Noup Head in Westray and launched a two-hour bombardment. The island folk didn't take long to realise that, perhaps ironically, the best vantage point for watching the shelling was from the war memorial on the rise north of Holland. There was no escaping the war for the people of Papay. For the sake of battle-readiness the island must have taken a bigger concentrated pounding, yard for yard, than any other part of the United Kingdom.

By the end of the autumn the log makes it clear that the brave boys of the Papay coastguard were in the thick of the action. Theoretically, the lookout hut, which now sits in Willie's back garden at Kimbland, was beyond the target area but a stark entry written on 7 October reminds us of the ever-present danger: 'Cruiser at practice; one shell passed 300 yards from the hut; two shells passed above us.'

You'll search the official records in vain for a bizarre incident which is now part of the island lore in relation to these troubled times. A codes list used in sending messages to Kirkwall was blown out of the hut by a gust of wind to glide off in the direction of the

Faroes. A search party eventually found the tattered codes on the clifftop at the very northern tip of the island.

Almost imperceptibly the activity of naval and air forces was being stepped up. By Thursday, 10 February 1944, an aircraft carrier, a battleship and four destroyers were sighted at exercise. Mid-April 1944 and the bombardment was intensified, the red flag being raised on a daily basis. Willie o' Kimbland, son of the wartime auxiliary coastguard, recalls a remarkable conversation he had in a naval hospital in the south of England in the mid-1940s. Willie, serving in the Navy, got talking with a sailor in the next bed who was struck dumb when told that Willie hailed from Papa Westray. The rating had been aboard one of the warships at practice around Papay and simply refused to believe anyone could have lived on the island they battered so mercilessly.

Everything seemed to be progressing smoothly until the old coo at Shorehouse was killed. Worse, Mrs Hewison came very close to becoming a victim of what is now confusingly called 'friendly fire'. The shell exploded nearby as she worked in the yard but the blast was carried away from her towards the unfortunate beast. When word got round about this all hell broke loose. The immediate reaction of the authorities was to suggest a complete evacuation of the island but the feeling among the folk on Papay was that if they left their homes they would never be allowed to return. Papa Westray would become an uninhabited bomb range for evermore; St Kilda with shrapnel. Eventually a compromise was reached and people at the northern end of the island went south when an exercise was signalled, sleeping in the school or with friends and family.

By the first week in June there was a sudden lull. The weather on 6 June 1944 was showery on Papay with a force 5 wind out of the nor' west. On the 1200–1600 shift Thomas Groat recorded: 'Liberation forces land today in France at 0700.' The news suddenly made sense of Papa Westray's months of punishment. Before long seabirds returned to the North Hill and now only shallow depressions show where the barrage fell. Most houses have a bomb case decorating a windowsill or garden wall and shrapnel is widely scattered across the bleak headland.

Chapter Three

Raiders of the Last Auk

FLUFFY FLEETS AND STUNNING THE SCARFIE

Are you acquainted with the big gormless bird which occupies a prominent spot at the entrance to the ornithology section of Glasgow's splendid Art Galleries and Museum in Kelvingrove Park? Before we face a seaborne invasion from the museum custodians' union, I should make it clear that this particular bird is a rather scruffy, stuffed specimen of the great auk; a flightless, penguin-like bird hunted to extinction in the first half of the nineteenth century.

There are many features of our beautiful island of Papa Westray of which local people are justly proud but every little community has a few skeletons rattling around in its collective cupboard and it's a sad but inescapable fact that up at the north end the last great auk in the British Isles was killed in 1813. It was battered to death with an oar, and it's no consolation to remind ourselves that the very last great auk of all was done to death by hunters in Iceland in 1844. Around the world there are said to be 80 stuffed specimens of the great auk and 75 eggs – a sad legacy for a species that once numbered many millions. They were large birds, some nearly three feet high, with a black back, white breast and flipper-like wings.

In the seventeenth and eighteenth centuries mass killings of great auks took place at Funk Island off Newfoundland; their meat, eggs and feathers being highly prized. Demand for feathers to fill bedspreads and mattresses also saw widespread slaughter in Scotland and Ireland. When a collector named Bullock came to Orkney in 1812 he wanted the Papay auk – already recognised as the last in the British Isles. To our further shame, its mate had been killed by stoning the previous year. For several hours Bullock pursued the auk in a six-oared boat but the bird, known to the islanders as King Auk, was such a splendid swimmer that he could not be shot.

Eventually, though, he was bludgeoned to death for the collector and subsequently purchased by the British Museum for £15.5s.6d. The Natural History Museum still regards our King Auk as one of their prize possessions. So much so that he is kept in a locked cupboard at Tring. An ignoble end for such a splendid bird. However, don't let's write off King Auk quite as easily as that. During the past few years in an almost mystical manner, his spirit has resurfaced on Papa Westray. By turns he seems to be prodding us into an awareness of the fragile environment in which we live; he has taught a few earnest Fleet Street scribes not to take themselves too seriously, and most recently gave endless hours of enjoyment to the island children who staged a drama about his life and death.

Aided by 27 visiting children – members of the Orkney Field Club – local youngsters erected a stone cairn up at Fowl Craig, the barren cliff where the last auk had his perch. Inside the cairn, anchored on the blustery clifftop, the children left a time capsule with a poignant message for future generations: 'We wish there was still a great auk to see. We hope that people won't have to build more cairns like this to remember things we see alive now. We humans gave a name to this bird, now only the name is left. If you who are reading this message are not human, remember us with kindness as we remember the great auk.' Well said, the wee ones!

A year or two earlier the auk reappeared in much more bizarre circumstances. A whisky company decided to brighten up our lives by setting modern daredevils the ultimate challenge, and the bold lads of the Findhorn yacht club rose to the occasion by suggesting an expedition to the wilds of Papay in search of the last great auk. Occasional stories had been filtering south, or so it was claimed by the intrepid mariners, that King Auk (or at least a descendant) still survived in the vast caves at the Craig where the waves surge back into the echoing darkness.

Whether these stories were encouraged by islanders looking for some extra visitors or whether it was simply a piece of imaginative and wishful thinking, matters not; we'd like to believe these ungainly birds might just have survived. It was a nice idea, a bit of fun, and the expedition was on. A party of journalists joined the adventurers for a day or two on Papa Westray and what resulted was nothing short of farce. It rained non-stop. The cynical – some would say realistic – reporters were content to enjoy the facilities at the guest-house, presumably having checked to ensure that the chances of finding the great auk were on the narrow side of non-existent. However, some of the Fleet Street team were not amused.

Then, when they were summoned through a rainstorm to the beach at Moclett to watch a papier-mâché auk dance unconvincingly on the edge of the surf, it was the last straw. The party returned home in disarray; one London columnist even felt compelled to describe in a long and bitter article how these hard-bitten newshounds had been conned into thinking the auk was still alive. Ah, well.

For months the auk was my constant companion in the little garret where I work at my writing. Here I put together the thoughts of the schoolchildren of the island and moulded them into a play titled 'Raiders of the Last Auk'. No' bad, eh? It tells the story of the last days of the auk and puts over a gentle environmental message. His final hours, translated into a dramatic setting, remain indescribably sad. The children, I think, have shared in the moving realisation that he will never return to the crags and can now see the auk in the context of an earth plagued by blooming algae, global warming, vanishing forests and man's greedy carelessness with the natural world.

From time to time, working at the creels a hundred yards or so from the slippery sandstone perch where the auk had his roost (fifth cave along if you're interested), I could swear I've seen a big black shape on the rock. Light can be very deceiving in the shadow of these cliffs and common sense tells me it's an oversize, overweight scarfie. King Auk may be gone from Papa Westray and the planet forever but if I've got any say in the matter, he'll never be forgotten.

You are conscious of birdlife everywhere on the island whether it's a huge backie with a metre wingspan flapping menacingly above the dog's bowl in the yard in search of scraps or the snipe dumped at the back door as a morning offering by our regiment of marauding cats. Hardly a day goes by without an entry in the School Place diaries on an ornithological note:

> Life and death, the never-ending cycle, can intrude even into early morning walks to the Old Pier with the dog. This morning I almost stood on a sparrow which refused to move from the road beyond Daybreak. It soon became apparent

that its mate had flown into a passing vehicle and lay dead at the verge. How swiftly this little explosion of life must have been snuffed out.

But new beginnings are everywhere. Below Skennist the first of the eider ducklings are out and about. They bob along in single file behind mum and are an entertainment to watch as they dip up and down practising their feeding technique; so fluffy and buoyant that they have terrible problems getting beneath the surface.

Again, during the worst of the winter of 1988–89:

Over at the Links to feed the horses we came across an injured grey heron (probably swept into the telephone wires in yesterday's blizzard). Our first inclination was to carry the bird to shelter and try to care for it. Then all the practical difficulties began to make themselves obvious – we have no outbuildings to speak of, no reliable supply of fresh fish. What trauma this free spirit might undergo being surrounded by people and bumped along in a Land Rover, God only knows. Should we try to get him into Kirkwall; more problems. The bird was silver grey and at close quarters was larger than I would have expected with a bright yellow beak and beautiful penetrating eyes; we postponed a decision and when we returned after giving hay to the horses, it was gone. Simply exhaustion? Perhaps.

Our feathered friends are liable to pop up just about anywhere on the isle, as Morag and I were to discover when we headed for Mary's Geo at the south end of the island with an old settee, chairs and assorted bric-a-brac for dumping – the product of our half-yearly clear-out at School Place. The cleft, the island's official rubbish tip, was quite full. In fact, a good-going storm was needed. Although the sea literally did a smashing job during the winter, serious consideration was then being given to a more efficient and environmentally friendly way of disposing of our refuse.

That particular afternoon one seabird certainly agreed on the need for improvement. The light metal tube from our old vacuum cleaner was lobbed into the echoing hole and a crash was followed by squawks as a scarfie emerged at a fast rate of knots and made for the open sea. Obviously, the bird had been poking around in search of scraps when this alien object plunged out of the heavens.

The bird made plenty of noise and I surmised that it was not injured, merely offended.

By 1994 household rubbish collected in the skip on the back of Alex's tractor was being taken into Kirkwall weekly by steamer, old cars and defunct agricultural equipment are shipped out every year or two and Mary's Geo is already the haunt of seabirds again, unmenaced by falling household appliances.

Strictly as an amateur, you understand (I've no ambitions to be a twitcher), I have come to recognise most of the island birds during my years here but one of the most moving sights is the geese heading south at the end of the summer. One morning while atop a ladder picking the west wall at Daybreak in preparation for harling, a skene of noisily honking geese appeared out of the north – about 50 birds in a splendidly formed 'v', exchanging leadership as they went and pressing on south over the loch. Didn't I end up in a heap on the grass, having peered too far round the gable to watch them go!

THE BLETHERING PIG

There's an extra snout in the teatime trough at School Place these days. Clarissa, having eaten her fill, settles down in front of the fire, trotters outstretched, and grunts contentedly. Doubtless she'll be dreaming of some backyard in Hanoi. And out in the byre, last time I looked, old antenna ears, Edward the donkey, who stares out at the world from beneath carpeted eyebrows, slumbers. In his reverie he surely wanders the dusty slopes of the Sierra Nevada. A cosmopolitan menagerie and no mistake.

Certainly I like to cultivate a mildly eccentric Doctor Dolittle image, although it must be said that it is daughter Katy who does most of the talking to the animals and, more importantly, the muckin' oot. However, the growth of our extended family of animals seems to have gained a sort of momentum of its own in recent years, and I blame the festive season. A few weeks before Christmas, when Morag starts to scan the small ads in *The Orcadian* and talks about a shopping trip to the town in the steamer, the alarm bells start to sound. Next year I must remember to lock her in the goat shed and throw away the key.

Appearance of a livestock item for School Place on the steamer manifest always causes a stir amongst the stevedores at the pier. There are knowing smiles as the crate is unloaded. First there was

Solo, a half-Arab, half-Highland garron, a powerful horsey mix; then the pig; and the donkey and the goats and, well, need I go on? These newcomers joined our flock of sheep, Sam the Alsatian, the other horses, Niry and Rhu, and a dozen assorted cats.

The pot belly, so I'm told, has become the latest trendy pet – all the rage around the Manhattan penthouses. I can see why. Clarissa runs to meet you, is easily house trained, enjoys a wee walk and has a range of grunts which makes you think you should be trying to arrange classes in Pot Belly so you can enjoy a blether. *chat*

But this is not Manhattan, nor yet suburbia. Pigs have never been pets, pampered or otherwise, out here. Innocently, Clarissa snorts her greeting to passers-by on the track or halts her rooting among the dockens to pose theatrically for a group of visitors hanging over the kirk dyke with their cameras, unaware that the fate of her race hereabouts was to be eaten or shipped. To have one as a friend is to stray around the margins of insanity.

The slaughtering of pigs on Papay followed a well-established pattern. Brought in as piglets from Westray, the animals were fattened up and killed at the start of winter – sticking a knife in them and letting them run around a bit seems to have been the formula. Salted, the pork provided variety in the diet during the long, dark days. As you wander the island every derelict house seems to have a broken-down pigsty at the bottom of the yard.

Temporary escape from the knife might be achieved if the pigs were shipped by steamer to the mart in Kirkwall, providing a few precious extra pennies. Islanders recall with a smile, even today, how the merchant at Backaskaill a century ago would use the broad back of the most convenient pig as his writing desk while he put together his order as they were being rowed over the surf to meet the steamer.

NO DONKEYS HERE, SIR

But what of Edward? I consulted the island sages in an attempt to track down the last member of the donkey family to grace these green acres. I'm afraid even old Johnny from North Rendall, whose memory encompasses most of this century, was stumped. However, I did turn up one lovely anecdote about an island doctor who really thought he'd encountered an island donkey.

In an article for the *Sunday Gleaner* in Kingston, Jamaica, I related the tale:

This talented GP, who doubled occasionally as a vet, had not yet become tuned to the local dialect. One day he had a visit from a farmer from the north end who wanted medicine for his ailing daughter. Shortly after his departure the doctor mentioned to someone that he had been surprised to learn that there was a donkey on the island. 'No donkey here, sir,' he was told and asked to explain. The farmer wanted a powerful potion, said the doctor, for his 'small ass'. Aghast, the doctor was told he had been asked for medicine for a 'sma' lass'! A speedy trip north avoided catastrophe.

Tommy of Clestrain, a wee house near the end of the north road, is said to have been the owner of an old white pony, the most stubborn piece of horseflesh ever to set hoof on Papay in the middle years of this century. Old Tommy's answer to this obstinacy was to rig up a block and tackle on the cart which allowed him to haul the old nag in whichever direction he wanted to go. Although Tommy was not thought to have been an animal rights campaigner, he was certainly one of Papay's many mild eccentrics.

Tommy would buy a hundredweight of sweeties at a time, usually the famous multi-coloured oddfellows and dish them out in one-pound bags to all and sundry. He owned a three-wheeler bike which made him a bit of a mobile celebrity as he moved about the island. Once, he failed to take the sharp bend at the New Houses (now the shop/guest-house) and overturned, cutting his head. The doc stitched him up but when the time came for the removal of the stitches Tommy decided on a do-it-yourself job. He used an old pair of pliers to haul out the stitches and when he couldn't get the last one to budge, he went to a neighbour and, to the man's astonishment, handed him the rusty pliers to complete the job.

In the 1870s, during the construction of the new school, the islanders had their first opportunity to see a new-fangled gadget called the bicycle which had been brought out to Papay by Mr Kirkness, the builder, on the steamer. One afternoon the old lady from Roadside arrived in a right tizzy at her neighbours'. When she got her breath back she said she had seen the devil speeding doon the road on wheels but 'he hid the face o' auld Kirkness'.

Anyway, from obstinate cuddies [ponies] we move to the amazing microscopic world of insects. Papa Westray is teeming with activity, summer and winter. An unexpectedly sunny and warm November day brought one of the most spectacular sights I've been privileged to witness since venturing to this island – and there have been many.

Crossing the field west of the roofless farm of Sunnybraes, I was suddenly aware that a large part of the Deichens, a boggy piece fenced off to give the marsh birds sanctuary, was undulating, shimmering like a golden pond. In fact, an area covering some three acres was cloaked in a vast diaphanous web, creeping right over the dyke in front of me and progressing across the field in which I was standing from docken stalk to tuft of grass. The whole sheet moved gently in the breeze, replete with ripples and waves, and the sun, as it dipped below the hill, glinted across this splendid piece of insect engineering. On closer inspection I could see an infinity of tiny money spiders busily engaged in extending and strengthening the structure.

Each little worker on this incredible building site was going about certain of their task – no conflict or doubling up on jobs. The web was literally growing before my eyes. This, I reckoned, was no hunting expedition but some instinctive territorial expansion on an enormous scale. An hour later, it only took the slightest of showers and a modest evening breeze to put paid to the miracle of the Well Park.

Such fragility of the environment, whether it be our fractured sandstone, our long-lost auk or the vanishing web, is a constant cause for concern. I recounted a strange nightmare in an article in 1991. In retrospect, if we're taking a pessimistic line, we might even call it a premonition:

> It was only a dream after all. Too outlandish and far-fetched to worry about. Crowds of tourists streaming back to meet the steamer. Down the hill from Sheepheight and round the arc of the bay they came, like the Philistine horde with their plunder. All wore a satisfied grin and their rucksacks, holdalls and suitcases were stuffed to overflowing with clumps of our precious island flower, the Primula Scotica, Papa Westray's pride and joy. One lady was even wearing a string in her hair. The dream was fast becoming a nightmare; trailer after trailer filled with the primrose trundling down the Sandy Road.

What a relief when a new day and a *pet* caddie lamb bleating for her breakfast dragged me from that troubled sleep into the workaday world. At the time I had absolutely no doubt what had prompted this unsettling dream. For weeks I'd been reading with growing alarm of how our Highlands and Islands have become a target for wildflower thieves (£30 is the going rate for a water lily, for example). These yobs find a lucrative market in the south for their spoils in the same way that their egg-thieving counterparts have done for decades. Organised crime of this bizarre botanical character has not yet reached Papa Westray – or Orkney for that matter – as far as we know, but in the past couple of years there have been worrying signs, indicators that the plundering time may not be far removed.

Primula Scotica, of which Orcadians generally are justly proud, is found in Orkney, Caithness and Sutherland – and nowhere else in the world. It is the most delicate of plants, seldom reaching five centimetres in height; a stunning purple flower with a yellow heart. It's most at home on the grassy clifftops where compact colonies can be found braving the gales. When I first heard tell of the Scots primrose, my confidante, singing its praises, added the throwaway line that it had probably survived the last Ice Age by nestling in ice-free pockets among the huge glaciers which covered Scotland. Alas, the number of sites where the primula is found have probably halved since the Second World War, although a series of mild winters has meant that individual colonies are blossoming. The Primula Scotica is one of 16 flowering plants which occur only in the British Isles.

The main concern among plant experts is the disappearance of the very special habitats in which the plant thrives. Too late for many colonies it was discovered some years back that the use of slag or shellfish waste as fertiliser quickly eliminated the primrose. At the 1992 Chelsea Flower Show the primula featured as part of the theme 'Glorious Scotland'. These plants, which had thousands of weekend gardeners entranced, are now being cultivated by nurserymen. This in itself has caused a bit of a stir among Orkney's flower people. The commercial availability of the primrose, they fear, is at best a distraction from the main issue of saving the habitats but is also an incentive to folk to come here and help themselves to the little beauty, free of charge. The truth is – for any would-be primrose pirates – our plants never survive long away from their home ground. The test-tube primrose is obviously here to stay but there is no substitute for conservation of the plant in the wild.

Every so often stories do the rounds in Orkney which give some idea of the growing pressure our wild flowers are under. For example, a busload of German tourists were seen on Orkney Mainland digging up clumps of thrift. Here on Papay we have our own horror story. A visitor on a guided tour of the North Hill (a site of Special Scientific Interest) was shown an interesting orchid and, as the party moved on, he produced a machete-like knife and started to dig up the specimen. During a recent summer on Hoy there was a mysterious rash of wooden stakes, plant markers it seemed. Strangers were sighted digging up plants. Scientific expedition or commercial raid, this secrecy prompted one islander to start using the stakes for kindlin'.

This incident highlights the dilemma. Should the primrose locations be kept secret or should people be able to visit, perhaps with some sensible restrictions on access. I'm sure here on Papay we'd argue for the latter. You've simply got to trust people. We also have to be realistic. Anyone wishing to plunder our primula colony would have no trouble locating the site, even on the expanse of the North Hill. Hundreds have already seen the plant on the heath. Word is well and truly out. In that case we should be ready with our own measures to ensure the plant's survival.

When Rab McNab, a Papay immigrant from Lanarkshire, left the army to settle here I don't reckon he ever imagined he would be toting a firearm in earnest again, except perhaps to keep rabbits at bay or to down a few clay pigeons. At the moment he's somewhere off Rockall at the fishing but I'm seriously considering putting his name forward as the ideal man to carry out North Hill security duties. The man fae Holytown would give the botanical bandits plenty to think about. But, then again, perhaps that's taking things too far. After all, it was only a dream.

ORCAS AND BLASTED BUGS

Perched in the cab of his roosty red tractor on yet another grand, even glorious, morning, Bill o' the Links scanned the field of Sunnybraes, master of the wee bit he surveyed; he was thinking hard. There's no rushing the sage of the east shore when he's in one of his contemplative moods, ask a wheen of radio reporters and writers who've tried to probe his innermost thoughts.

So, reversing my baseball cap, I propped one foot on his front tyre and followed the cotton-wool vapour trail of the jet crossing the deep blue arc of the sky from south to north. I'd just about worked out that the airliner with the miles-high club munching their breakfast rolls must be heading over the North Pole for Tokyo, when at last the oracle spake.

Pushing his bunnet to the back of his head and scratching his broo, Bill concluded: 'Yes, best summer in 40 years, no doubt about

it.' We had been discussing the marvellous season of growth on the island before he went into his meditative mode and now the sage, having scrolled through the memory banks, had rubber-stamped what the islanders had suspected for weeks. It was a record-breaking summer – officially.

Normally, here on the lip of the Atlantic, we count ourselves blessed if May and June are pleasant but for the past few years it was almost a weary succession of sunny days from April right through to September. Any rain fell considerably at night and puddles on the track evaporated as the daytime sunshine transformed the School Place back-lot into an Amazonian forest – beanstalks reaching for the stratosphere, onions the size of footballs, and turnips, well, our neeps were so splendid it would almost gar ye greet.

Most summers there is something memorable on the wildlife front but 1994 was just that little bit special. We were visited by two unfamiliar species of beastie which couldn't really have been much further apart on the physical scale.

At the microscopic level it was the bug E Coli, a tiny organism which thrives in nasty places and which found its way into our drinking water. It was unquestionably Papay's most unwelcome guest in many a long year. Tests betrayed its presence after it had somehow found its way into the water from the artesian well which feeds the guest-house, school and the Hewitson household among others. Successive chlorinations left us feeling internally cleansed but failed to eradicate the wee buggers. Boiling water became second nature and sales of bottled water up at the shop must have quadrupled. The water was eventually given the all-clear after the installation of ultra-violet lamps at the wellhead had chased away the wee coli.

In the big league, however, came the orcas, brief but spectacular passers-by. Throughout the islands during the summer there had been excitement over the appearance of a pod of killer whales among the bays and sounds. Most sightings for the privileged few were around Mainland shore but, lo and behold, one late summer day, as Bobby from the shop took a party of day-trippers up the North Hill, they appeared close in below the cliffs at Fowl Craig, harrying the seals.

Everyone was suitably stunned but one visitor had his video camera to hand and these magnificent creatures – a dozen whales, adults and calves – sliced through the water, giving him some of the most memorable holiday footage imaginable.

Certainly there are times out here when we humans feel very much like guests in a kingdom that truly belongs to the birds and the beasts. This not only occurs when Jenny and Rebecca escape from the manse field and are discovered munching old Stuart Gray's much-cared-for vegetables at Bilbo' or when a herd of cows from the farm of Holland go walkabout in the school yard, nor yet when Sam our Alsatian, oblivious to our commands, takes off across the marsh at Hookin' in pursuit of a rabbit. You sense it through day-to-day events. Crossing by boat to school on Westray, my children were soon on nodding terms with the local porpoises. It's that sort of place, but the balance is very delicate.

Take the summer of 1991. As always, the May fogbanks rolled in across the North Sound. Down at the pier the boys waited with their cattle for the steamer to emerge from the gloom when someone picked out a familiar high-pitched screech, then another and another. Up on the tattielands coastguard Jim Davidson stopped the engine of his tractor and listened. Across the Links at Charleston old Jess halted in the yard and looked skyward. The whole island knew something was afoot. Soon the air would be filled with a squawking symphony – the cries from the vanguard of a great, feathered air force sweeping in over the New Pier. The Arctic terns were returning.

That year we had awaited the sudden, theatrical return of our world-famous colony – a signal for the start of the short Orcadian summer – with more than the usual anxiety. We watched as the birds settled on the North Hill sanctuary and the other beautiful but deserted corners of the island, returning, incredibly, to the same clump of windswept grass where they were born and where they will raise their own chicks. Our concern centred on the fact that during the previous two summers the colony of some 5,500 pairs managed, due mainly to bad weather and predation, to raise only *two* chicks. A unique bond between island and bird was threatened.

Since before the Vikings hauled their longships ashore in the South Wick a thousand years ago, the terns have, according to a local tradition that has proved uncannily accurate, arrived on the first foggy day in the second week in May. After they left in that summer of 1991 I was pleased to report the elements had been kinder and the terns departed with a nursery of several hundred healthy chicks. Further improvement was noted the following year with Sean the birdie man anticipating up to 600 chicks. For an expectant father with these sorts of numbers in mind he looked remarkably calm on it! The immediate crisis seemed to be over.

The story of the Arctic tern is an astonishing one, especially for a city dweller who, up until the age of 16, thought the only birds in the world were sparrows and pigeons. The tern is a delicate little bird, weighing in at just a few ounces, with its black head, blood-red bill, grey-white plumage, distinctive forked tail and almost transparent wings. Each year it makes an amazing round trip of more than 14,000 miles between the South Atlantic and Papay, and for a few short summer weeks the great, grassy bowls around our North Hill are filled with noise and excitement as nesting gets under way.

Before the words 'conservation' or 'protected species' were ever heard some island folk used to plunder the nests on the North Hill; it was almost a Papay tradition among the youngsters, who had to be cunning because not everyone smiled on this pastime. The boys would wear big, skipped caps in those days and the older folk remember how quite a few of the delicate tern eggs could be stored under the skip. They were said to be sweet and flavoursome but it took several to make a decent mouthful.

One of the bravest of the few adult egg collectors was a chap who stood six foot six inches in his stocking soles and made an easy target for the dive-bombing terns. Legend has it he needed 16 eggs to make a meal.

For my American audience, this is how I described the emotional departure of the terns:

> After a few brief weeks on Papay, through long days and nights that are never truly dark, the terns leave, just as suddenly and dramatically as they arrived. A whirr of wings over the taing and they're gone. This year I was out after lobster on an August evening when the last of the squadron departed. They danced towards us as we splashed among the creel ropes, circling the boat, dipping low over the swell and hanging in the air in the last aerial ballet of the season. Fanciful, I suppose, but as they peeled off across the Sound towards the cliffs of Eday on the first leg of their journey to the bottom of the world, I wondered if they had stopped off for a moment to say goodbye. More likely they were after bait scraps – but you never know.

Whether the omnipresence of the natural world played a part we can only guess but Lindsey, our eldest daughter, is now studying zoology at Glasgow University and Katy moves towards the end of her secondary education determined also to be involved with animals. Opportunities to learn, to get in tune with the natural world, were always available, and some bizarre little cameos come to mind. I recorded one such in the School Place diaries:

> A team of Jehovah's Witnesses appeared off the boat this morning and a cheery couple eventually arrived at the back door. In bright sunshine we chatted about Judgement Day, the weather and watched the antics of a young sparrowhawk who has made the area around the house his temporary home. He hangs precariously on the phone wires or rocks to and fro atop the telegraph poles before launching off into his erratic, swooping flight. He has landed more than once on the track but our sunbathing cats don't know what to make of him. I think they know instinctively that he would be a different proposition from a snipe or blackbird.
>
> The Witnesses bade farewell when Katy asked if they would like to help muck out the goat shed!

Along with the seals and the terns, puffins are invariably on the 'must-see' list for visitors to the island. Alas, there are usually only a handful of pairs nesting up near Fowl Craig so a sighting is never guaranteed. However, on a trip to Westray I took an old friend, Dave Mathie, along the cliffs to the Castle of Burrian, a precipitous rock stack and site of an early Christian hermitage. Hundreds of puffins were in residence, rafts of birds clearly seen on the offshore swell and scores were popping in and out of their burrows on the stack itself. They really are the most inquisitive of birds and we got within a few feet of one chap who seemed determined to stare us out. David's camera was on overdrive.

NEW FRIENDS/LONG MEMORIES

A secret ambition which up until now I've only whispered to the breeze came a step nearer realisation, thanks to the unpredictable habits of my old armour-plated adversary, the North Atlantic lobster. Since I regard you all, rightly or wrongly, as friends and fellow conservationists at heart, I can surely let you in on my dream that one wonderful day I'll feed the seals of Papa Westray with fishy morsels, by hand.

There were times a few years ago, of course, when there were serious doubts about whether there would be any seals in the azure waters and secret shoals beyond the Old Pier to develop a relationship with. The virus which killed 3,000 selkies threatened our colony of grey and common seals, and daily we watched with concern for the coughing and spluttering and lazy reluctance to take to the water which marked out victims of this horrible illness. It's pleasing to report that we escaped more or less unscathed.

Credit for bringing us so much closer, physically and spiritually, to the seals must, however, go to the lobster, crusty old *Homarus Vulgaris*, the lad who adorns the posh dinner tables of the Parisian boulevards.

The gently sloping west side of the Holm, our calf island, is at first glance a barren and uninviting place. But in comparison with the east-facing flank of the isle, with its jagged cliffs and surf-pounded geos, this is a sheltered and peaceful location. Within the crooked finger of Sooth Croo, with its sandy, crescent beach, we had occasionally left a few creels. You might find the odd lobster on a solo outing wandering into the creel but they never gathered there, in our experience, in any significant numbers.

Early in the season we had tried all the familiar spots at Surhoose Taing, Weelie's Taing, below Cott, at Alskar, in the Bay of Burland, at Mill Point; we even ventured a shoot below the cliffs at Fowl Craig. We toyed with the South Craig but memories of losing creels there to an unexpected summer storm were fresh and kept us out of that tempting little corner.

Rab o' Windywalls, Nurse Fiona's hubbie, who was off at the deep-sea fishing with one of the Westray boats, offered us some of his steel creels for the summer and they worked well. Our normal creels are rectangular and wooden with a bow-shaped top. Sturdy brutes, they are weighted with concrete or a slab of sandstone. One or two eyes in the net allow the lobster and other marine dwellers to enter and approach the bait which is suspended on a string in the heart of the creel. This type of trap only came into use on Orkney in the early 1800s; before that a circular device, like a bicycle wheel, which was lowered into the water and whipped up to the surface when a lob was seen to jump aboard, was in widespread use.

But back to business. The black-enamelled bastions of the deep were coming along at a steady, if unspectacular, rate. Early on the partans were plentiful and it was a pleasant nuisance to have those big, pink lads skulking among the stowed creels, pincers poised, ready to make a leap for freedom aboard a spiralling, seabound rope. But the lobster was our principal target and as June moved into July we had tried most of the permutations with our 50-odd creels without the return we had hoped and planned for. That's when we chanced a line on the west side of the Holm, in the shadow of the chambered tomb, down past the sandstone shelves and into the shelter of Sooth Croo.

The 20 creels were well spaced and as close in to shore as we dared. At low tide we were dodging and fast-revving among the weed-covered rocks, lifting creels in a variety of unorthodox styles from water which often looked shallow enough to paddle in. A severe test for yours truly, the fastest wet ropeman in the north isles. At low tides we were perilously close to grounding but faint heart never won a lobster and, as always in fishing – as in life, I suppose – the return is commensurate with the risk.

The Holm that year was simply a revelation. It was good to us, producing fair-sized lobsters when other grounds let us down. An encouraging sign was the numbers just under size which we returned to the deep. On the Eastern Seaboard of the States they've taken this a step further and are even returning the berried females as a conservation measure. Although lobsters are basically home-loving creatures they can travel many kilometres away from their native ground. What dictates these movements, water temperature, light or dark, feeding conditions, tidal factors, is part of a greater mystery. Whatever the reasons, the Holm had suddenly become a popular hang-out for the lobsters and their presence in turn meant that at least once daily we were in among the seals who cherish the tranquillity of this desert island.

At first they were nervous at the arrival of the *Valkyr* and in a splashing panic young and old alike took to the water, the little ones bumping along the shingle before sliding into the surf and dipping below the waves. Then, after a week or so, only a few of the more nervous specimens would make that mad dash. The others relaxed and scratched happily in the sun, keeping one eye on us from their rocky perch 30 or 40 feet away as we hauled, rebaited and gently lowered the creels back into the transparent water, watching them settle on the bottom, a couple of fathoms below. Dark shadows darting below the boat let us know that the seals were keeping an eye on our activities both above and below the surface. Another few weeks and the seals, who we were beginning to recognise as individuals, swam out to meet us as we rounded Cairn Heid. They dived around us, ever more daring, ever closer to the boat.

This is how I described our growing friendship with the seals for readers of *The Inverness Courier*:

> There was the little fellow with the gammy flipper, old grandpa with the big moustaches and the grumpy expression, the tiny white pup who was always last in the water and mum with her angelic face and elegant, unhurried swimming action. Now, as we work, they lie contentedly or play around the creel ropes. I suppose they come regularly within ten feet of the boat, a great achievement in itself. We've offered mackerel scraps but they inevitably give us that faraway, knowing look and slip beneath the swell.

It's as if the selkies were telling us: 'Have patience, give us a chance to get to know you.' And, of course, they're right. How quickly we humans forget the Orkney seal cull. Perhaps my dream will be fulfilled next year. Perhaps.

Geirbolls, recently renovated and home now to a settler family, was a collection of ramshackle buildings on the road down to the west shore, a perfect set for anyone trying to recreate the squalor of a medieval Scottish village. Incongruously in the derelict front room of the old house sat an antique juke-box and a pool table. The proprietor had an ambitious plan to transform the place into Papay's hottest night-spot but, like a lot of ideas I've heard mention hereabouts, it never quite came to fruition. Witness the 'in the public' plan for the community to band together and buy the Brent Spar platform and use it as an offshore floating casino.

I digress. It was at Geirbolls, within the arm of the treb-dyke, an ancient land boundary which cuts across the centre of Papa Westray, amongst the half-buried farm equipment, head-high dockens, swaying nettle forests, roofless sheds and Alice's predator chickens that we stabled Katy's horse, Solo, in preparation for the birth of her foal. Solo had gone off to the stallion in Elgin and, according to despatches, after violently rejecting his initial amorous advances, settled to the job in hand.

On her return we began crossing off dates on the calendar, doing all sorts of complex calculations and watching the phases of the moon in anticipation of the birth of the first foal on Papay for a decade or more. Geirbolls had to be made passably wind and watertight. Cracks between the heavy sandstone roofing slabs were filled with cement; big, gusty holes in the west wall were plugged with old copies of *The Herald* (a perfect windbreak, as it happens); and generations of compacted sharn were scraped from the flagstone floor until the place was looking magnificent – well, much improved.

Eventually, as the worst of the winter arrived from the west, great battlements of cloud towering out in the Atlantic, we separated Solo from her equine pals, Niry and Rhu, up at our 10-acre field. No place for the boys when Solo, a flighty individual at the best of times, was engaged in such important business. Companionship for Solo during her confinement came in the decrepit form of Champion, North Rendall's old white sheltie. Mostly, Solo treated him with studied contempt and the occasional impatient nip but, if he happened to stagger away through the ruined buildings out of sight as she overnighted in the stable, there would be a helluva fuss. For his part Champion went his unhurried way, totally unconcerned about his role as custodian, contentedly chewing the long grass and sheltering from the storm beside the chickens in the dripping outhouses, generously sharing his nightly neep with the flock.

Mucking out became a daily routine as did feeding Solo with a basinful of magic oats-and-barley mix to build up the mare as she progressed through her pregnancy. Then there was the udder controversy. As Solo grew plumper it became a constant source of amazement to islanders accustomed to seeing enormous cow udders that the horse should be sporting what can only be described as a streamline version. 'It'll be a while yet before there's milk,' we were told by the island sages. They were still saying that the day before the birth.

Interminable – that's how the pregnancy seemed – 11 months felt like 11 years. As the big day neared, Morag and I began to make regular post-midnight trips down to Geirbolls to ensure she was safe and secure. A stack of stable management books on the kitchen table told us that chances of actually witnessing the birth were slim. The horse would pick her own time and most likely look for a bit of privacy. The books, of course, proved correct. One drizzly Saturday afternoon Bobby o' Whitehowe arrived at the front door in his rust-eaten yet immortal Daihatsu van to tell us in the calm, collected way that Orcadians have when speaking about everything from the price of beans to the collapse of civilisation that there was action down the road. Pressed a little further, he admitted, with a gleam in his eye, 'Yas, the foal's there noo.'

We all piled into the van and sure enough, in the middle of the meadow below the telephone exchange, mother and newly arrived daughter were getting to know each other, the wee one drinking in her surroundings and making preliminary forays in search of mum's milk. Once she sorted out the front from the back, the milk bar opened for business.

The foal was the same lovely soft-brown colour as her mother and was, frankly, all legs. She was soon away exploring the field and, within a few hours, was sprinting up and down like a filly preparing for the 1,000 Guineas, spinning at the far wall, as often as not ending up head over heels. Books suggest that this early activity relates to an ancient need to escape predators. Maybe so, but you also get the strong feeling she was glad to be alive. It's a wee touch ironic that the girls decided to call the foal Eclipse because she was born in the week of that unusual solar event. Far from casting a shadow over the land she brought a burst of bouncy sunshine into the island's long, dark winter.

MURDER IN THE MAYBO' MARSH

A less happy tale is to be told across the island at the marsh o' Maybo', with its half-submerged fence posts, waving grasses and mysterious mound. It is a lonely and, since a couple of summers ago, a gey sinister place. Within a few yards of Tommy's caravan, shielded from the gales by breeze blocks like some lonely outpost on a forgotten frontier, a foul murder was committed and the victim, horror of horrors, was dumped in Tommy's bedroom. If you promise not to shop us to the animal rights heavy mob, I'll tell you the sorry tale.

A bit of background might be useful. Did you know that the corncrake, once commonly found throughout Scotland, is one of 24 species of bird listed as being of global conservation concern. In Scotland they are now restricted to the western mainland, the Western Isles – and Orkney. So anxious are the conservationists to halt the decline that farmers are being offered grants to leave the cutting of hay meadows until August and are encouraged to cut from the centre so that the birds are chased outwards to the field edges. Nowadays, however, silage is cut early and often twice yearly. In the past 25 years breeding males throughout the UK have dwindled from 3,000 to 448. Sorry, as you were. After the incident at Maybo', you'd better make that 447.

The shyest of creatures, the corncrake arrives from Africa in the spring and is rarely seen. Counting the males is done by identifying their rasping two-syllable 'krek-krek' which has been compared to a comb being grated over the striking surface of a matchbox.

I first heard the corncrake one tranquil summer evening here on Papa Westray when I was showing an American journalist round the kirkyard. Suddenly, sounding out across the field from the direction of Kimbland came the distinctive call. Our visitor had been all over Scotland and this was also the first time he had heard the strange sound. The siren song of the mermaid could not have been more enchanting.

For the past few summers one or two corncrakes have been identified here on the island and I heard at least one of them on my daily hikes, mainly in the rough grass shoreside of the farm at Skennist. The corncrake at Maybo' marsh fell victim to Jack, Tommy's black cat, who returned from one of his nightly patrols beside the reed beds with a unique trophy.

Says Tommy: 'I was sound asleep when the cat brought the bird up on to the bed and dumped it on my pillow. I switched on the flashlight and I knew right away it was a corncrake. It was a shame, yes, but the cat looked so proud o' himsel'.

'The bird was smaller than I remember. In my young days I saw them many a time running in and out of the hay. At that time they just seemed to be everywhere. Of course, in those days harvesting was done at a slower pace and the birds got a chance to fly away. You'd sometimes see them rising straight up at the last moment as the harvester reached them.'

Jack comes in and out of the caravan through a broken window and it seems possible that he heard the bird calling and went out on the prowl. Cats aside, Tommy agrees that the old farming methods gave the birds a far greater chance of survival: 'In those days on Papay we cut about a fortnight later, well into July, so that gave the birds a better chance. Hopefully, it's not too late for them.'

One feature of the corncrake initiative led by the Royal Society for the Protection of Birds is to offer bells to farmers to tie to a cat's collar and alert the corncrake to the feline presence. Jack and Tommy tell me they are not impressed.

Between the wars, old-stagers on Papay remember, the raucous chorus of the corncrake from May onwards was a herald of summer on the island. Today, it is more commonly the stench of slurry. A world changing for the better? I wonder.

Chapter Four

Where the Action Isn't

Strange and colourful visitors, usually of the feathered variety, are blown to our inaccessible shores each year. But one summer a light so' easterly scarcely more than a zephyr, brought Papa Westray its most sensational guest in decades. It's open to question whether the landing in the school playing-field of a photon-drive starship with its crew of wee green guys would have caused a bigger fuss.

She came unheralded out of a quiet Sunday afternoon, emerging from the backdrop of the low hills of Sanday, looking head-on for all the world like a runaway oil production platform. I saw her first from the top road when she was still probably 10 or 12 miles east, cutting towards us through the North Sound. The tall, top-heavy superstructure confused us until she turned more broadside on to the island. It was an aircraft carrier. We began to make out the dipping blades of the helicopters and the sleek profiles of the Harriers on deck. From School Place we followed her progress, David stretched out on the flagstone roof of the goat shed while I balanced precariously on the dyke by the front door. By this time a score of spyglasses on Papay were fixed on the warship.

At any moment we expected her to veer off towards Norway but, amazingly, she kept coming and it became clear that Papay was her preferred destination. Jumping aboard the Land Rover, we made for the southern tip of the island and the New Pier. We watched in wonder, narrowly missing the ditch at the top of the Sandy Road, as the vessel slipped partially out of sight behind the cliffs at Sheepheight. Her grey funnel and radio masts moved oddly along the landscape behind the unconcerned cattle. By this time the remarkable island communication network had established that the vessel carried the legendary name of *Ark Royal*, pride of the fleet. Most of the islanders had gathered at the pier by the time she dropped anchor half-a-mile offshore. A fast, semi-inflatable with a team of life-jacketed seamen conducted a quick 'recce' of the pier to establish its suitability for the liberty boats, a tannoy on board sent orders echoing off across the bay and, before we knew what was afoot, the friendly invasion was under way.

The *Ark Royal* is an impressive war machine. Smaller than her illustrious predecessor she nevertheless dwarfed the little boats which scurried around her. On deck we could plainly see five helicopters and a couple of Harrier jump-jets. During her brief stopover a fitness fiend could be seen pounding the metal track of the landing deck; punishment or self-inflicted exercise we never did discover.

About 100 young men – officers and ratings – came ashore. They were all, of course, sworn to secrecy but between you, me and the gatepost (and at risk of breaching the Official Secrets Act) our islanders, thirsty for information, found out that Hamburg had been her last port of call, she had a crew of 1,200 and that she was taking part in a NATO exercise. Yes, you'd better swallow this despatch once read.

Our Co-op bus was drafted into military service for the afternoon, the shop was opened specially and tea and biscuits served to the crewmen at the guest-house. Whispers about the whereabouts of the nearest pub from some of the boys had to be discreetly ignored although there was a nasty story doing the rounds that senior officers went to the hotel in Pierowall for lunch and, more importantly, for a 'wee swallie'. A roaring trade in sweeties and postcards, souvenir sweat-shirts and the ever-popular Papay mugs ensued. It was unquestionably the shop's busiest afternoon of the year. One intrepid pair of matelots brought their golf clubs ashore and were seen swinging their way across the machair at Moclett. Those pioneers would be interested to know, I'm sure, that there's now a nine-hole golf course at this site, the main hazard being Jim o' Sheepheight's black sheltie Perky who grazes the greens.

The pay phone in the guest-house was kept busy as sailors tried to contact wives, pals and sweethearts, and one bloke was delighted to get through to a relative on our neighbouring island of North Ronaldsay, which lies on the horizon way to the east. In early evening the *Ark Royal* moved off majestically towards Fair Isle.

A couple of centuries ago the reaction of the people of Papa Westray to such a visit would have been very different. Men of Orkney had a grand reputation as skilled sailors having served around the world – from whalers in the Davis Strait to clippers in the Indian Ocean. Thenadays, most would have been as familiar with the sea as they were with the land. True to a lesser extent even today. Consequently, they became tempting targets for the Royal Navy's press gangs.

Tricks adopted by the men of the north isles to avoid the gangs have become the stuff of legend and even when capture was inevitable they didn't run short of ideas. As the press gang closed in, one man removed his clothes, rolled in a bed of nettles and threw his clothes on again before the sailors rounded the corner of the byre. He came up in a fearsome rash and was sent packing by the ship's surgeon as an infection risk. Others would play the fool, feign deafness or epilepsy rather than serve. We haven't completed a head count of islanders in the aftermath of the *Ark Royal*'s visit but has anyone seen John David Hume, bold skipper of the lobster boat *Jacinth*, in the past week?

Over the years my diaries record similarly odd encounters. For example, in the autumn of 1990:

> On my way back from the Post Office I was met by a quite remarkable sight – a helicopter parked in our back garden. In fact, the Royal Navy Lynx had set down just over the wall in John Bill's field and the navy men were paying a PR visit to the school. These fly-guys let the children sit at the controls and although free trips were ruled out, they staged an impromptu air display before heading south. Scotland beat Rumania 2–1 at Hampden. Enough excitement for one day, methinks!

In summer, apart from visitors arriving by scheduled air and steamer services, the occasional yacht anchors in the South Wick and the seafarers wander like R.L. Stevenson on his South Seas isle, drinking in the atmosphere. From time to time a light aircraft will touch down at the airstrip and very occasionally a small cruise ship calls by. All of these comings and goings, of course, are signalled by the Viking trumpet and even the police and TV licence people, on their occasional forays north, can never count on the element of surprise.

Visitors are often stunned to learn that the nearest police officer is 30 miles away in Kirkwall. Although we do have two special constables on the isle, their main duties centre on the polling station at election times. In fact, uniforms of any sort, apart from Jim the postie, nurse Fiona and the smart fluorescent waterproofs worn by David and Bobby up at the airstrip, are a rarity.

Crime has been virtually non-existent and, for as long as anyone can remember, front doors and cars have been left unlocked and keys rust happily in the ignition. Self-policing has, until very recently, been the name of the game – witness the parish handcuffs in the bothy museum. However, the world seems to be much more with us of late (petty thefts have been reported) and islanders speculate about just how long this utopian state of affairs can persist.

One cutting which I cherish from an English regional newspaper looking at life on Papay describes how the island is 'where the action isn't'. Perhaps this is not quite as accurate as it was ten years ago.

The most recent criminal case involving Papay folk that I can uncover and which went as far as the court in Kirkwall takes us back nearly 40 years to a simple assault – a £5 fine eventually being imposed. It's interesting to learn that the accused was an incomer and the victim an islander, and no surprise at all to find that the incident was the culmination of a long-running feud.

When witnesses were being ferried out to board the steamer *en route* to Kirkwall for the trial, the animosity, apparently, was almost tangible and the different factions sat at opposite ends of the boat. Fearing a rammy, one of the boatmen had wisely stowed a table leg beneath the floorboards of the skiff.

Another case heard at Kirkwall indicates that islanders were just as capable of fighting amongst themselves. Just before the outbreak of the Second World War an assault took place. A lobster fisherman was accused of interfering with a neighbour's creels off the Backaskaill jetty. He reacted violently and several blows were struck. A £1 fine with an alternative of 10 days in prison was imposed.

One, possibly apocryphal, story about an islander called to appear in court as a witness bears repetition. The disgusted sheriff, eyeing this dishevelled and seldom-washed farmer, asked: 'How long do you wear that shirt?' Quick as a flash came the reply: 'An inch above me bum, yer Lordship!'

Police officers are more regular visitors to the island now, principally to check gun licences, but once the ground-to-air missiles have been stowed in the loft and the older cars revert to hay stores or hennie hooses, the encounter is usually a pretty amiable one. We're exempt from the MOT test out here (because of our isolation from the nearest test station, I'm told) but road tax, even for vehicles which only use our four miles of metalled road, is obligatory, if maybe a wee bit unfair.

Believe it or not, on a visit to the school a year or two back the young constable gave the kids the standard chat about not speaking to strangers. When we first came here I actively encouraged my own children to talk to visitors to the island, to make them feel at home. Sad to say, in this changing world, the police may now have the rights o' it.

FROM CHALK TO CHIPS

The way Katy, our youngest daughter, returned from school, made herself a jeely piece and settled down to listen to the Lemonseeds (or was that the Lightning Heads?), you wouldn't have reckoned that she had been making history. As a quaintly styled 'wet weather child', occasionally stranded on Papay by winter storms, she had been reaching her classroom in the secondary school across the way in Westray through the miracle of an electronic writing board which had been set up in the wee primary school across the dyke.

Children and the new technology, they go together these days like wellie boots and puddle-splashing, don't they? In fact, they're inseparable. Most experts speak of society today as an electronic village where even the most isolated farmstead can become a telecroft, linked to the outside world through a telephone/computer system. Talk in Scotland is increasingly of home working, bits, chips and modems, and the implications for a dispersed community such as Orkney are obvious.

A quiet revolution, the use of these electronic writing boards in education has been under way in Orkney since the beginning of the decade. A hi-tech scheme which links our remote islands is set to spark a profound change in rural education, probably right across Europe. In time it may even be possible for pupils to complete their secondary education from home.

The so-called whiteboards, used in conjunction with fax machines and an audio link, all working through the standard telephone lines, allow the teacher in what is termed the 'main station' to write on a board with an electronic pen which causes the script or diagrams to appear simultaneously on monitor screens in a number of 'out stations' – the remote schools. Correspondingly, the students' work can be observed and corrected. God only knows how incredibly sophisticated this system might become in the next decade.

Changed days indeed from that famous occasion in 1877 when the pupils filed out of the old school (now our home at School Place) and marched behind their teacher, Mr Pyper, round the corner, past the kirk and into the new building. Incredibly, the long Victorian classroom, which now consists of four rooms and forms the north wing of our house, accommodated scores of children, from tiny tots to teenagers, sitting at long benches with their chalk and slates.

The teacher's desk was on a raised dais at the south end, the walls were neatly stencilled and halfway along the east wall was set a peat-burning stove – the kids probably brought fuel to stoke the flames as part of their tuition fees. The teacher's study and sewing-room is now our spacious lounge. There's an odd thing about this room, though: situated at the quiet end of the house, everyone who sits alone, reading or simply daydreaming, has this strange compulsion to tut at nothing in particular. A psychic, ghostly legacy of a long-dead school ma'am fretting over the careless needlework of her girls? Who knows?

Nowadays, after a primary education on Papay our children have the option of going to the secondary school on the increasingly prosperous island of Westray or direct to the Grammar School in Kirkwall where they either stay with family or board at the hostel.

There is much to be said for the smaller schools. And there is no doubt that they are popular postings for teachers. Christine Hopkins, our teacher, arrived in 1990 having fought off the challenge of over 50 candidates from as far away as Saudi Arabia. The presence of the school certainly slows the drift of young families away from the island and while sometimes the children miss youngsters of their own age group, they have almost one-to-one tuition and can proceed at their own pace in a relaxed, almost family atmosphere. Nowadays regular trips into Kirkwall, made possible by the improved air and ferry service, mean that they miss out less on the educational visits to theatres, museums, swimming-pools and exhibitions which are taken for granted by kids from the more populous areas.

Balanced precariously on a knife edge between prosperity and population decline, the certainty that education can be made available on Papa Westray through new technology, come what may, is a big plus and may yet prove to be the single biggest factor in securing the island's future. But I often wonder what Mr Pyper would have made of all this electronic wizardry? His modest requests for the opening day of the new school were a blackboard, two coal scuttles and one box of prepared chalk.

Recently, through a newspaper clipping which arrived on the island and was passed along to me, we made the acquaintance of one of Mr Pyper's predecessors at School Place. George Pottinger, his wife, Isabella, and their four children eventually settled in British Columbia in 1864 and made a successful new life for themselves. Born in Westray he began teaching here in the 1840s. By the winter of 1849 his school roll had touched 90 and, with the help of a female assistant, he was able also to operate an evening class for 20 students. Although he received a small annual allowance from the Free Church (£1 when he began teaching) this was supplemented by one shilling per head, per quarter, from each pupil.

Class sizes seemed to vary dramatically over the years, however, and writing in this article in the *Victoria Times-Colonist* John Adams suggested, very logically, that poverty as well as the demands of seasonal labour on Papa Westray were probably at the root of these fluctuations. On one occasion, George, accompanied by his oldest son, James, went to visit a Papay family whose son had been regularly absent, probably because they were destitute. The two boys played happily together while Mr Pottinger and the mother talked. Finally the boy asked his mother if the Pottingers could stay for dinner. In a hushed tone she is said to have replied: 'Ach, we canna do that, since we hae but one small dove for our ain meal.'

Such abject poverty may now be blessedly absent from the island but involvement with your children's education here can still have unexpected complications and adventure. In my diaries for the winter of 1988 I found the following entry referring to a trip to the secondary on Westray on the school boat *Amarinth*:

> Parents nights were never like this in Glasgow. With the fire stoked and the dog walked we set off on the morning crossing to Westray with the kids in relatively calm conditions. Rounding the point of Vestness, Tommy the boatman took a heading for Gill Pier and we spotted, right on cue, two larger than normal waves which the children – now seasoned travellers – say are always met just there. An

odd oceanographic phenomenon. In Westray, apart from the official business at the school, we had the incredible luxury of a meal out at the Pierowall Hotel . . . the famous haddock and chips, so enormous that the fish spilled over the edge of the plate. A rare treat!

I remember on that self-same expedition being taken to the rear of the hotel and shown a recently landed halibut on the flags; it was five feet long and about as wide. A few fish suppers there, I reckon.

In their turn the children have to be ready for just about anything. When the 'pierie' men arrived in the summer of 1992 to begin a six-month contract carrying out remedial work on the New Pier (starting point for the school boat), they brought with them a crane, portacabins, heavy vehicles and a huge metal barge. Divers had found most of the metal pillars filled with thin air instead of cement. Anyway, it was chaos at the south end for days and inevitably it was the children returning on the *Amarinth* who were among the first to negotiate this construction yard. They arrived home claiming they had had to complete the last leg of the journey to shore in a bathtub; it turned out that this was the contractor's flat-bottomed dive boat.

PULL UP AN EGG BOX!

How do the citizens of Papa Westray spend their leisure time without the joys of cinema, pub, theatre, pool hall or amusement arcade? It's an important question, I think, when we're trying to gauge the health of the community. Unquestionably the most serious pastime on Papay is exchanging information, testing the water with new topics most recently emerging 'in the public' and passing on any suitable titbits. In less enlightened circles it might be called gossiping.

The greatest social crime on the island is surely not knowing what is going down – who has taken the huff with whom, the state of play in the current feuds, the life histories of visitors to the guest-house or B & Bs, how many lobsters each boat landed the previous day or how many young, unattached female backpackers had come off the morning plane. Interestingly, we menfolk can often be bigger 'sweetie wives' than the women and are always keen to get the pleasantries about the weather out of the way so we can get down to the social nitty-gritty.

Sociologists tell us that this gossipy buzz is a very necessary release valve in a community such as ours, which is too small to allow discord to die a natural death. Gossip may even act as a restraint on anyone either involved in, or contemplating, some sort of unacceptable, anti-social behaviour. However, I know from experience that gossip can often gain a life of its own and build, with camp followers worrying away at each other on the flanks, until every couple of years a crisis is reached.

A lot can be read into the most innocent of activities. Scan the property section of the paper and, before you know what's hit you, you'll allegedly be moving on to pastures new.

Activities at the Co-op, the focus of so much of importance to the community, are naturally an almost bottomless trough of gossip. I remember one particular set-to, a mini-palace coup, which involved a change of control up the road, a redistribution of the workload. Factional bitterness was at a new high. By coincidence it blossomed on the same day as Saddam Hussein announced that in the event of war he planned a missile attack on the Israeli capital of Tel Aviv. Giving peace a chance seemed to be on no one's mind either internationally or locally that day.

Unfortunately, the latest furore on the Papa Westray front developed after I had already filed a despatch to *The Washington Post* about the beauty and tranquillity, the community spirit and comradeship of life on a small Orkney island. Apparently it was being flagged in Washington as part of a 'Peace on Earth' special. Self-consciously I noted in my diary: 'Button yer lip, Jim – and take the dollars!'

Within a few months of first coming to the island I was to discover that a popular forum for exchanging information – in addition to the pierhead or the airstrip – was around the till in the Co-op shop of a Saturday night. It's an island tradition that the shop is always open this one night weekly; a legacy, I supposed, of the Saturday night opening of the island's first shop down at Backaskaill. I found the men would meet up for a blether and an ice-cream. I never got much involved in these sessions because, if the truth be told, after a couple of choc ices, I tend to get outrageous.

Equally, there are many other social activities, particularly in the winter months, which help draw the community together in a more constructive and meaningful way. A turnout of a dozen or more islanders allows the organisers to mark it down as a success. There's the lifeboat guild, the occasional community meals (chippie nights), women's groups, the camera club, craft classes, the youth club, the old folk's 'Thursday' club, bring-and-buy sales, fund-raising coffee mornings, seasonal parties and, of course, the famous Papay dances. Even the occasional roup or public auction, often after a bereavement, can become a bit of a social event. The largest in recent years was down at Fulmars and lasted fully six hours. People came and went throughout the day to bid for 400 assorted items including such gems as a three-quarters-full packet of soap powder!

Weddings naturally provide a rare highlight in the island's social calendar. Most recently Mike and Marina were married down at St Boniface with a reception in the Holland loft. Towards the end of 1991, Jim o' Backaskaill, this time wearing his registrar's hat, was given the go-ahead to conduct civil marriages. Rather a token gesture you might suppose, bearing in mind our small population and remoteness. But, lo and behold, within a few weeks Tim the birdie man (RSPB summer warden to the uninitiated) arrived from Edinburgh with Jennifer and a couple of plane loads of relatives. The first civil marriage in Papay's history took place in the school and the happy couple left to join a wildlife project in Zambia with the strains of the Eightsome Reel still ringing in their ears.

Interestingly, down towards the loch, just below the school, is a field where tradition places an Odin stone. Young lovers clasped hands through a hole in these pagan monoliths and pledged their devotion to each other. It's a notable fact, certainly worth remarking on in these unstable days, that there has never been a divorce in the annals of Papay.

On a more sombre note, anniversaries such as Remembrance Day still provide a focus for the older members of the community. In the autumn of 1991, I introduced a syndicated article on the annual remembrance service thus:

> At the eleventh hour of the eleventh day of the eleventh month the view from Papa Westray's modest war memorial, on the gentle rise north of Holland, is exactly as it has been these 70 years past, as tranquil and pastoral as you could wish for. A patchwork of fields studded with squat sandstone crofts, narrow tracks leading to crescent sands and the grey-brooding sea. It's the sort of peace, beauty and continuity that generations of men from our little community have felt worth fighting for.

Those who gave their lives are remembered on the polished pink obelisk. No VCs here, no national heroes, just a few ordinary lads doing a dangerous job. Among the names was that of Thomas Miller of Daybreak, the first islander killed in the Great War. A private in the Gordon Highlanders, he vanished during intense fighting at the Battle of Arras. All that was ever found of Tom was his paybook. Gunner David Irvine from Hinso was with the Royal Garrison Artillery (the big guns) on the Western Front. His gun post took a direct hit in December 1917 and he was killed along with two others in his platoon. His family treasure a letter from his sergeant speaking highly of David. An old clock stopped on the day of his death and hasn't gone since.

David's brother, Thomas of the Seaforth Highlanders, who spent long months in the front line, came home to die of trench feet and is buried in the St Boniface kirkyard. Another Seaforth, his neighbour Willie Tulloch of New Houses, was killed in the Mesopotamian campaign and his last resting place is under the skies of Iraq. Worlds apart, yet together.

Other local men died on 9 February 1918 when the coaster SS *Express* was run down by a British destroyer in the Pentland Firth – William Foulis, John Rendall and George Foulis are recalled on the memorial. Two cousins from the Groat family, Stewart and William, were killed in separate but remarkably similar incidents in the Second World War. Stewart, a merchant seaman who had survived the rigours of the North Atlantic convoy crossings, was killed at Glasgow docks during the blackout when he fell 40 feet into a hold. William received fatal injuries on a freighter at Fraserburgh. And so the list goes on. Papay has paid its price. War reaches out to touch even the remotest of communities.

As the generations pass you can argue the rights and wrongs of any conflict. But the fact is that millions made the ultimate sacrifice to preserve places such as Papa Westray. Surely neither the sacrifice nor what they fought for should ever be taken for granted. As the minister, Mr D.A. Cameron, said on an August Sunday in 1924 when the memorial was dedicated: 'When will their memory fail? If we allow them to grow dim, the glory of our land will depart from us.'

COWES IT AIN'T

One of the least known and perhaps most surprising aspects of social life is that we have our very own yacht club here on Papa Westray, complete with rules, regulations and a commodore. For most of this century the young and not so young men, their boat-building skills no longer required for the skiffs which once fished as much as 30 miles away from the island, began to construct model yachts and race them on St Tredwell's Loch. Sadly, there are no longer the numbers that once competed but a few enthusiasts keep the event alive and several homes still have yachts lying in the byre or attic so there is always the hope that the club may yet regain some of its former status.

The rules of the regatta are impossibly complex, shrouded in an almost Masonic secrecy, but they seem to consist of three races, each made up of three legs, providing the weather holds, no one goes down with hypothermia and the numbed audience don't drift away to replenish the hip flasks. The yachtsmen, some wise souls in rubber leggings, other dafties in shorts, plowter around the marshy margin of the loch rescuing their vessels from mudbanks, angry birdlife or barbed-wire obstructions.

You can just about determine when a race has begun but to say conclusively when it has been completed is impossible. As the last bedraggled skip sees his yacht make port there is a great consulting of notes, starting and finishing times, handicaps, signs of the zodiac, then almost miraculously, a result is announced. It's fun, but Cowes it ain't.

As always the races are followed by a dance and the prize-giving. A quick glance at the prize list – for 1991 as it happens – shows just how tight-knit we are as a community. George Rendall Memorial Cup: 1, Johnny Gray; 2, David Hewitson; 3, Peter Miller. Tankard: 1, Peter Miller; 2, Johnny Gray; 3, Jim Rendall. Barometer: 1, Peter Miller; 2, Jim Rendall; 3, Johnny Gray. Strange to find our builder Peter Miller involved in any sort of race. He's the most thoughtful, deliberate Orcadian you're ever likely to meet, the very personification, in fact, of Papay's phenomenon of slowed-down time. But Peter has hidden depths.

Boat-building, I'm pleased to report, although no longer geared to the extensive fishing once found around the island, is not yet a lost art thanks to Peter, who shut himself away in his shed a couple of winters ago and emerged having constructed a smashing wee lug or dinghy. Papay sent two crews to the Westray Regatta in 1995 and swept the board in that section. John o' Holland with Bill o' the Links as crew sailed across the Papay Sound, and Peter recruited Paul from the Glasgow University ornithology team as his crewman. The Papay boats won a race each and the fact that they were the only entries in the category concerns no one, particularly on Papay.

We've seen how technology is in the process of revolutionising the way the three 'r's are taught but it has already had a profound effect on the way the people of Papa Westray amuse themselves. 'Steam' radio and the gogglebox, which arrived in the 1930s and 1950s respectively, subtly altered a social scene which must have remained unchanged for centuries previously. In the 1990s video recorders and satellite dishes have begun to put in an appearance.

In years past islanders manufactured their own entertainment, visiting friends, enjoying songs or hymns and stories and, naturally, the latest gossip. The fiddle and the squeezebox would have been produced and what we now would call craftwork – chair- and basket-making, modelling from wood or simply fashioning and repairing gear used around the farmstead or at the fishing – would have been considered a suitable way of relaxing. The working day was often long and arduous and leisure time something of a luxury.

As far as I can discover the first radio to appear on the island found a home right here at School Place where Geordie Drever had his merchant and cobbler's business in what is now the Hewitson kitchen. Geordie, remembered as a dour, but severely honest, individual, used to sit of a morning, straight-backed, cap in hand, arms folded, listening and meditating on 'Thought for the Day' before beginning his labours. Woe betide anyone who disturbed these moments of tranquillity.

Television arrived in the 1950s and the first set is thought to have been plugged in down at the farm of Whitehowe. One early programme which the whole island wanted to see featured Dan Kirkpatrick, cox of Longhope lifeboat, who was to lose his life in the 1969 disaster. Unfortunately, I'm told, the failure of a power plant put paid to the night's entertainment.

One chap who vividly recalled the island before the advent of television was Sandy Wylie. He was roving projectionist on behalf of Orkney Islands Council and brought feature films, national news, as well as films of local events such as the Ba' Game, agricultural shows and the Miss Orkney contest to remote corners like Papay. Once again School Place comes into the equation. For three decades from the late 1940s it housed the island cinema. From the earliest days Sandy joined the steamer north with his heavy box of camera equipment, each circuit of the far-flung isles taking a fortnight.

His first memories of Papa Westray are of finding the most restrained of audiences. Folk sat where they could – on egg boxes and benches and even on some old bus seats – children at the front, older ones and rascals to the rear. Said Sandy: 'It was often as much fun to watch the audience on Papay as it was to watch the film.' He remembered that our islanders seemed awestruck by their first encounters with the moving pictures. 'Most people on Papay had never seen a film before and sat very quietly. It took a wee while before they would laugh, even at Popeye.' Huckleberry Finn was the first film screened all those years ago and received mixed reviews among the island folk, some finding the Mississippi backwaters just too far removed from the well-kent corners of Papay, others relishing a chance to see even a fictional portrayal of life in a distant land.

One early adventure which was screened on the north isles circuit featured the explosion of a ship's boiler. When the blast finally came Sandy recalled how three men on a bench in the back row got such a start they fell over backwards, legs in the air. One of our island matrons, still concerned that these moving pictures might be tools o' the de'il, was eventually persuaded by some visiting relatives from the south to go along to School Place where *The Blue Lamp*, the Dixon of Dock Green classic, was being shown. As police cars, sirens blaring, came racing down the screen towards the audience, this lady was seen dippin' and a-duckin' to avoid the oncoming traffic.

As a lay-preacher, Sandy was once asked during a weekend visit to stand in for the minister at the Sunday service next door at St Ann's. 'I chose the theme Let there be Light,' Sandy recalled. An appropriate topic you'd think for a projectionist, but halfway through the sermon the rattly generator gave up the ghost and the congregation was plunged into darkness. Islanders deny to this day that the breakdown was greeted by a traditional, rhythmic stamping of feet.

Perhaps the highlight for the Papay cinema was the screening of the Coronation film, *The Crowning of a Queen*. The tour schedule for this film was the tightest ever. Everyone wanted to see it and Sandy could only spend a couple of hours on each island. John Rendall of Holland remembers: 'We were singlin' neeps when Sandy arrived off the steamer. We downed tools immediately and went, mid-afternoon, to see the film at School Place. It was unheard of to stop work in the middle of the day. It has never happened before on Papay and I don't suppose it will again. It was a very special occasion.'

Bill o' the Links, a youngster on that famous day, has another, quite different memory of the film show. 'Some old folk were disgusted by the unpatriotic behaviour of young men who smoked during the screening. It was a sort of outrage.'

Papa Westray had a very special place in Sandy's affections, partly explained by an incident during a snowy December visit. The roads were impassable because of high drifts but a group of children arrived at Holland with their sledge and offered to take Sandy and his gear overland to Moclett where he was to be rowed out to meet the steamer. Across the fields the strange party went, unloading and reloading the sled at each dyke. After a heroic two-mile trek they made the boat. The film show of the previous evening surely inspired the Papay children in this adventure – it was *Scott of the Antarctic*. Can the self-centred pleasures of video viewing or surfing the satellite channels ever match the simple, communal fun of a couple of hours at Sandy's trail-blazing cinema – ah hae me doots.

Sadly, in December 1991, only a few short months after our chat, Sandy Wylie died and with him a unique chapter in Orkney's story.

Without street corners to hang around or pubs to frequent it has always intrigued me as to how the young men of Papa Westray let off steam in their later teenage years. An anonymous informant, after much cajoling and suitable lubrication, was eventually persuaded to part with a few secrets of mischief-making on Papay.

Stappin' lums was, and remains, a peculiar Papay pastime. The technique was to select a house, clamber across the flags to the

Andrew Seatter, a steady hand at the tiller

Papay heroes of the Badger *rescue (1906)*

The Orcadia (built in 1868) at the Old Pier in the early years of this century

Pupils and teachers at the Papay school in the early 1930s

The Bellavista aground at the north end (1948)

Two John Hourstons, father and son, at the grindstone, Vestness

A huge haystack under construction at Holland farm (c.1920)

The busy interior of St Ann's kirk just after the Second World War

Baiting fishing-lines by the east shore in the early 1930s

Davie Groat's shopping 'van' calls by Nouster in the 1930s

Postie and mail pony at Backaskaill Post Office around the turn of the century

Working kelp on the shore below
Cott in the 1920s

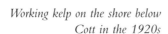

Mary and Robbie Rendall
and cow at Nouster c.1950s

Building the stack at Cott in the 1930s

Aileen, *the doctor's boat at the turn of the century*

chimney head and jam the lum with a wad of hay. Retreating to a safe distance the rogues would watch from behind a dyke until the occupants, coughing and spluttering, would burst out of the smoke-filled croft. Rare fun. This particular technique reached the heights of sophistication when one of the young blades managed to force the corpse of a seal down the chimney pot.

Another popular jest was to remove a section from a haystack, trundle a convenient cairt inside then carefully fill in the gap. To all intents and purposes the wagon had vanished from the face of the earth. Pulling a haystack apart under cover of darkness and resetting the stooks in the field was also considered good for a laugh. The effort involved must have been enormous. Some of these leisure pursuits were conducted to the accompaniment of a shared half-bottle. Yes, boys will be boys, even on the outer edge.

Today, occasional concerts up at the guest-house and open-air services during the summer months at St Boniface may not quite have the same appeal as these nocturnal exploits. By the time young folk are into their late teens nowadays they are usually furth of the island.

Country and western singers always seem to find a special welcome and have become adept at dealing with song requests which can range from 'Flower of Scotland' through to the 'Grand Coulee Dam' and 'El Paso' to 'Murder in the Chipshop'. If we're looking for a folk hero for the islanders then Daniel O'Donnell certainly comes into the reckoning.

A much more adventurous and lavish event was the concert in Holland's grain loft during the winter of 1989–90. Despite some confused mutterings about highbrow culture being imported to Papay, Jocelyn from Micklegarth pressed ahead with arrangements for her friends and international celebrities, Anthony Rooley (lute) and Emma Kirkby (soprano), to venture out to Papay.

Alas, the weather couldn't have been more unkind and it was something of a miracle that the boatload of early music enthusiasts made it at all. World renowned they may be but Anthony admitted freely that the loft was possibly the most unlikely setting in which he and Emma had presented their haunting Baroque and Renaissance music. The Wigmore Hall, it ain't. The wind howled round the old loft, rattling doors and windows as the performers treated us to a repertoire ranging from the 'Suffolk Owl', which had the kids hooting with delight, to 'Hey Johnny Cope'.

Thankfully, the doubters who feel more at home when the artist is wearing a Stetson, were won over – at least for the day – and a good turnout of curious islanders allowed the concert to proceed on a positive note. The old loft has seen weddings and harvest homes over the years but surely nothing like this. Since then, Emma and Anthony have become hooked on Papay and in a hectic schedule which sees them tour the world, they usually manage to spend a few days on the island most summers.

To Jocelyn also must go credit for one of the island's most innovative sporting developments. On the back green at Micklegarth you'll find one of the most northerly croquet lawns in the United Kingdom.

From time to time this quest for a sporting challenge and a day out combine, and Papay sends a team to the North Isles Sports.

TALKING BACK TO THE MAN IN BLACK

Midway through my third cold sausage roll in Sanday's community hall, the call to arms came from Neil of Holland, who was acting as press gang sergeant for the Papa Westray team. It's a long tradition of the North Isles Sports that folk are hauled out of the ranks of spectators and sandwich-munchers to make up the numbers. Papay, smallest of the competing islands, needed someone with magic in his feet and, despite the threat of chronic indigestion, I was that footballer.

When I discovered that kickba' on the islands is of heroic proportions – five-a-side on a full-size park – I almost turned on my heels and retreated to the sandwich boards but Neil was lurking in the background and looking mean. At the end of an epic day's competition, Papay (with the benefit of the unique handicapping system) finished third with 40 points. We were well pleased and the fact that we are gifted 35 points before the contest opens is neither here nor there. The boys and lassies, as usual, done good.

After ten hours on windswept Sanday one or two aspects of that particular contest still caused concern for the Hewitson clan:

WOULD a drugs scandal break over the north isles when it was discovered that Morag had taken a couple of blasts from her inhaler before the netball contest?

WOULD anyone notice that my eldest daughter, Lindsey, who had to relinquish her girls' championship, despite winning both sprints, had Papa Westray inscribed on the trophy in her name last year when officially she was running for Westray?

WOULD my argument with the referee mean a trip to Park

Gardens to debate the four-step rule as applied to goalkeepers in a five-a-side tournament?

For 40 years the far-flung northern isles of Orkney have competed in this highly original sporting fixture. In the earliest days of the sports Papa Westray joined in enthusiastically. Then came a 20-year gap before we resumed the fray in the mid-1980s. These were to be our glory years. In 1984 the tug-o'-war team won their event but this was just a prelude to greater things and in 1985 there was much rejoicing by the shores of St Tredwell's Loch as we landed the North Isles trophy for the first time. The boat journey back from that marvellous success and the tales of the great feats of athleticism that day will live in Papay folklore forever.

The year I got the call the island had an injured and unavailable list which made the Scottish team manager's job look easy. Marion from the shop had a bout of tonsillitis, Bobby from Whitehowe and brother Philip o' Newbiggin' were on the sick list also and our tug-o'-war anchorman, Rab o' Windywalls, was sidelined with a bad back after his car tried to follow the Loganair flight over the dyke at Tirlo.

This meant that team preparation and planning was dramatic, last-minute stuff. Climbing the gangplank on to the *Orcadia* at a ridiculously early hour, Johnny Gray of the Caravan and Alistair o' Cott were still debating tactics and team selection while the netball ladies got in a huddle in the saloon and, with only half a practice match under their belts, sensibly planned on a containing game. It almost worked. They lost 16–0 and 6–0 showing, according to commentators, vastly improved form in the second match.

The Westray team had been first aboard the *Orcadia* and there were further stops at Eday and Stronsay before we all spilled ashore at Kettletoft on Sanday and started the trek to the school and the traditional pre-contest dinner. On the field of battle the last smirr of rain moved off nor' east towards Start Point lighthouse. As ever, the afternoon was spiced with close decisions and not a little controversy. The team-colours rule was being openly flouted and in one confusing 400-metre race five of the six runners were wearing the yellow of Westray. There were murmurings, too, about the poor condition of the tug-o'-war track where one pulling area was firmer than the other.

As the afternoon progressed the stronger teams overhauled Papay's enormous 35-point advantage. We kept in touch with a couple of hard-won points in the relay; Alistair Hourston surprised himself by taking third place in the long jump and Jon Symonds was on the scoreboard (actually it was a blackboard) with a point in the 400 metres.

Then came my summons to the football field. We talked tactics; it was about letting the ball do the work, dictating play, hitting on the break. Fine, except, when the whistle sounded, the plan went oot the windae and we all charged madly upfield. I don't know about the opposition but it certainly stunned me. An early goal was lost and after half-time I missed a clear chance (bad bounce, unlucky deflection, caught by the wind; select any two from three) and we went down 0–3.

In the second match against Stronsay we were doing much better. It was 1–1 when the referee, who took himself far too seriously, pulled me up for taking more than four steps. I should explain that by this stage my team-mates had decided I was a better bet between the posts. Anyway, I know all about the four-step rule, but I ask you, in five-a-sides, on a playing-field which stretched forever? I thought it was ludicrous and told the ref as much. I was immediately substituted. If I could have found a dressing-room door, I would have kicked it. We lost out in this match, too, but only after extra time and a penalty shoot-out. Yes, even this questionable aspect of the modern game has filtered out here.

On the three-hour sail home thoughts turned to the old *Orcadia* which was soon to head to retirement in warmer climes. Sports days are no longer the same without her. Penalty shoot-outs may come, well-loved old steamers may go, but I suspect the delights of the North Isles Sports are here to stay.

MAKING DO

Among the saddest losses in the past century for Papa Westray has been our once proud claim to self-sufficiency. We no longer produce our own bread (the old mill lies derelict and stone bases are all that remain of the once plentiful domestic threshing mills). There is no home-produced cheese or butter since there isn't a single milking cow to be found, and the bulk of foodstuffs are now imported through the Co-op shop or direct from Kirkwall. Winter vegetables, shellfish, salted fish and a few splendid wild mushrooms in the season are really now the island's only products, consumed locally. What a contrast with a century ago when salt and peat would probably have been the only imported necessities.

It's rather too easy to glamorise the fact that people filled the larder in the 1800s through their own efforts. The truth is that their diet was disastrous. There were carbohydrates aplenty but precious few vitamins. Malnutrition was rife and in its train came tuberculosis, a scourge which for decades must have been present on Papay and carried off entire families. Young people, aged between 12 and 20, seem to have been the principal victims, partly because they often inherited the cast-off clothes of relatives who died from the disease.

By gathering together accounts of life on Papa Westray it's possible to get an idea of the daily diet of these self-reliant people last century. An article in the now defunct *Orkney Herald* provides the best summary.

> In the morning porridge, often with weak ale or cabbage juice from the previous day's dinner, was served for breakfast. Then about midday a light snack, consisting of bere bread and light ale, corresponding to the modern coffee break, was enjoyed. If the household was busy in the fields then one of the children or the grandpa would carry the bread and ale out to the workers. This snack was called the 'beulie'.
>
> Some time around 1.30 p.m. the main meal of the day was eaten. It usually consisted of dried salt fish and potatoes, or cabbage which was boiled with pork and potatoes until all the vitamins had been destroyed. For tea the Papa Westray crofter ate suir cuithes or even sour skate. These fish were not salted but were hung up on a wall until they were in a half-dried condition, or placed under straw in a pot until they were beginning to breed maggots. At suppertime clapshot was often served up, or dried cuithes were cut down from the side of the open fire and eaten. A favourite way of eating clapshot was to take it with sour buttermilk.

There were milk cows but the art of cattle rearing was only imperfectly understood and the cows often yielded milk for only a few months annually. Often the best milk cows had to be given to the laird to pay off debt or rental.

High feasting in Papay took place infrequently when a pig or sheep was slaughtered or when a large quantity of home-brew was prepared. As well as lacking nutrition the diet was, to say the least, uninspiring and monotonous. As Bill o' the Links once summed it up for me: 'One day they had fish and tatties, the next day they had tatties and fish.' Perhaps there is something to be said for the freezer units up at the shop.

DEMOCRACY ON THE WILD FRONTIER

Euro-voting in the outlands of Oz began so slowly that the presiding officer began to wonder if he'd got the wrong day. Had the voters forgotten the road to the primary school polling station? It looked that way. Quaintly titled 'Orkney and Zetland' (OZ in the ballot box shorthand) the Northern Isles are part of the sprawling Highlands and Islands constituency which, according to folk who know about these things, is bigger than Denmark.

One of the most outlandish outposts of democracy in this vast bailiwick is Papa Westray. Generally the island is Liberal in outlook but there has been a good deal of confusion over all the Euro fuss.

It became apparent early in the 1989 campaign that Papay wouldn't figure high on the visiting list of the five candidates in Britain's most northerly EEC constituency. However, we did have a visit from that venerable Highland bulldog, Sir Albert McQuarrie, who arrived for lunch at the guest-house having arranged for his agent to pin a notice in the shop offering to meet islanders at the airstrip for a blether. Shrewd political observers on Papay were agreed on three aspects of the Tory stalwart's stopover: (*a*) he was here because Papay was the only place in the north isles of Orkney where he could get a decent meal; (*b*) his PR people had bungled by choosing the day of the inter-island sports to grace Papay with his presence when half the island was in Westray; and (*c*) he flew off towards Fair Isle in a red (sic) helicopter. Not a good set of omens by any standard, but at least he came.

If you believe in such signs from the gods, then try this one for size. A day or so before the vote, I passed a pleasant few minutes chatting with Cott's new piglet which was relaxing in the back of Alistair's hatchback outside the Post Office. He was the first piglet on Papay for a few years. The significance of this may be a little obscure but bear with me. In the 1920s the fledgling Lord Boothby stood as MP for Orkney and Shetland and found his way out to Papay with his electioneering team. He was introduced to the party faithful down at the house of Links. There he shook the bloodstained hand of one of the women of the house who was busy at her morning chore, disembowelling a pig on the kitchen table.

Black puddings and trotters wait for no man, even would-be politicians. Boothby, a star of the future, did not win the election but left Orkney more worldly-wise and perhaps with a stronger stomach. How much of his later success can be attributed to this experience, who can say?

Had it not been for a previous encounter with a Tory candidate I might have been tempted to put a few quid on Sir Albert on the basis of the pig omen. At another recent election an enthusiastic young Tory candidate stepped ashore from the steamer to greet folk on the pier during a 20-minute turnaround by the *Orcadia*. When asked what brought him campaigning to Papay the tweed-suited zealot replied earnestly: 'It's the only way to get to Westray.' Surprisingly, I know of at least one islander who voted for this man despite his tactlessness, but only because the election agent bought him a drink in the bar of the *Orcadia*.

Party meetings were occasionally held on the island in years past and there again the Tories took the honours. The chairman of the meeting was always an islander who received 10 shillings for his trouble. This was enough to keep him in tobacco for the entire winter, so he entered the election arena with great enthusiasm.

Prior to the 1930s, voters who wished to exercise their franchise were obliged to take the steamer across to Westray. The trip, of course, was free and an election was seen as an excuse for a day out. After casting their vote the doondies would retire to the cluster of shops in Pierowall village, the homes of relatives or, in the case of the more spirited young men, to the local hostelry for a jar or three. A treat, even today. One chap got so carried away with the all too infrequent celebration of freedom and democracy that he had to be helped to the steamer in a decidedly over-tired state. He was hardly up the gangplank when he drifted into the galley and in his confused state planked his bum on the burning stove. The boat had to make an about-turn to allow for some delicate doctoring.

Long-time MP for Orkney and Shetland, Jo Grimond (later Lord Grimond), was a frequent adventurer to Papay during his days at Westminster. He had, it seems, a special affection for our silver shores, having been piggy-backed ashore through the surf by the island's former special constable, John Henry Rendall of Newbigging. Grimond's successor, Jim Wallace, flies out to hold regular surgeries in the guest-house.

But back to Euro-day. It was a 15-hour vigil for Jim o' Sheepheight, the presiding officer, and his wife, Phemie, the clerk. But after the first voter arrived at midday there was a steady trickle and at the end of the day 27 islanders had cast their vote – a poll of over 38 per cent. A straw poll suggested that everyone expected Winnie Ewing to retain the seat for the SNP (as she did comfortably) and there were a few interesting whispers for the Greens. So the school closed and Jim and Phemie went home. The ballot box was seen safely away on the morning plane. That evening there was graphic footage on TV of the carnage at Beijing's Tiananmen Square in the quest for greater freedom of speech; suddenly the little electoral pageant which had unfolded on Papa Westray could be seen as part of an important global drama.

Our ubiquitous postie, Jim Rendall, despite all his other commitments, has run twice in Orkney Islands Council elections in the past decade, failing on the first occasion to be elected by a few votes for Papa Westray and Westray then being thumped by Westray farmer Stephen Hagan who has gone on to make a real impression in Kirkwall. Despite demands on his time, he is always mindful of the issues affecting the smaller island.

Service to the community and the nation at large remains an important Papay tradition. The big news on the first day of 1992, apart from the overnight gale which tore the school gate off its hinges and put the phones out of commission, was that John Rendall of Holland had received the British Empire Medal for his role as key-keeper of the ancient dwelling at the Knap of Howar. He joins Willie Groat of Kimbland who got his award for long service with the coastguard and Jim Rendall, holder of the BEM, who received his for work in the community. A case of gongs galore by the Papay shore.

Chapter Five

Tattie Planting for Beginners

AREN'T WE ALL JUST TENANTS?

Along the line of the bottom wall which separates our field from the marshy edge of St Tredwell's Loch the fulmars skim past, straight-winged, banking at the last moment to avoid the seemingly inevitable collision. This is their territory and they make sure everyone knows it. As we labour on the adjacent drystane dyke, shadowy spectres, equally at home here, share our toil.

Coaxing the fallen stone from the turf and setting them back into the three-dimensional sandstone jigsaw, I'm conscious of the Papa Westray men who first built this wall as one of the feudal duties owed by the islanders to their Traill landlords. I can sense those long-departed builders nodding in approval or frowning in turn as our amateurish efforts progress.

The dilapidated central wall is the field's distinctive feature – a legacy of the days in the last century when the laird wanted his land to be neatly edged, improved according to the style of the times. This wall, between three and four feet in height, splits the field into two oblong blocks of around five acres; we knew when we bought the land that the main task would be the restoration of the dyke which had been breached at several points by stone-tumbling ewes.

Halfway down the slope from the impressive twin-pillared gateway, known among the crofts as Johnny Hourston's slap, a ridge of sandstone breaks the surface of the ground at right angles to the wall, effectively quartering the field. Rough pasture is the kindest description for the land but, despite the shallowness of the soil, it has proved ideal for our three horses and handful of cosmopolitan sheep. There is no record or memory of there ever having been a dwelling on the ten acres, but on an island with such a vast span of human habitation, who knows? It's difficult to imagine that someone hasn't found the site appealing; well sheltered from the westerlies and looking out across the loch to the cliffs of Eday, 15 miles away. Certainly, there are one or two low turf platforms which seem to attract rabbits and suggest fallen flagstones below.

In the season the field is a nesting site for snipe, oystercatcher and lapwing, larks trill high above the grazing sheep and the fulmar squadron make their home among the wild irises on the far side of the dyke which runs along the loch shore. Up and down the fields gallus bunnies, knowing they can outrun our dog from any part of the field to reach the security of the partly fallen dyke, hop with confidence around their domain.

The field is bare, apart from the pile of oil drums, palettes, poles, pipes, milk crates and rubber tyres which the girls use to construct their gymkhana during the short summer. Just below the central ridge we have constructed a stone enclosure to give the tough old cuddies some shelter for feeding during the worst of the winter. Our faithful old Land Rover has been built into one wall to provide a useful hay store and, as we built the north wall, we placed an ice-cream box with a few memories of 1990 – coins, newspaper clippings, the usual stuff. Actually, come to think of it, the plastic box may say more than its contents about life in the 1990s.

In vain, as we picked our way through the fallen stones, sorted them into heavy boys for the basement, elegant uprights and infill, I looked for some trace of those Papay builders from centuries past. It's clear that the only tangible mark they left on our island landscape has been their craftsmanship and the simple gravestones in the kirkyard.

Right at the bottom of the field a metal gate gives on to the loch and from here our kids launched their dinghy for a summer afternoon's adventuring to Frenchman's Cove or Skull Coast; a packet of digestive biscuits and a bottle of ginger being the only sustenance required for pirates bold.

The purchase of this field had brought sharply into focus what, for me at least, is one of life's great myths . . . the ownership of land or property. Brought up in a tenement building, the idea of property ownership when I was a child seemed a remote one. The houses, backcourt, stairs, communal bin and wash-house belonged to everyone, or so it seemed. Even when my father got a step up and we flitted to a comfortable bungalow in the foothills of the Kilpatricks, it was a concept I found great difficulty dealing with. When I went on to own my first home – a long-wheel-base Land Rover as it happens – then to the more traditional flats and houses, the problem persisted. No matter how often I studied the deeds, walked around the garden, let the soil run through my fingers or stood like a laird at my front door, did I feel I had any genuine claim to the property. This feeling of unreality was only heightened when we purchased School Place (for a sum the islanders thought ludicrously high but which today wouldn't buy you a lock-up in Glasgow). *GARAGE*

Here in Orkney we moved into a house which had been a focal point of the island community on and off for more than two centuries. This building, of which we are but temporary occupants, belongs, in truth, to the island itself; to those wee ones in Victoria's time who sat at their benches and scratched chalk alphabets on their slates; to Geordie Drever, the merchant and cobbler who had it as a shop; to the marines billeted here during the Second World War; to the teachers who have occupied School Place over the years.

But the field, more than anything, brought home the sheer folly of imagining that ownership of land or property is real, in any sense at all. At most we are guardians of something precious, irreplaceable, just for a little while. As time passes the land, unaware of legal entanglements and human ambition, lives, breathes and endures . . . patiently awaiting the next tenant.

Interestingly, it's possible, I think, to date quite precisely when the crofters of Papa Westray, among them the builders of our dyke, finally emerged from their almost medieval servitude into a bright – well, brighter – new tomorrow. On 11 September 1888, with security of tenure already in place, the Crofters Commission, on circuit in the Highlands and Islands, opened a session in the Westray UP church to examine the Papa Westray rentals.

A boatload of crofters attended and it was learned that, in a bizarre twist, the Traills, their fortunes taking a downward turn, were in fact in debt to various islanders to the tune of £400. When the agent for the Traill trustees suggested that kelp gathering and fishing yielded fortunes for the folk of Papay there was laughter from the body of the hall. Agents for the crofters, on the other hand, said that rents had increased progressively on Papa Westray beyond anything that had been seen elsewhere in Orkney and that the old feudal services persisted.

One Papay witness, David Groat of Howe, said that people were still obliged to work the kelp for the Traills because if they did not they were 'badly liket'. Each crofter gave evidence and at the end of the three-day session rents generally had been halved. Holland land near St Tredwell's Loch, including what is now our field, was allocated to various applicants who were owed money by the Traills. The once all-powerful Holland estate today consists of one derelict house by the east shore.

Perhaps the most interesting development in relation to land use on Papay since the war has been a recent deal between the islanders and Scottish Natural Heritage for the management of the North Hill. The site, bleak moorland dotted with freshwater pools, occupies the northern third of the island and, as well as being an RSPB reserve, was also designated a Site of Special Scientific Interest. Together a programme has been worked out which restricts the use of this traditional common grazing to allow plant and birdlife to flourish.

Money flowing in from this arrangement has, among other benefits, helped with the construction of a new slipway at the Old Pier, allowing lobstermen in our little fleet to haul up their boats more speedily when storms come thundering in from the Atlantic. Surely this is a useful example of how conservation can work to protect the human, as well as plant and animal environment. Papay, I'm told, is considered one of the jewels in the SNH crown – a place where people, plants and pickieternos can all find their space.

It did take time, however, for the Hewitson family to adjust to requirements of life on an island where the pace of things is dictated by factors other than traffic reports on the radio, train timetables or the opportunity for late-night shopping. Diary entries during that first summer of 1988 emphasise the transition:

> Harvest time – and I feel I should be writing wonderful prose about the hope that had been sown in the spring being wonderfully realised, of the fruitful black earth of Papay, of blue skies, and happy, shorn hillsides . . . but, in truth, I'm knackered. While stacking a thousand bales at Sheepheight, I think we stumbled across another of life's great puzzles. Why should the last bale in a load be the heaviest? This enigma surely comes from the same mystical source as the experience I had as a young reporter in Glasgow – I discovered that if you were sent to interview anyone in a tenement they always lived on the top floor (and had a big, vicious dug!).

Really, as incomers and particularly as former toonies (I tell folk my background is in Ayrshire farming but usually omit to mention that this was almost two centuries ago and that there is family talk of sheep stealing) we can hardly begin to understand the bond that exists between the farmer, his land and his animals. Subsidies, EC regulations, fluctuating prices, changes in demand and escalating freight costs may have changed the profession out of all recognition in the past 20 years and have created new stresses for the farmer on Papa Westray, as elsewhere.

Nevertheless, I like to believe, perhaps naïvely, that daily contact with the land and the animals surely helps to keep the candle of hope flickering even through the difficult times. This relationship with the natural world is at one and the same time a privilege and a responsibility but is something denied to so many locked into a soulless urban setting where despair can be the constant companion.

A couple of years after we settled here I was to read, with a lump in my throat, the following paragraph in *The Orcadian*: 'Forward for sale at Kirkwall Mart were 81 cattle, comprising 7 prime cattle, 16 prime heifers, 41 store cattle and 17 farrow cows. A feature of this sale was an outstanding cross Charolais steer from T. Mackay, Mayback, Papa Westray. The steer, the last to be sold by Tommy as he has now retired from farming, was, he said, the best price he had ever received during his farming career – 620kg, selling at £751 to J.C. Irvine of Sandwick.'

Gone for Tommy were the long nights of sitting up fretting over an ailing beast, or the sweat and anxiety of a difficult calving in the cramped wee byre at Maybo'. Tommy will maybe tell you he's happy cultivating his tattie patch and that he doesn't miss all that hassle – but I wonder.

Soon we were beginning to touch the realities of rural life, the comedy and the drama, the sadness and the satisfaction. Morag, along with Anne of Cott and Marina of Charleston, made arrangements for the temporary import of a billy goat from Sanday to service the female goats of Papay, including our Jenny. The girls were warned that he was a sturdy character with a good track record but a bit on the small side – so much so, that he would probably need a box to stand on to perform his duties!

Then there was the lambing. The island soon got to know that our Katy and Lindsey had a kind of magic touch when it came to seemingly lost causes and in the spring our porch became a clearing house for sick and infirm lambs. On one occasion the girls returned from a hard day's work at North Rendall with three poorly specimens. One lamb died, slipped away within the hour, the second, an orphan but a big bruiser who had been separated overlong from his mother, made it with large doses of milk substitute and lots of TLC. The third was a scrawny, pathetic wee creature, a lost cause if you ever saw one, which, we understood, had been blinded by a *gull backie*, hoisted in the air by a hind leg and dropped. In my diary I remember noting it would be a miracle if she survived.

But miracles do happen. She, too, pulled through and joined our flock. The girls christened the larger lamb Dopey while the gull-attack victim turned out to be a beautiful lamb (blind in only one eye, lame in only one leg) and carries the undistinguished title of Limpy-Blindy. The latest recruit is a lamb with a penchant for trying to put his head through any available door – he has been nicknamed The Battering Lamb.

It should be pointed out that this naming of sheep, or any animal for that matter, is regarded by islanders as the first step to madness. Yet it does seem to be a trait of soothmoothers. Even the tysties on the Holm which have been under scrutiny by a team from Glasgow University – including oor Lindsey – for the past few years, have their pet names. Among the recent handles – Linford and Smelly. However, the names given to the seaweed-eating sheep who also decided that they enjoyed nibbling the plastic cable covers running from the TV monitors at the nests are not repeatable.

[handwritten margin note: black Guillemot]

It's strange how, after a few years on Papa Westray, our perspectives began to change. In 1992 the BBC drama series Strathblair, set in a Perthshire farming community just after the war, was watched with great interest by the islanders. The scenery, of course, was marvellous, the storyline reasonably interesting, the acting a bit wooden. However, I found myself in complete agreement with the panels of critics up at the shop who homed in on the big flaw in the production. Everyone had noticed how clean and tidy the farmyard was. Where, oh where, was all the glaur and gutter we know so well on Papay? Is it really that much drier in Perthshire, or maybe they simply don't work as hard?

In my writing, I found myself turning increasingly to issues concerning land-ownership, 'white settlers' and the like. And every so often knowledge of our place in the scheme of things was added to by the most unlikely sources. In 1992, for instance, we learned that Papa Westray is the 69th largest island in the British archipelago. Who said so? None other than Norris McWhirter, he of *Guinness Book of Records* fame who paid us a brief visit. He had two reasons for his Papay pilgrimage – he wanted to make the one-minute hop on the world's shortest scheduled flight between here and Westray (a distance shorter than the main runway at Heathrow!) and he was gathering facts for a new book on the islands of Britain.

Papay's position in the premier league of Britain's thousand-island chain surprised a few people. If we've achieved such an illustrious slot then the best of the rest can be scarcely more than sea-washed reefs.

Big or small, the islands of Scotland continue to hold a fascination for people from the south who see them, quite rightly, as a haven from the madness of urban life and a place where it's possible to gain a foothold on more solid emotional ground. Fine. Island life is much more complex, of course, but the basic premise is correct.

Broadening the topic in one of my *Glasgow Herald* 'World Apart' columns, I wrote:

> Writers, particularly from the Celtic fringe, have once again become jumpy about 'white settlers', colonists with computers and green wellies who breenge in, buying up houses and appearing anxious to steal, or worse, submerge our heritage under an avalanche of shallow, southern values. But why so nervous? Scotland has been a mongrel nation for centuries and we've been able to absorb fresh blood and turn new talent to best effect without losing our identity.

Certainly, here in Orkney you get some whispering behind hands, maybe a wee bit of resentment, and talk of too many English accents in positions of power. But the arrival of the ferryloupers has also sparked an interest in the old Norse language, made Orcadians look afresh at their remarkable heritage and where on earth they are headed, and enlivened the social scene as well as the letters page of *The Orcadian* (always a good guide to the vitality of a community).

Once, I had a boss who was a Grand Master in the school of creative friction. Granted, he took this abrasive philosophy to extremes which occasionally involved pieces of office furniture hurtling around. Head wounds you might have died of, boredom, never! He believed in interaction, and it did, I have to admit, bring results.

The big danger in being over-critical of the up and at 'em brigade from the south is that we ignore the important lessons they can teach. They provide a catalyst for change, not necessarily for loss of Scottishness. Without change Scotland as a nation will surely stagnate, culturally, socially, intellectually. Okay, their way of doing things is not Scottish. It's up front, tell-it-like-it-is tactics. The Calvinist 'be seen and not heard' approach is not for them. And do you know something, this confrontational style is not all bad. It can get things done. Sit back and wait for the world to change for your benefit and you may have to wait a while. Ask the crofters of Assynt.

The main role for native Scots, anxious about their national integrity, must be to educate themselves in their history; to ensure that they remain in control of developments, whether in farming, fishing, industry, tourism; and, perhaps even more importantly, they must exercise a tight rein over the pace of change. You see, our friends from the south will, given half a chance, hurry things through at an unseemly pace. But that isn't the Scottish way and God forbid that it ever should be. Speed does not always equal achievement. Lose those sanctions and the citadel will indeed have fallen: culture and history sent tumbling and the social weave rent asunder. In places, alas, this process may already be under way.

But let's not get too hot and bothered about accepting newcomers into our world. It's up to us to ensure that we as individuals, our children and our grandchildren, from whatever part of the nation we hail, never forget our multi-faceted Scottishness and show our 'guests' that they are right to think that something special lingers north of the border and especially out here in the windy isles. Our land is simply the best and we should be prepared to share what's on offer, providing it's on our terms.

Over the seasons, as we got to know our new home, we gathered a whole new range of agricultural skills and experience. Some back-breaking primitive, nay Neolithic, procedures – like filling fish crates with stones from the field – I took to as if born to the task. Did you know, apropos of nothing really, that you can clear a field of stones as thoroughly as you like after ploughing but next year there will be just as many clogging the clay. It's a fact. And the reason for this? The centrifugal force which is created as the earth spins is constantly pushing chuckies towards the surface. Well, that's my theory anyway.

Stone lifting is one thing. Set me in a field with plenty of empty boxes to fill and I'm as happy as a Cro-Magnon in coo sharn. When

wow! (handwritten margin note)

COW DUNG (handwritten note)

it comes to marginally more complex matters like tattie planting I'm struggling. This business requires initial concentration and, more worryingly, common sense and the ability to separate mind from body. In the shadow of North Rendall's traction engine, one of Papay's more bizarre landmarks, I perch on a board at the rear of the tractor with a box of seed potatoes in my lap, dropping them one by one into the drills. When a little bell rings on a rotating disc attached to the tractor that's the signal to fire a spud into the furrow down a narrow metal tube. By now you'll have gathered that, like many mechanical devices on the island, this is a Heath-Robinson, haun-knittet apparatus, but the generally held view is that this is one of our more effective creations.

Once I'd negotiated the apprentice's initiation (Alice told me to ensure that the spuds landed with stalk uppermost, shades of the legendary Clydebank shipyard tin of tartan paint here, methinks) it became pretty numbing, repetitive work. Having counted the oystercatchers in the next field, hummed a few choruses of 'We Plough the Fields and Scatter' (the good spuds on the land) and examined the bumps on the back of Alex's head, the only relief, I found, was to attempt various mind-expanding exercises such as trying to get the potato down the tube without it touching the sides.

Unlikely though it may be that you'll ever need this information here's the trick – drop the spud towards the front of the tube to allow for the forward motion of the tractor and it will plop cleanly into the furrow. Another device is to anticipate the bell, the spud actually dropping as the bell rings.

Then there's the technique of grabbing a handful of potatoes by the stalks and trying to release them one at a time. Although this is fun and certainly breaks the monotony, invariably you're going to coup some over the edge of the tube. Random shaws make for an untidy field and if the boss sees this procedure, we're talking jotters for sure. All this brain strain for a midwinter plate of chips. Mind you, it may just be imagination but if you've planted the spuds yourself they do seem to have that added flavour. Anyway, my reputation as a patient and unflappable tattie operative soon spread. Within 24 hours Bill o' the Links had recruited me and we were soon working his plot north of Daybreak. I'm promised row 11 (some earlies, some lates) as reward for my efforts.

OUR UNPRODUCTIVE MENAGERIE

You've learned a little about our lambs, but what future is there for an Alpine goat ordained to spend her days among the gently rolling contours of Orkney where anything above 20 feet is a veritable Matterhorn? More than you might imagine. The trick seems to be to make the very best of every available climb. This much became clear when I discovered Jenny perched confidently on the apex of the goat shed roof, neck stretched, beard waving in the breeze and looking for all the world like an advert for Swiss dairy produce.

She was born along the east shore at the farm of Cott, overlooking Surhoose Taing. Under Mima's gentle care Jenny spent her first days in a tea chest, venturing out only for a stagger around the living-room and a spray of the carpet. For days the children worked to clear out years of accumulated junk from our wee byre.

The walls were whitewashed, a straw bed covered the cobblestone floor and a manger was cleverly constructed using the bottom of an old Welsh dresser. I played a minor role in this project, rigging up the electric light which gave the old byre a warmth and comfort I would scarcely have imagined possible.

Jenny was a Saanen, Swiss in origin, with a dazzlingly white coat, pink-rimmed eyes and a plaintive bleat. Odi, a pet lamb, had refused to take his milk from anything other than a vodka bottle. Well, Jenny was clearly from a very different cultural background. Cognac was her choice. The milk substitute came off the steamer along with the niftiest set of teats you've ever clapped eyes on. A rota was organised for four feeds daily, with each frenzy of sooking and slurping followed by an irresistible desire to leap around (the goat, that is!). I don't know what it is about the sheep and goats on Papa Westray but these animals seem to make grand sookers. Must be something in the air.

Jenny's athletic prowess and her mountaineering abilities were soon apparent. The three-foot fence between her little paved courtyard and the garden proved no obstacle at all. We suddenly experienced the curse of the headless daffs. She visited Morag at the school kitchen next door, having scaled the dyke and soon developed a technique of circling the house by balancing on the window ledges.

Within a couple of years I was clearly beginning to get a bit self-conscious about our menagerie. An extract from a despatch sent to the *Sunday Gleaner* in Jamaica:

> It's difficult to know what the islanders think of our burgeoning collection of animals at School Place, or the Ark, as I've heard it whispered. People here like the beasts well enough but keeping animals for pets is non-profitable and, in some ways, an unnatural pastime. In centuries past every creature had a job to do, whether it was the sturdy oxen in the field or the mice-harrying moggies in the barn. I suspect folk consider us a bit soft, feeding animals and getting nothing in return save companionship and loyalty.

Take Asia for instance. He was the only Siamese cat on Papay and flew in from Kirkwall after Floyd, big cuddly Floyd, the children's favourite kitten, went to meet his ancestors under the wheels of a car outside the school. He hadn't, I'm sure, used up any of his nine lives so that piece of homespun philosophy can be consigned to the scrapheap where it belongs. Asia's great grandpa, Adoneam Indigo Firefly, was twice a grand champion and there were another five champions or grand champions among his forebears. Our choice of Asia as a name now seems singularly unimaginative with such an impressive pedigree. He was the consummate thief, aristocratic and

fierce when it took his mind. Woe betide the brave feline who meddled with his chicken leg. Out shot a silky paw and the villain was grasped by the scalp and held fast. All done without missing a chew.

Siamese cats are one thing – Siamese rats quite another. Polly and Sybil occupied a rabbit hutch in the backyard and it was no use telling folk these smashers were once worshipped as gods. Rats are bad news in a farming community. However, I would have taken Basil too but I was certain to be accused of attempting to set up some kind of rodent stud. Their arrival was a clandestine affair. Some kind soul brought them to the shop where they were handed over to Katy, the only comment being: 'Yer hamsters huv arrived.' Katy, discreet little soul, said nothing.

Dogs can swim. Fact. Seals can swim further, deeper, faster and longer. Another fact. The problem is that no one told our family Alsatian Sam this basic law of the wild and as a result he caused us considerable angst. Firstly, let me declare my affection for the seals. Anger and outrage over their culling (why can't we just admit it's killing?) of the selkies has always seemed to me to be the correct response. They are gentle, thoughtful, otherworldly, yet friendly and inquisitive. They enjoyed a fish diet long before man began to plunder the seas and blame its less profitworthy occupants for depletion of fish stocks. Statistics to prove these allegations are anxiously awaited.

In summer, when the light in our northern isle has a clarity unmatched anywhere in the United Kingdom, the seals laze on the skerries, lolling from side to side on the weed-covered sandstone, catching the sun and watching the world go by. If you venture too close to family groups they simply flop into the sea and wait unconcerned until the passers-by are on their way. That spring our resident colony of grey and common seals, now numbering over one hundred, had something out of the ordinary to amuse them. With four legs, a bushy tail, a desire to swim and a curiosity matching that of the seals, Sam arrived.

On his first excursion along the sands of the South Wick he seemed at first unaware of the sea creatures bobbing along a few yards offshore, intent on his every swerve, sprint and jump. Sam, for his part, was concerned only with his rubber ball which bounced crazily off the jagged rocks and splashed into the pools. Then, out of the corner of his eye, he suddenly noticed a multitude of heads watching him from the shallows . . . 30 pairs of eyes, black and beady, fixed on him. For a few moments they studied each other, creatures secure in their own environments. This first encounter was brief and unremarkable, simply a sizing up. In no way did it prepare us for what was to follow the next day.

To our amazement the dog made straight for the water's edge. Having spotted the seals, he paddled into the chilly tide, performed a few lazy strokes amid this army of new acquaintances and then swam off in the direction of Holm, half a mile away across the inlet. Soon only a head, a thin pointed head among the Roman noses, was discernible. Then the shallow swell hid them all, only the occasional barking of a seal and a slapping dive betraying their whereabouts. Was Sam never to return? Had he been spirited away like a lost sailor charmed by the mermaids? We sat on the sand and peered helplessly across the bay.

Certainly the hunky bull seals could have disposed of him with one dunt if they had had a mind to, but it had been some comfort to see the way they were diving and carousing around him as they moved away from shore. Dog owners carry an awesome burden of responsibility. There are fights to be avoided, pavements to be kept clean, busy roads to negotiate. But surely here was something new – kidnap by seals. Trying to call him back had proved useless. He was under the spell of a unique experience. Going where no dog had gone before. Water: the final frontier.

Twenty minutes later, as Morag worked on a form of words to explain his loss to the children, a familiar head appeared in the distance. He was swimming much more slowly, battling against the tide now strongly on its way out, but heading steadily, with a weary determination towards the sandy sweep where we waited. Padding up the beach he stopped to shake himself and although a bit shoogly on the old pins, he recovered quickly enough to want the ball thrown again. He had returned unabashed by his adventure and we didn't have the heart to ladel into him for his disobedience.

After this incident was related in one of my columns, the London press took an interest in this unlikely tale from the modern Orkney sagas and big money was mentioned for a re-enactment of Samson seal-swimmer's epic voyage, this time for the cameras. We decided not to push his luck.

Eventually, there was a column to be written which I'd always dreaded. Sam, bought in the bar of the Castle Inn, Dirleton, and brought to a life of splendid freedom in Orkney, my companion of a thousand beachcombing expeditions, went to meet his pointy-eared ancestors. For weeks it had been obvious that he was failing. A leg injury which he had sustained in a sprint across the links after his ball had never repaired itself. His joints were stiffening, he was deaf and his eyesight was failing. Although of an indeterminate age – Sam was at least twelve – it was a good innings for the breed, the vet told us comfortingly.

The pair of us had become a familiar sight along Papay's muddy tracks. But the days had gone when he could leap like a fawn into the back of the van. The so'-westerly gales which he had defied for years now buffeted him mercilessly as he staggered across the field o' Sunnybraes on his morning walks. These walks, once long, rambling affairs by the tideline or along the marshy margin of the loch to the tumbledown chapel had been curtailed to a quarter-mile trek to the Old Pier and a sniff around the broken-down farmyard at Nouster. His days as top dog on Papay were past. Great battles were forgotten and the sheep and chickens now treated him with studied contempt. Even the bold bunnies in our field strolled across his bow. A sad state of affairs for an old hound.

When the vet left School Place for the Westray boat I carried my old pal round to the garden where we'd booked a spot for him in the shelter of the west dyke. A sharp wind whipped in over the kirk wall as it had done on the day of our arrival on the island. Memories flooded back. Sam's introduction to Papay saw him staggering around the tiny carpark at the airstrip, knocked stupid by sedatives which had kept him calm on the flight north from Edinburgh. Then there was the night he had returned home disgraced, having come off second best in a scrap with a *blind* Labrador! Sam carried the scars of many a scrap; he loved people but hated dogs. In his early days on Papay he would go courting to nearby farms, once chewing his way through the shed door to begin his amorous adventures. On that occasion he trapped Alice in her kitchen and she was found trying to calm the savage beast by feeding him scraps through the window.

Once he climbed unseen into the back of nurse Fiona's car for a bit of hanky-panky with her Labrador, Bess. A litter of Albadors was anticipated. Small for an Alsatian, we always suspected he was the runt of the litter. Perhaps that was why, as a misfit, he found himself so much at home in the occasionally crazy, always confused, life at the Hewitsons.

Small of stature he may have been but he was a brave heart. One particularly fierce January day we walked south through a blizzard to carry hay to our horses. The return leg was simply hellish. In whiteout conditions, with snow freezing on our faces and the initial sense of adventure fast turning to genuine apprehension, Sam paced back and forward, his coat caked with snow, shepherding the family through the drifts and down the hill to the safety of our own fireside.

It's strange not to hear his warning bark when Jim the postie turns up the track or to hear him reminding me it's teatime by playing keepy-uppy with his tin bowl. Already his den under the stairs looks awfy empty. Latterly he was slow, stubborn and, it has to be said, a bit smelly. We'll miss him, but we're a big bunch and there is no time to stop and stare – horses wait for their hay, the donkey and goat will want down from the manse field to their wee byre and there's a regiment of cats to be fed.

It wasn't too many weeks before the children, seeing me pine, arrived off the steamer with a sheepdog called Spot and together we follow the well-worn tracks through the fields and along the shore which I wandered with Sam. Spot has to forgive me if I find myself inadvertently calling him 'Spam'.

BEWARE THE PAPAY PECK!

Sheep take a bit of watching, we learned very quickly after our arrival on Papay. Up at Sheepheight I recall helping with a set of these unpredictable woollies as 89 lambs, eight of them belonging to the School Place flock, were being readied for shipping to the mart.

Jim had devised a new handling system which worked pretty efficiently, allowing us to filter the sheep through for counting and marking. The casualty list that day included Phemie (mainly through pride I think) who had the feet ca'd from her by a lamb (bit of a misnomer because by this time they were sturdy buggers) and I sustained a couple of bruised ribs when one of the over-excited creatures flew at me through the air like an all-in wrestler in a woolly jumper.

Alas, when we had successfully moved them down the hill and thought we had them securely penned on the pier, they made a desperate break for freedom and, despite a frantic, last-minute round-up, with the steamer already on the horizon towards Eday, we were only able to recapture 31 in time for shipping that day.

The slaying of Sylvester is assuredly the saddest and most dramatic of winter tales concerning the woolly ones of Papay. Sylvester was a Holmie and a much-loved companion of Pam Gould. Since she left the island Sylvester had been tethered around

Sheepheight, swiftly becoming as much a part of the scenery as the abandoned cars, assorted items of ageing farm equipment, cats, dogs and peacocks.

Jim's plan had been to use him to train his new sheepdog, Bouncer, but this imaginative proposal was not in Sylvester's stars. His fate was sealed when we ran him with the rest of the flock through yet another sheep handling system which Jim had cleverly improvised from staves, wire, metal, palettes and the old gangway from the pier. (Shh! Don't tell the shipping company.) Sylvester had been moored to a heavy iron hoop on the green beside the pens; this gave him plenty of freedom but stopped him wandering off towards the craigs.

First the ewes were steered on to the green, then enter the four rams which we'd coaxed up the steep brae from the links. Almost immediately, amid the mêlée, Sylvester collapsed in a heap. It didn't take a 'tec to solve this hot-blooded slaying. One of the huge Suffolk rams, ignoring Sylvester's fine set of curving horns and fearing a bit of opposition, I suppose, in the servicing stakes, had floored the old Holmie with a devastating head butt; a 'Papay peck' as one insensitive wag would have it. As Sylvester was dragged to the sidelines, Jim leaned on his crook and shook his head ruefully. His observation had a simple beauty: 'Did ye see that? One dunt and he wis deid!'

And there was another problem. In a few days Pamela was due to make a brief visit to the island. She would be inconsolable, we thought. All sorts of panic measures were considered. Could we prop Sylvester up at the far side of the Gayfield Park and offer Pamela a quick glance through the binocs or would Katy don sad Sylvester's coat and horns and munch with the rest of the flock – a Trojan sheep – in some distant and inaccessible corner of the farm?

The next day, while Jim was pondering this dilemma and drafting an explanatory letter, an amazing thing happened. Home-made greetings cards arrived at several homes on the island, including Sheepheight. They were from Pamela and the front carried an atmospheric photograph taken at the north end of the island under sombre, snow-laden skies. Posing confidently in the foreground was the late-lamented Sylvester. Beneath ran the text: 'A righteous man regardeth the life of his beast'. Was Pam psychic? Was the cosmic joker at work?

Whatever, Jim had to lie down for a few minutes to recover from this thunderbolt before redrafting his letter in much, much more sensitive terms. Fortunately, when Pamela did arrive, she adopted a philosophical approach to the loss and concentrated her affection on Perky, the Shetland pony. Jim was relieved.

Omens and dark prophecy played no significant part in my childhood in Clydebank, the only worthwhile forecast in those far-off days was that, if the polis caught you playing football against the metal doors of the biscuit factory, you'd get a cuff round the lug.

However, edging up the road one afternoon from the Old Pier using Dixie our Jacob ewe as a shield against her fearsome, horned hubby, one-eyed Jack the Lad, I had this recurring vision of model sheep. If I'd just remembered earlier how the sheep on my model railway layout simply refused to stand upright, I might have read the runes and saved myself a lot of heartache – ewe-wise. As for Jack, he was, as our island predecessors might have said, 'a mad etterkep o' a ting'.

We had a brief but eventful relationship. Morag had returned on an expedition to Kirkwall with the ewe and two lambs. They were a smashing trio, alert and affectionate with the distinctive brown and white blotches of the Jacob breed. They settled in well on the little park between Daybreak and the school. Morag had some vague notion that we would become millionaires by selling the fleeces after a breeding programme.

In the quest for a ram, lengthy negotiations were conducted over the phone with a Westray gent who rejoices in the name of Long Dod o' the Ring, a man who chooses his words carefully and very, very slowly. When the ram arrived he was just as fascinating as his owner. Jack was sturdy, blind in the left eye and possessed the most menacing set of scimitar-like horns.

Unfortunately, Dixie was not enthusiastic about his amorous intentions and a break for freedom was on the cards. One morning they were gone; over or under the wire, it mattered not. A search was immediately organised with Morag taking the Land Rover south while I headed off in the direction of the Old Pier with Sam. It was in the abandoned front garden of Bayview that I found the pair munching on the lush grass. The ewe, tempted by a pocketful of goat feed, was quickly lassoed and came quietly but Jack got nasty and launched a series of charges.

I managed to haul the ewe around and progressed back up the road keeping her between myself and surly old Jack, who had the occasional sideswipe at Sam. The dog hadn't had this much fun in ages. We made a very strange quartet that winter morning. Rearrangements had to be made and the ewe and lambs went over to our field by the loch and Jack found a new home in Sandwick. I can testify to one certainty. Working with the sheep of Orkney during the day makes counting the brutes at night to aid slumber quite unnecessary.

HONG KONG AMONG THE HOLMS AND SKERRIES

Reminiscing over past land use on Papay or speculating about the future can, from time to time, prompt bizarre notions. In *The Inverness Courier* I indulged myself in what can only be described as an Oriental flight of fancy.

Recent events in Hong Kong had set me thinking that we might be a trifle cagey, unambitious and restrained in our efforts to develop the island's economy. However, if we're determined to enter the race for commercial success on a broad front then we must ascertain what is our greatest asset – it's the land, of course. Let's not be half-hearted or shilly-shallying, let's go for broke, as our American guests have been heard to say.

Our commonwealth compatriots in Hong Kong, or at least a substantial number of the 3,200,000 British passport-holders will, we are told, soon be looking for new homes with the handover to

China. So far, however, the Government seems to be shutting the door in the faces of all but a select few.

Recently the Adam Smith Institute – the occasionally over-imaginative right-wing think tank – suggested that the Western Highlands could be the location of a new city to house these refugees. But I believe they are being unfair to our Gaelic counterparts in the west. They are not equipped to absorb alien cultures in the way that Orkney has done for centuries, millennia even. Perhaps the Hong Kong problem can be solved at a stroke.

I'll whisper it so no one here on Papay gets prematurely concerned but if the Government is set on denying hospitality then let the island of Papa Westray open its green acres to this legion of would-be settlers. Anyone with a calculator will tell you that squeezing three million people into six square miles scarcely leaves enough room to swing a wok, but the whole point of this exercise is to make the Hong Kong evacuees feel at home. We'll build up the way, with perhaps a little more flexibility in the tower blocks than normal to allow for winter gales.

Our topography may not be identical to the island of Hong Kong but I feel there are enough similarities to make the idea work. We have the North Hill with ample room to reassemble the Peak where better-off residents could lounge on the terraces of their penthouses and watch the birdlife pass by. We will find an Orcadian equivalent of Kai Tak in the valleys above Hundland and Bewing. The floating market of Aberdeen should present no problems. The Bay of Moclett is a sheltered anchorage and could provide moorings for as many junks as care to make the journey from the Orient. We'll simply have to ensure that there's enough clearance for the steamers to squeeze into the pier.

The teeming fruit and vegetable markets could be recreated in Holland's walled garden while banking and commercial premises would be based around Bill Irvine's front room at Links where flying bankers already conduct their business once monthly. Stocks may have to be increased at the Co-op shop. To have only three bags of rice available at any one time may prove insufficient and surely someone is bound to make a killing in the lychee import business. Government House may present problems but the community rooms at the school might fit the bill and Jim Rendall (he of the Chinese blood, you'll recall) would seem the obvious choice for governor.

Frequency of air services would certainly have to be increased and a strict control exerted over the sheep and cattle which wander the runway. Yes, indeed, on close examination the problems seem small and the potential enormous. Could Hong Kong really come to Scotland? Well, didn't Birnham Wood, much against expectations, eventually come to Dunsinane? Come to think of it, I might go into the restaurant business myself. With some suitable piped music and a few lanterns my goat shed would be just the ticket.

SERENADING THE SELKIES

One of the privileges of living on an island which can provoke so many imaginative ramblings is that from time to time we get to play host to visitors and to see this very special place anew, through their eyes. To show off a little. And do we get our share of interesting visitors? You bet your sweet bippy we do.

I remember the New Age man who arrived in kaftan and flowing locks to be ferried across to the Holm where, perched on a rock, he produced a flute and started to serenade the seals along the shore. Such esoteric, spaced-out behaviour does not tend to impress the hard-working, practical folk of Papay and Rab fae Windywalls brought him back to earth with a bump when he demanded on the return crossing: 'Can ye play the Sash on that thing?' You can't keep a good Lanarkshire man down.

A surprisingly large number of level-headed visitors do indeed seem to be overtaken with this crazy urge to serenade the seals. Drawn mysteriously to the shore, a quick glance around, no one in sight and a couple of quick choruses from *The Sound of Music*. None of you will admit it, I know. But you know it to be so.

Still on a musical theme, in the summer of 1993 we had a visit from a gent who brought along his bagpipes and was also soon under the spell of Papay. He was a bit of a showman I should say because he'd hardly unpacked his bags before he was marching up and down in front of the Co-op, giving it laldie. However, he couldn't compete with Edward our donkey in the adjacent manse field, who, on hearing the skirl of the pipes, set up a braying din which echoed around the centre of the island and drowned out the disgusted musician.

And then there was Pete, the urban cowboy. Stepping off the afternoon flight into a steady drizzle, he halted on the pad to get the traditional photos of the pilot signing the cargo manifest. It was at this point that I noted that our guest, a Paris-based American writer, was wearing cowboy boots. Not just a battered pair of cowpuncher buits, you understand, but fine, embossed brown leather specimens with pointed toes; the sort of stylish gear I would have sold my *Pop go the Beatles* tapes for in the sixties.

From the Place Vendome to Papay's North Hill is the sort of quantum leap that really demands appropriate footwear. Baccy-chewing, Marlboro County boots which would raise gasps of admiration at an Elysee Palace news briefing or nods of approval at a rodeo in Wyoming are, I fear, simply non-starters for Papay's boggy acres. Out came the reserve wellies from the back of the car and Pete was ready to go. He also borrowed a baseball cap from the Hewitson hat-rack. Talk about coals to Newcastle. Out here on the last frontier we have improvisation honed to a fine art.

Travel writer and stringer for an impressive list of big-name US journals, Pete has a Scottish pedigree, his grandfather having emigrated from Edinburgh. Quietly Pete confessed that on an earlier visit to Scotland he had a mystical experience, an encounter with something that wasn't there in the physical sense. Now, I've found that the Papay home-brew can have the same effect but Pete has been sold on Scotland ever since that odd event. Having searched for his indelible-ink pen and wiped the rain off his glasses, Pete interviewed the airstrip personnel, David and Bobby from Whitehowe, who have fielded more questions over the years about the famous short hop than they care to remember.

Checking in for his overnight at the guest-house, Pete tiptoed past the dining-room. With the journalist's nose for news he'd landed on Papay on an important day for the community. A delegation from Orkney Islands Shipping Company was 'in town' to debate our sea links with the mainland. Islanders, councillors and officials were hard at it by mid-afternoon. Meeting up in the shop, Pete whispered conspiratorially in my ear: 'Milk deliveries seem to be the big issue.' Ah, Pete, if only it were as simple as that.

The rain showed no sign of letting up so, heads down, we plodded along the North Wick with Sam diving in and out of the surf. Pete lit up, with difficulty in the buffeting wind, offered me a fag and shrugged with resignation at my refusal: 'Ah reckon I must be the last person in the world that smokes.' Come to think of it, a week trying to light cigarettes on the wind-blasted North Hill would be enough to turn anyone away from smoking for life.

But our short-stay guest was inhaling more than tobacco smoke he was breathing in the tranquillity. We passed the mysterious

paved causeway which stretches out below the sand at Hundland and clambered over the rusting metal from the wreck of the *Bellavista*, and along the lonely beach at Neil's Helly where thousands of giant boulders, each weighing a ton or more, fringe the shore.

On the precarious sandstone finger, which gives an awesome view of the rock tenements where the kittiwakes nest at Fowl Craig, we paused. Walking up on to the hill we talked of many things – of tourist development, of the subtle differences between the tourist and the traveller, of trips in glass-bottomed boats in Canada to view the seal colonies (scope here, methinks, for some local entrepreneur). We spoke of the royal family and their

Rainier family and *Paris Match*, of Paris during the war and of Clydebank during the blitz.

Up on the heath, as we searched more in hope than expectation for the first of that year's crop of the Scots primrose, the sun burst through the towering grey clouds. 'I know why you're up here, Jim,' he confided, 'it all makes more sense.' Next morning Pete pulled on his cowboy boots and flew back to Kirkwall. The Viking trumpet tells me that he mistakenly got out at North Ronaldsay, thinking he'd reached Orkney mainland. But I know better, he simply wanted to ease himself back into the hurly-burly – one step at a time.

Chapter Six

Beneath a Wall of Water

A BASINFUL O' PARTANS

The Bay of Burland is a deceptive and dangerous place. For good reason it is known to the islanders of Papa Westray as the 'graveyard'. A few hundred yards along the shore at Hookin' a rough mound marks the last resting place of perhaps a dozen or more seamen who were drowned last century when their sailing ship came ashore at the tail of the Holm. Treacherous territory, indeed. Today, however, as we round the Mill Point and make for the line of bobbing buoys, the bay wears a tranquil face, waves splashing gently on the rock shelves below the abandoned farm of Blossom.

Mind you, as the first creel clatters aboard with a disappointing cargo of ware and velvets it's difficult for Jim and myself to forget that only a few yards from here we received a hard reminder that creeling is not an easy calling. The fruits of the deep are always hard won. Too early after an unexpected summer gale which devastated our fleet of creels we ventured out on a recovery mission. From his kitchen window on the morning after the storm, Jim scanned the east shore and spotted a tangle of ropes and buoys in the middle of Burland. We knew there was still a powerful sea running but the wind had dropped and halfway through the lobster season we couldn't afford to lose a single day.

Out in the bay, having lashed one of the slippery creel ropes to the middle bench, Jim sent the *Valkyr* charging off in an effort to pop the shattered creel out from under the rock ledge where it lay jammed, fathoms below us. We were in the middle of the third charge when a series of half-a-dozen waves came sweeping into the bay towards us. Immediately, we freed the rope and turned to face them, riding the first two waves with ease. However, at the back of the pack, still some 50 yards off, a huge bottle-green wall was a-building. It seemed to grow before our eyes and held us transfixed as it rose to block out the eastern horizon. It was probably only 15 feet high but looked easily twice that. There was nowhere to run. I braced myself against the seat while Jim crouched in the stern, keeping the engine turning over and muttering under his breath. He is not an over-religious man but I suspect a little prayer found its way to his lips at that moment.

In retrospect, I should have been afraid, terrified even. But the truth is that I gaped open-mouthed as it bore down on us. My memory of those amazing few seconds was of being filled with wonder at the enormity of this lump of water. The wave curled above us, ominously beginning to crest at its peak. The *Valkyr* ran straight up its face, straight up towards the sky, the bow impossibly high above our heads.

Half a degree to port or starboard and the force of this monster would have spun and capsized us for sure. Jim's seamanship was sorely tested. We seemed to climb for an eternity before, outboard screaming, we sat atop the wave; then we dropped through the air to land with a crash which sent the timbers shivering and would surely have shattered a lesser boat. We left the creels in Burland for another day or two. Nothing is that urgent.

Today, the enigmatic bay is an altogether friendlier place and we push on towards the wreck of the trawler *Nousy* on the north side of Burland. Working around the remains of the skeleton of the old *Nousy*, who came to her final rest on Papay on a filthy night in the 1940s, is difficult. Shafts of steel, still below the water at most tides, guard her and only on a couple of occasions have I seen the tide low enough to expose the bulk of her weed-encrusted boiler. But the lobsters who lurk in her remains can be formidable specimens and emerge as if half-cooked, with a distinctive reddish-brown tinge acquired from the rusting metal around them.

It's poor fare in Burland today, I fear. We decide on an ambitious plan, taking the creels two miles north to the caves at Fowl Craig. A foolhardy move, perhaps, for two men who lost half their fleet of creels to a summer storm but you don't catch lobs by sitting around waiting for them to pay you a visit. They have to be hunted. At Fowl Craig we are only a few hundred yards from the Bore which guards the northern passage around the island; the backwash from the cliffs is always troublesome. So we ca' canny, Jim watching the movement of the swell as it climbs hugely up the guano-stained cliffs while I feed the creels rhythmically into the deep. Fingers crossed that we find some productive 'bottom' at this spectacular site.

Moving into the shadow of the rock tenements, home to a township of kittiwakes, guillemots, shags, cormorants and puffins, the stench is unmistakable. Great echoing caverns have been gouged into the overhanging sandstone mass; waves crash into hidden walls way back in the darkness; only with the gentlest of seas and absence of swell dare you enter these awesome stone cathedrals. Birds dive and swoop around us and the guillemots show their underwater agility, zipping through the cold, lime-green water beneath the *Valkyr*. One last look at the line of buoys, a reassuring glance at the sky and we're under way again on the half-hour run to the Old Pier.

I was soon to realise that for every successful session at the creeling or for each expedition after bait there would be a wheen of frustratingly unproductive days. Female lobsters breed every other year, laying many thousands of eggs. More than occasionally, as an empty creel emerges from the deep and is bumped aboard you do wonder where the hell they've all got to. It's worrying Orkney fishermen too, and all sorts of conservation measures are now being considered.

In the summer of 1989, after a run along our line of creels at Mill Point, disappointment was noted in my diary:

> A cold sea washed in to the South Wick today and from 20 creels in the vicinity of the Mill we got a basinful of partans, an octopus, two huge dog whelks and an undersize lobster. Out at the Shooders, bait proved equally elusive. The tide was running so strongly that despite the weights the long lines were almost breaking surface. As much chance of catching a cormorant as a cuithe!

The cuithes, or coalfish, make excellent bait for the creels, halved and used either fresh or salted. Using hand lines with up to six hooks on each line is the traditional method of fishing for cuithes hereabouts. It's an extraordinary feeling to run the line down into the heaving darkness and sense the hooks being jerked, then taken one after another as the line passes through the shoal. Then you haul the jumping, silvery catch on board and try to unhook them.

On a productive day this can be a mad and dangerous scramble – the bottom of the boat awash with tumbling fish and bare hooks spinning around.

Sometimes we would be accompanied at our labours out on the swell by a pair of passing porpoises, dipping and diving elegantly and occasionally surfacing close by for a look-see with a distinctive whooshing sound. With these sleek anglers around a modest catch was the best you could hope for.

Unexpected difficulties also arose. Pondering the wisdom and the necessity of wearing glasses out at the creels, I found myself confessing to my diary:

> Windscreen wipers would seem to be the order of the day at the creels if this drizzly weather persists. Between salt spray and rain I found it well-nigh impossible to guide the *Valkyr* among buoys and around the submerged, seaweed-cloaked edges at Alskar, a circular reef in the North Wick. As Jim lowered the creels, I pondered the possibility that specs and shellfishing might not sit easily together.

A similarly downbeat entry reported how we had to free three young blackbirds from the stacked creels at the Old Pier before we set off . . . a considerably better catch, I noted bitterly, than was to materialise during the next couple of hours. You see, it wasn't always bulging creels and dancing hooks.

Our disappointment at the creels is as nothing, assuredly, compared with the hardships endured when every family on the island had a boat and the Papay fleet ventured out over the horizon in search of fish. Over a glass of home-brew Bill o' the Links was reminding me of the way the sea can wreak terrible havoc in such a small community. There are plenty of sad examples. The three men who drowned in 1882 after crossing to Westray to be measured for wedding suits or the story of Willie o' Kimbland's grandfather and two uncles who drowned off the North Wick in 1904, seemingly within easy reach of the shore, when their boat capsized and disappeared on the way back from the fishing. Their bodies were never found. That day, a group of island youngsters making their way home from school along the east shore were told in passing a farm steading to keep their voices down – 'The boat o' Kimbland is lost'.

On a less sombre note Bill informed me that, for some inexplicable reason, the hardy men of Papay found it difficult to pass water when they were out at the fishing. The cure for this strange malady (prepare to be stunned) was to cut and carry a slab of the emerald green turf of Papay in the bottom of the boat on to which the fishermen were apparently able to pee, nae bother. A quick check of the diary confirmed that 1 April was still some weeks away.

SHIPWRECKED ON CANNIBAL ISLAND

Around AD 84, according to the historian Tacitus, a Roman fleet circumnavigated Orkney. This must have brought them very close to Papa Westray. Tacitus mentions a particularly fierce tidal race and I like to imagine that this was the 'Bore' off Mull Head where the Atlantic and North Sea crash into each other in a frenzy of creamy breakers. From archaeological evidence we know that our island was a busy place around that time. Perhaps the islanders, from the safety of their brochs, watched the Roman galleys with their golden and red sails pass menacingly and majestically by. Then again, there may be Roman timbers and wine jars among the tangles on the bottom somewhere offshore because the rugged coast of Papay has, over the centuries, claimed many vessels, the old *Nousy* at Burland being just one of a sunken fleet.

One of my favourite spots on the North Hill is Ned's Cott, a couple of shallow depressions above the shore, just beyond Fowl Craig. The abandoned and roofless goose pens, owned last century by a kirk elder by the name of Edward Thomson from the farm of Breck on the North Wick, afford shelter from the winds which cut across the heath and offer a spectacular view out towards Norway. Near here on the rocks the freighter *Bellavista* was wrecked in 1948 and at the pens a fire was lit to warm the distressed mariners who were brought ashore by breeches buoy. Among the foreign crew, according to island tradition, were two African seamen, one of whom reached safety holding his trousers aloft to keep them dry and wielding a meat cleaver because he feared he would be eaten by the savages of this remote island!

On a beautiful summer's afternoon with the South Wick mirror-still it's difficult to believe that the coastline of this small island is studded with wreck sites. The truth is that in winter this can be a fearsome place.

Somewhere off the point of Vestness in the 1790s, says island lore, a vessel called the *Peggy* went down with her cargo of slate.

Impregnated with iron pyrites (fool's gold) the slates can still be found from time to time along the desolate Vestness shore, near where a summer tinker encampment used to be located. North by, at a wild piece of shattered rock and swirling seas called the Floodnisses, old shoreline fishing sites, is the spot where the trawler *City of Lincoln* foundered with the loss of six lives. Here again a boiler can be seen at the lowest of tides, I'm told.

Over on the east shore there are equally sorry tales of vessels which have been thrown on to the Papay shore by the anger of the sea. Only a few of the more recent wrecks have found their way into the island annals but names along the shore occasionally harken back to a wreck – the Skold near Fowl Craig, for instance, being named after a Norwegian ship which was lost there.

In the year 1805, with a ferocious storm blowing out of the south-east, a Swedish vessel with a cargo of beer was thrown up on the far side of the Holm. The ship split in two and the barrels were washed up on the main island. As ever, the man of Holland, on this occasion George Traill, insisted that the booty was his and his alone. Despite his keen eye, the crofters were not about to miss the chance of a lifetime and considerable quantities of the beer were spirited away to caches on the hill or hidden in the rafters of the byre. It's said that the winter of 1805–06 was Papay's happiest in living memory.

February 1853 saw the *Antelope* of Bergen wrecked on Weelie's Taing during a northerly gale. The ship broke up and although most of her crew escaped, the captain, Rasmussen by name, elected to stay on board his ship until it began to disintegrate. Clinging to a mast, he was swept round into the South Wick and came ashore at Maybo'. Sadly he died and today the location of his grave by the shore is forgotten.

The *Antelope*'s cargo of timber was eventually auctioned on the island for the princely sum of £475.19s.8d. This windfall of cheap timber encouraged the islanders to extend and improve their homes and to make new furniture. However, when the Traill laird noted any improvements, the rents were increased accordingly.

Many improvements in the domestic architecture of Papay can be traced to such wrecks. The top floor of the house of Nouster, down near the Old Pier, is said to have been constructed from the timbers of a target ship used by the Royal Navy during the First World War.

There are also stories of local heroism. In 1906 the men of Papay's lifesaving team were called out to help in the rocket rescue of the crew of the Aberdeen steam trawler *Badger*, which had grounded on the Bow Skerry across on Westray. The Papay men rowed the doctor's boat *Aileen* to the scene and using their newly acquired lifesaving apparatus brought eight men, one by one, from the stricken vessel. The significance of this rescue was that it was possibly the first time that a rocket rescue had been attempted from a boat. The crew of the *Aileen* were commended at the Kirkwall inquiry into the wreck.

With this sort of heritage, the island is ever on its guard and respectful of the sea, although much of the rescue back-up falls to the helicopter service these days. Even on the calmest of evenings there can be problems. I recall getting word that John David of Sooth-hoose in his lobster boat *Jacinth* had stuck fast on Surhoose Taing in the gathering gloom. His shouts had been heard at Cott. Tracking his position on the reef by his yells we were able to take the *Valkyr* with her shallow draught out on to the taing, Jim carefully edging her between the sandstone ridges.

We pinpointed the *Jacinth* in the distance with the spotlight and found John David leaning disconsolately over the gunwale. He was persuaded to temporarily abandon ship and the *Jacinth* was refloated on the morning tide, apparently undamaged. Today the *Jacinth* is one of only half-a-dozen small boats regularly in use around Papay and based on the island. What a contrast with 1870 when it was reported that Papa Westray had 254 boats, almost one for every inhabitant!

Outwith the calm weeks of summer the struggle with the elements seems a constant one. In the autumn of 1988 I recorded:

> The equinoctial gales are with us. Listened on the VHF to the dramatic helicopter rescue of crewmen from a freighter which threatened to run ashore below the Noup Head cliffs across on Westray, only a few miles from us. In fierce northerly gales, with white-crested waves ringing the islands, four men were winched to safety from their 900-ton vessel. The problem had been engine failure and we heard the helicopter pilot suggesting to no one in particular that a return to the days of sail might be overdue. I fear his workload would be much increased were that to happen. Engines on the cargo boat were finally restarted by crewmen who had remained aboard.

Beachcombing is a secret joy of Orkney strangely absent from the tourist literature. Yet few people who come north for the fishing, scuba-diving, birdwatching or the archaeological glories feel their stay is complete without sampling the delights of our tidal ponds or weed-fringed strands. My own meanderings along the rock ledges and tide lines of our isle over the years have yielded much strange fruit.

Our kitchen fire is nurtured still by the remains of a pile of 500 pit props, part of a vast deck cargo, bound for Wales from Scandinavia, so we learned, which was set adrift one wild night from a struggling freighter. That year the tattielands were abandoned and the howking temporarily forgotten as the whole island, men, women and bairns, lifted logs for a day or two.

On a less dramatic scale you'll find a rusty German helmet from the First World War which is now a hidey-hole for the kittens at the front door; in the porch sits a lump of driftwood, which looks for all the world like a great whale twisting and diving; and perhaps most tantalisingly, on the hall cabinet lies a small, white, screw-on number plate – number 14 in fact – from the cabin door of some stricken ship, surely.

Thanks again to my diary I can pretty accurately date the start of this obsession with the edge of the sea. In the autumn of 1984:

> Wandering along the curve of the North Wick today huge waves rolled in, white-capped; spindrift rising out on the taing. Black clouds north towards Shetland. The beach was unusually cluttered with litter – jetsam from some passing freighter in the Fair Isle channel perhaps. Here a cardboard milk carton, tin cans, the inevitable plastic bottles and there, among the seaweed, a cormorant, his fishing days over.
>
> Scientists tell us (don't ask me how they worked it out) that some man-made items decay faster than others. A movie ticket (a collector's item in its own right up here) takes only two weeks; a woollen sock up to a year; a tin can takes 100 years and a plastic bottle up to 450. Does this mean that the plastic fruit juice container at my feet had been around since the Reformation? Scary!

The craft of beachcombing is not the haphazard business you might imagine. There are rules and regulations. Woe betide the wanderer who lifts someone else's salvage, hauled up above the high-tide line. Once the seasoned campaigner has single-mindedly dragged his spoils through the seaweed tangles and up on to the security of the banks he or she should be able to collect it at a later date, knowing it has been formally claimed. On an island where you're never more than a few hundred yards from the sea and the shoreline is a constant pull, it's no wonder that beachcombing has developed into a skilled trade.

West-facing shores can be expected to capture occasional gems swept here by the Gulf Stream from the US or Canadian tidewater and from as far south as the Caribbean. Drift seeds, which may have been in the water for years, their vital life centres protected by a thick shell, occasionally turn up on our beaches. I'm told they can be coaxed out of suspended animation in the warmth of the porch, a world away from their sun-kissed home beach.

Every one of our households can produce some seaborne treasure for the interested visitor – a lump of pumice, froth from a lava outburst, a float launched into the St Lawrence seaway by oceanographers or a selection of beached bottles with messages from a Swedish schoolchild or a lonely fisherman in the Faroe Islands. Unquestionably the most famous message in a bottle reputed to have come ashore on Papay was launched from the ill-fated Franklin expedition of 1845 which shortly before had set out from the Orkney port of Stromness in search of the Northwest Passage.

East-facing shores, looking out to the grey North Sea are more likely to receive the flotsam of Scandinavian and Baltic countries. But nothing is certain in this strange pastime; tide and wind can play odd games. After listening to the shipping forecast, shorelines must be carefully selected; anticipation grows of surprises lurking below the banks after a night of storms. The daily expectation is for a sack of driftwood to stoke the fire. It's seldom, alas, that the comber, peering into the pools beneath the cliff face or sifting seaweed under towering Orkney skies, will find the Holy Grail, the dreamed-about windfall. But the tantalising possibility is always there and it is this which keeps you trudging on when the rain drips down your neck and the west wind smacks you around.

The value of the discovered objects is very much in the eye of the beholder. I wouldn't swap my German helmet for anything . . . except perhaps that beautiful bronze plaque which, I'm told, hangs at the back of a barn at the north end and is etched with the Stars and Stripes.

Shipwrecks are, of course, the ultimate experience for the beachcomber. In the Orkney of not so many years ago these were a target for gentry and peasantry alike and the successful plundering of vessels could set families up for life. Although simple beachcombing, the snapping up of unconsidered trifles can become an obsession for island folk, summer visitors take it all a bit more lightly. It's now an established tradition that people who stay with us at School Place take part in a trek around the fringe of the North Hill, a hike enlivened by a keenly fought contest to gather the most unlikely objects from the shore. All sorts of categories exist, the more obscene they are, the more popular they seem to be with the children. Points are awarded and prizes given.

Generally we're looking for the smelliest, most useful, smallest and, of course, the best living or formerly living object (that one is almost sure to get the parents raging). By evening, as the weary walkers return in ones and twos, the porch is littered with plastic floats, chains, assorted balls, perhaps a Norwegian milk carton or a Russian fly spray, assorted lumps of wood, metal, bone, unspecific organic matter and a selection of deceased wildlife or parts thereof. The presentation is made and the treasures spirited away.

Once I saw a vision of beachcomber's paradise. Martin Gray, one of our neighbours on North Ronaldsay, showed some slides of a trip to Arctic Norway, including the vast desolate island of Spitzbergen where the beaches are littered with a veritable forest of tree trunks, giants which have floated down the rivers of Siberia. Were we able to transport even a fraction of these to Papay it would solve our kindlin' shortage at a stroke!

If you've never known the joy of plucking a fish box from the swell or the elation of unearthing a German soft-drink container from the sand then a whole new experience awaits you. Ah, the delights of beachcombing. There's a Force 7 out of the so' west tonight. The peninsula of Vestness beckons in the morning. Slip on the wellies and join me in the surf.

Traipsing along the beaches can involve some unexpected encounters. For instance, measuring a whale, even a youngster with a yard or two to grow, is not the simple, straightforward business you might imagine. You must have had the same difficulty last time you produced a tape and stretched it along the sleek, black length of the *globicephela meleana*. This is the great sea creature known variously through these isles as the ca'in whale (because it was driven ashore for slaughter, as it is in the Faroes to this day), the blackfish or the pilot whale. Knowing exactly where to place the tape measure at the beastie's snout is the trick. You see, a difference of a few inches and the whale ceases to be the responsibility of the coastguard and becomes a problem for the local harbour authority.

Anything over 18 feet, apparently, and the coastguard can pass the buck.

Experts tell me that the pilot whale is the most common species found in the north isles but, for a Clydebank boy who sat in the stalls at the Regal, Dalmuir, and watched, white-knuckled, as Mad Captain Ahab clashed with Moby Dick, there is absolutely nothing common about a whale, no matter its size or species.

So when Jim, in his coastguard capacity, got a call from the north end to say there was a whale stranded on Savil Less below Bewing, the whole family agreed it was an opportunity not to be missed. Eighteen species of whale have been identified in Orkney waters over the years and recently we had the sad beaching of a family group on Sanday. More positively a pod of whales, who misread their route map, got stranded in Scapa Flow. After much effort they were ushered on their way. In the early 1980s a huge specimen, possibly a sperm whale, came ashore at Backaskaill and the children were pictured in the local paper scrambling over the enormous corpse (until the stench forced a retreat).

Most fishermen will tell you that there is no more awe-inspiring sight than a whale as it broaches a dozen yards from what is suddenly your frail little craft. I've heard the word 'unforgettable' used more than once. It leaves an impression which never fades and surely helps man remember his place in the scale of the natural world, reminding us to go easy with the technology of death which we trail around the oceans and hurl at these gentle monsters.

We left the cars at the bottom of the road to Bewing, scene a few days before of another minor Papay drama when Tommy o' Maybo', having returned triumphant from an operation in Kirkwall, inadvertently steered his tractor into the septic tank. A dripping Tommy wisely resisted the temptation to dive for his missing rubber boot. It's said the folk from Bewing took him back along the shore to his caravan on the tail of the longest trailer they could find. He did, it seems, smell a bit. It's impossible to believe that Tommy's toothy grin didn't penetrate the grime.

But I digress. Jim, two-way radio in hand, took the lead, the rest of us scrambling in pursuit across the slippery rocks, having first negotiated the rusting sections of the *Bellavista* on the foreshore. Sad debris cast ashore by half a century of gales. Down near the water, tidal pools forced us off our direct route to the black hulk we could now see lying half-in, half-out of the water, being rocked back and forward by the surf. It was clearly dead. Nevertheless, the children were fascinated to be so close to an animal of this size and stroked its flanks, carefully tested the rows of little teeth in the half-open mouth and peered into the blowhole. For me, seeing such a magnificent creature dead on our shore brought a mixture of emotions. A sense of achievement at having come so close to one of the creatures of the deep was mingled with dismay at seeing it devoid of life, out of its natural environment, cast up on a strange shore. It was impossible to say at first glance what had brought about its untimely death because Jim was convinced that it was a youngster.

These days, even in the crystal-clear waters of Orkney, pollution springs immediately to mind. However, its jet skin was unblemished save for a few lacerations where it had been thrown against the sandstone shelves. The mystery will remain forever, the corpse was gone on the next tide.

For the people of Papa Westray the sea is their place of enchantment, where mysteries lurk as they do further south in forest glades, mountain passes, even in the tumbled inner cities. Big sea beasties have always played a central role in Orcadian folklore with the most sinister by far being the Stoor Worm, the Northern Isles equivalent of the World Serpent. A huge creature, the Worm has bad breath and needs a feed of seven maidens each weekend to keep him cheerful.

Sea serpents, mermaids and fin folk also figure in the tales. But the whale – here was a living, breathing denizen of the deep, nothing intangible or otherworldly about him. This was a beastie over which man could, on occasion, achieve mastery. He might never capture the Stoor Worm, but its cousin the whale could be given a severe seeing to. Oil for the lamps may have been a secondary consideration in this conquest.

My favourite Orkney tale of the whale is set on Westray where a local farmer making a coffin for his newly deceased wife heard the cry go up: 'Whales in the bay!' He set off immediately for the killing grounds. The laird, there to supervise an equitable division of the spoils, was amazed to find the bereft farmer at the shore. But the man explained with a cold logic: 'Ah couldna' afford to lose baith wife and whales in the same day.'

THE REEK O' KELP

Patrolling the grassy banks of Papay, scanning the water margin for potential treasure, you'll occasionally stumble into shallow, overgrown circular depressions, maybe seven feet in diameter, just

above the rocky foreshore. These are the kelp kilns where seaweed was burned to produce an alkali used in glass and soap making. This process was the mainstay of the Orkney economy for a century from the mid-1700s. On Papa Westray kelp gathering was one of the duties owed to the laird and no money changed hands for the back-breaking work, goods were doled out to the value of the kelp collected. It seems likely that there was always a substantial profit for the Traill family.

Seaweed was also used as manure and when a northerly wind tore large quantities of tangles from the seabed out beyond the Mull, the entire island made for their allocated section of beach and the tangles, the stems of these sea plants, were piled high above the shore. When the burning time came in late April or early May quarrels were frequent, thefts were reported and the laird was called in from time to time to arbitrate.

Our island folklorist John D. Mackay offered this description of the burning season:

> The entire coast of the island seemed shrouded in mist as the smoke from over 100 kelp kilns was wafted out to sea by spring breezes. On the island itself this smoke found its way into the houses where it changed the taste of food and clung to clothes and furniture so that people smelt of kelp for weeks afterwards.

Some of the islanders – most recently Willie o' Daybreak – still go to the shore in the winter months to stack the tangles in preparation for the arrival of the 'tanglie' boat in the north isles in the spring. Pulling seaweed off the shore is hard graft for what nowadays seems only a modest return.

SPOOTS, STEAMERS AND SELF-REPAIRING NEEPS

Another ancient Papay activity which you'll witness along the tideline to this day might initially have you shaking your head in disbelief. Little knots of islanders or lone rangers armed with buckets and forks trudge *backwards* along sandy stretches of Vestness and Surhoose Taing which are exposed only at the lowest tides of the year. They're in search of 'spoots' or razor fish, an island 'delicacy' but very much an acquired taste. The best way of eating this particular kind of shellfish, which looks like an albino version of *Alien*, is to boil them briefly; a moment too long and they're transformed into inedible lumps of rubber.

The 'spoot' tides must have been anxiously awaited, however, in years gone by as islanders tried to enhance their diet. Oh yes, walking backwards. After stepping on the sand above the spoot and taking a pace backwards you can see a movement as they head downwards; that's when you quickly get to work with the fork or the bare hands if you're so inclined.

I've heard it said that pouring a super-saline solution into the hole makes the shellfish leap from the sand but I can find no one who has used or will admit to having used this questionable procedure. I haven't tried it myself but, then again, I've still to acquire a liking for this odd creature.

As far as I can recall, I never saw spoots on the breakfast menu of the *Orcadia*. West of Shapinsay you were gently shaken from slumber by the persistent throb of the engines. A magical aroma of bacon and eggs drifts in through the cabin window from the galley next door. Time for a walk around deck and a quick glance at the map as the jigsaw of the north isles unfolds, then you could settle down for a leisurely breakfast in the saloon.

Unfortunately, such delights, redolent of an age when the fun was not in arriving but simply travelling, are over. The MV *Orcadia*, which for the people of these far-flung islands was for 30 years not so much a boat but more a way of life, has retired, replaced by two modern roll-on, roll-off ferries. For me, seafaring around the firths and sounds of Orkney can never be quite the same.

A journey on the *Orcadia* carried a status similar to a trip on the Orient Express; a touch less glamorous and exotic perhaps but certainly every bit as adventurous and colourful. I've already been inadvertently very close to doing the spectacular double. In the mid-1960s in Paris, having dwelt overlong in the pavement cafés, I boarded a train to discover, just in time, as we were pulling slowly out of the station, that I was on board the famed Orient Express, first stop Vienna, instead of the overnight to Barcelona.

But back to the splendours of the *Orcadia*. A laughingly small sum secured a double cabin. Boarding at 10 p.m. you slept through the early morning bustle at the pierhead in Kirkwall and woke with the three-hour journey to Papay well under way. The *Orcadia* was built in 1962 as a replacement for the sturdy old steamers *Earls Sigurd* and *Thorfinn*, romantically named after two tough Norse earls of Orkney. In a nice touch, the two new vessels were given the same names. History repeats itself. While the new ships – each able to carry 145 passengers and 26 cars – began their duties, the *Orcadia* was bound for the Caribbean. She left behind a flood of memories for thousands of Orcadians who regarded her as a lifeline between the more remote north isles and Kirkwall.

The shipping company manager, Alastair Learmonth, recalled that when the *Orcadia* first arrived in Orkney everyone thought her the last word in luxury and power. Her first encounter with the Eday tender is recalled with affection. Coming into Calf Sound for the first time, she threw up a spectacular wake, buffeting the little boat waiting to meet her. With a gleam in his eye the boatman told the proud skipper of the *Orcadia*: 'That's nae steamer ye huv there, it's a bluidy destroyer.'

The new vessels have a long and proud Orkney tradition to

maintain but they may take a little while to win folk over. Anything newfangled hereabouts is treated warily. There were, indeed, a few teething problems. Farmers were fuming when early shipments of cattle had to be abandoned when the animals were found to be slipping and sliding on the car deck. An emergency coating of epoxy resin was applied. The stairs in the boat are unreasonably steep, isolating older folk to the lower decks.

The final run for the *Orcadia* in the summer of 1990 was a kind of historic and sad day. She was scheduled to make her last call at Papay in the mid-afternoon but we miscalculated the timing and were still at the Post Office when we heard several loud blasts of salute from her hooter. No tears were shed that I know of but we were told the old boat looked grand, decked in bunting and sparkling on her departure. Later in the day while we were working in our field, the *Thorfinn* appeared through the Heads of Eday and a new era had begun.

For our old friend the *Orcadia*, however, retirement to the sun did not materialise as quickly as expected. The initial deal fell through and she lay mothballed for four years at Leith before being sold to a Florida-based company for £150,000. She now trades between the smaller Caribbean islands and along the Florida coast.

UP TO THE OXTERS IN SALT WATER

Apart from being an ever-present backdrop to life and sloshing around us year in year out, does the mighty ocean perhaps hold some therapeutic, even religious, significance? If I can just get someone's ear at Orkney Enterprise, then I reckon we'll be on a winner. Seawater might be Papay's saving. Fifteen million pounds, I reckon, would establish the Papa Westray Thalassotherapy Centre, a plush clinic devoted to letting the world at large share in the amazing health-giving properties of the sea and wind around these parts.

Site selection is almost complete. I've opted for a shoreline location overlooking the silver sands and slapping surf of the Bay of Moclett with the gentle hills of Westray slumbering in the distance – a panorama once compared favourably with the Bay of Naples. Appropriately, the site lies among the mysterious mounds which line the road to the New Pier. Cynics will tell you it's building rubble but I reckon there must have been the odd Viking sauna around here in the days of the noble Magnus Barelegs.

What are our credentials for such an ambitious project? For years I've watched our visitors arrive off the plane or steamer to wander the shores or range across the North Hill. After a few hours they are overtaken by an unexpected drowsiness. This is ozone overdose, and a heaviness of the eyelids is experienced. Do they sleep well? Don't they just! The mystical properties of Papay's sea air are at work. Seawater or thalassotherapy dates back to ancient Mediterranean civilisations and both Hippocrates, granddaddy of modern medicine, and Plato are said to have given it the seal of approval. Romans and Egyptians (when they were out of asses' milk) discovered the benefits of sinking the body in seawater which is rich in calcium, magnesium and bromide as well as sulphates and carbonates. By immersion the body absorbs all these precious salts.

Just like the ancients, getting seawater about your body seems to have been custom and practice on Papa Westray long since. Tommy o' Maybo' minds being sent to the shore for buckets of seawater which, when heated, provided joyous relief for his mother's chilblains. It was thought that bathing bandy-legged youngsters with seawater would straighten out their joints and islanders will tell you of old men who would wade out in the surf in their long-johns and emerge to let their clothes dry on them, declaring, rather incredibly, that it eased their rheumatism – a common curse on these damp islands. (This technique finished Rabbie Burns, if I remember correctly.)

Last century one old boy regularly waded out to meet the tender from the steamer without boots and returned home soaked to the waist. The salt water would be running across the floor yet this hardy citizen lived into his eighties and never suffered a cold. Then there was the bold sea captain who took to the water on the east shore every day for a swim and swore this relieved his asthma. People alone didn't benefit from the soothing properties of the sea; horses were often led into the water to ease leg inflammation or hoof problems.

What other evidence can we call on? Cattle kept in fields adjoining the island's west shore which is showered with Atlantic spray for more than half the year are said to be sturdier and more resistant to illness than the beasts on the more sheltered pastures to the east of the island's central ridge. Then there's the odd story of the 'staggers' – a magnesium deficiency in cattle. It was unknown on Papay until after the Second World War when islanders stopped using seaweed tangles in large quantities to fertilise the fields. Seaweed, as we've already discovered, is rich in magnesium.

Dulse or edible seaweed was once a favourite fruit de mer on the island and one of the delicacies conjured up by the womenfolk was a delicious seaweed pudding. It's not so many years since that seaweed was eaten regularly here, and not just in times of dearth when dogs are also said to have provided sustenance for the starving.

An indicator of the restorative power of the air is found in the strange phenomenon of the self-repairing turnips. If the beasts get in among them and the neeps are left half-eaten in the field they can, apparently, form a new skin. When salt was expensive, air-dried sillocks (young coalfish) were an important part of the diet – a washing-line of sillocks can still be seen on the island occasionally. Faroese fishing-boats calling in at Papay in the 1950s sometimes had a sheep carcass nailed grotesquely to the mast. The crew would carve a slice from the animal as they worked, the mutton being well and truly cured in the constantly salty environment.

But the sea as a saviour? That's more difficult to come to terms with. Yet it really is the only way to describe what happened in the winter of 1992–93 right on our doorstep. For days storm-force winds had thrown a curtain of spray across the island and wind speeds of 120 m.p.h. were being recorded. By the time of the calamity it was possible to scrape the wind-carried salt from the outside of the kitchen window. Fifty miles to the north those self-same Atlantic waves threw a giant tanker on to the rocky southern tip of Shetland, threatening Europe's biggest ecological disaster. It was the *Braer*. In everyone's mind were visions of the oil-choked beaches of Alaska after the *Exxon Valdez* incident or the seas of oil during the Gulf War.

But here a totally different and quite unexpected scenario unfolded as we prepared for the worst. The incessant gale-force winds and 40-foot breakers which had savaged the *Braer* as she lay in Quendale Bay – the very conditions which had thrown her on to the rocks in the first place – combined to disperse the leaking oil, some 85,000 tons of light crude. Hundreds of birds were oiled, many died, animals and crops inland were affected by windblown oil spray but the great catastrophe failed to materialise.

Certainly the oil did not just vanish, it must still be around somewhere in the water column and it may be some time before the effects are fully understood but it wasn't long before the religious and not-so-religious were offering up a prayer of deliverance.

The actual events which led to the grounding had, I remember, a sort of fatal inevitability about them. With the livestock checked, we listened anxiously to the radio bulletins in the kitchen, the wind howling round the house. It was a distressing progression . . . tanker in distress . . . crew airlifted to safety . . . firmly grounded . . . first oil slick sighted. Even the blouster out in the yard seemed to be yelling disaster. While all the talk quickly turned to compensation, flags of convenience, tanker design, crew training and tighter control of shipping in international waters, it's clear the Shetlanders can never have the same confidence in the commercial shipping which uses their stormy waters.

From Papa Westray, Shetland is just over the curve of the northern horizon, but we are always aware of the presence of our windswept neighbour on the Atlantic edge. Papa Westray nudges out from the fringe of the Orkney archipelago into the strait which separates the island groups. This passage, the Fair Isle Channel, gives access between the New World and Northern Europe, a route which avoids the overcrowding of the English Channel but where sea conditions can be truly hellish. Any day of the week out there on our horizon, the long, somehow menacing shapes of the tankers can be seen passing by. There's a lot of ocean beyond our North Hill but in recent years it has been noticeably busier.

The storms which brought the accident were not exceptional in terms of these Northern Isles. Early in the year, any year, the islands expect to be battered by Atlantic westerlies. However, circumstances combined on this occasion to produce the worst of scenarios – foul weather, a heavily laden tanker, and engine failure.

Although the oil in Shetland was dispersed by those mountainous seas which quickly transformed the tanker to scrap metal, the longer-term effects for fish-farmers and lobstermen are awaited. It's too late for the birdlife who died, however, and it took fully three seasons for Shetland's image as a tourist destination to recover.

On the day after the wreck of the *Braer*, I took my evening walk along the silver-white sands of our east shore. Storms were gathering in the west again, way out over the Atlantic. Our seals were lolling contentedly above the surf at Weelie's Taing and in the half-light a pair of redshank probed the sand along the water margin. Illogically, I found myself looking for dark, oily stains among the seaweed strands. When will we ever learn? Soon, I hope. It would be too much to expect the normally cruel sea to act as a saviour again.

Chapter Seven

Daddy's Home!

THE PHANTOM TRAIN

By now you will realise that Papa Westray in midwinter is a pretty rugged, uncompromising place. Great Atlantic breakers complete their voyage smashing almost gratefully on to the island's nor' west shore, up by Mad Geo and the Pow o' Keldie. Such is the thunderous, echoing force of their arrival that a stranger to the outer isles who was staying with us for a few days announced earnestly one morning: 'I heard a train last night. I know it sounds daft, Jim, but I definitely heard a train.'

The Scots writer Iain Crichton Smith captures this omnipresence of the sea quite beautifully: 'On an island the sea is always present. Always one hears the sound of it behind the painted day, a background, a resonance, the loved and feared one.'

Here in Orkney winter is the season when clouds scud past, our horses seek shelter behind south-west facing dykes and the wind slaps you mightily in the face as you exit the byre. We are reminded of the isolation of yesteryear without flying taxis and speedy ferries, of the need for self-sufficiency. For most islanders this is a time of partial hibernation, muckin' the byres and sitting snug by the fireside. We contemplate, as surely folk have before us here on the European fringe, the mystery of the dark months, the precursor of spring's fruitfulness. But all this introversion can put you in a kind of doleful, woebegone frame of mind.

I like the story of the visitor from East Anglia who paid a midwinter visit to one of our island's more sombre elder citizens. Together the old lady and her guest sat in the kitchen through an eternal silence watching the glow of the collapsing coals in the grate. Then, out of the blue, the matron announced, pointing to the fiery ingle: 'Yas, that's what hell will be like.' How's that for killing a conversation that never got started. The sequel to this tale is that the traveller phoned home and asked for a bottle of whisky to be despatched north post haste as an antidote to this melancholy encounter.

But let's not be silly. It isn't all doom and gloom. Occasional excursions to the shop, the pier and the airstrip offer the opportunity to catch up with island gossip which in turn can prevent the mind from seizing up altogether. As well as the summary of who's not speaking to who and the latest in the island's longest-running soap opera – 'Who's in charge at the Co-op?' – we are constantly searching for something to cheer us, to allow us to lighten up, if only for a moment.

A few winters ago it was the decision by Orkney Islands Council to provide each household on the island with a surplus Second World War stirrup pump for domestic fire-fighting which offered *the* fun moment. Received with ill-disguised merriment by the community, they were quickly adapted as bilge pumps and yard-cleaning equipment and Grampian TV thought the whole thing such a hoot they sent out a TV crew to film a staged attempt to douse an inferno in a pile of old newspapers down at Midhoose. Yes, winter can be the silly season too.

Here on the island with a population small enough now to squeeze into a double-deck bus, self-help is, and to a large extent will remain, the name of the game. Isolation is felt most acutely when the waves are breaking over the New Pier and the weather forecasters are telling us to expect a splatter of rain, which usually means a downpour for the duration.

Anchored where we are, ambulance, police and fire klaxons are familiar only from TV movies and news bulletins. However, by the end of 1993, we really did have something to cheer about, the Papay Volunteer Fire Brigade was up and running. With nurse Fiona and teacher Christine in the ranks, you're unlikely to encounter a more cheerful or cosmopolitan bunch of fire-fighters. In the midst of our tea one evening we learned they were operational in the oddest of ways. We were confused to hear a sound like someone throwing buckets of water against the window. That's one helluva downpour, thought we. Outside we discovered the new fire service team, resplendent in hard hats, wellie boots and waterproofs, testing the range of their hoses around the kirk.

Alistair o' Cott, a natural public relations man if there ever was one, posed happily for photographs while Rab, officer in charge, looked busy and seriously professional.

Up until the formation of the new team the only official fire-fighting gear on the island was the airstrip foam tender. A few weeks after the Hewitson clan settled here, I was burning rubbish in the backyard. I wouldn't say the blaze was out of control but the clouds of dense, black smoke must have looked ominous from most vantage points on the island. As I struggled with a lot of sweat and not a little swearing to keep the inferno in check my eldest girl, Lindsey, then 13, popped her head around the corner of the byre and announced sheepishly: 'That's the fire brigade here now, Dad.' What a torrent of abuse she got to the effect that if all she had to offer were smart comments, then she should clear off. Fire brigade indeed! Here, on the wild frontier!

Five minutes later as I emerged black-faced and triumphant from the yard, I found, to my eternal embarrassment, big Neil of Holland and David from Whitehowe out on the track, leaning on the foam tender. The fire brigade had indeed arrived but my outburst from the yard must have suggested that assistance would not be welcomed. 'You'll have everything under control then?' they asked, ever so politely. What do they say about wishing the earth would swallow you up?

CABIN FEVER

During the sombre, overcast months such moments are precious. Mostly, as the animals listen to the rain hammering on the roofs and gaze at the same spot on the byre wall, we humans strive, with greater or lesser success, to keep claustrophobia and scunneration *DISGUST* at bay, the expectancy of spring our only comfort. Often I've tried to make sense of this strange lethargy, the island blues which can overtake us in winter. It would be instructive to discover just how many of the islanders are on anti-depressants during the dark season. The experts will put it down to a seasonal disorder due to the oppressive lowering skies, the eight-eighths cloud cover for six months, a lack of sunshine, vitamins or whatever, but in an article for *The Herald* in 1990 I tried to take the argument a stage further:

> Do you remember Jack Nicholson, cut off with his family
> behind 20-foot snowdrifts, stalking the corridors of a vast,

empty hotel, axe on his shoulder in Stephen King's smashing, scary film, *The Shining*? Mention was made in that movie of a strange, claustrophobic condition called 'cabin fever' suffered by hairy frontiersmen who, cooped up for weeks with their unlovely companions behind the winter snow, started out carving twigs and ended up carving lumps off each other. Although it was something more sinister than monotony which possessed Jack in the film, the paranoia described strikes a familiar chord.

It's not that we're really isolated up here on Papay. Not like old Jack, anyway. The steamer gets in most days with a bit of nifty steering, even in awkward winds, and the Loganair pilots pride themselves on keeping to the schedules, notwithstanding the occasional tempest. No, the isolation is more psychological than physical. When the winter wind and rain has been sweeping in relentlessly over the North Hill for weeks, the day refuses to dawn, the sun skulks around the horizon and you can't remember the last time you saw a neighbour, then you really begin to feel cut off, out of touch – well, yes, out of touch with reality.

I know it can often seem just as isolated in a big city but there is something especially unsettling about bad winters up here. In those periods our only links with the greater realities, with the world out there, might be the lights of a trawler heading for the deep-sea fishing or the carefree smile of an unexpected visitor from south stepping off the plane. Such events can temporarily restore confidence. But the old imagination can play strange tricks. It's easy to feel closed in and to believe that out there something is going on and nobody's telling you about it.

Wait, I hear you protest, what about TV, radio and the phone? Surely these electronic links with the outside world assuage all those silly, unspecific fears. Perhaps. But machinery can be tampered with, ideas shaped, to give a picture of a world sailing merrily along . . . when, in fact, the ba' is well and truly on the slates. Bear with me a moment, all hopefully will become clear.

Take TV. I've become a devotee of *Neighbours* which only occasionally, very occasionally, raises issues fundamental to existence. If everything was so innocuous then my suspicions might never be heightened. But one Sunday afternoon I saw, or at least I think I saw, Nelson Mandela walk to freedom, apartheid crumbling in the sunshine. On its own that was fine. But a few weeks previously they appeared to be tearing down the Berlin Wall. A hard-headed frontiersman can only take so much of this fantasy. This is not the tough, withering world which I left behind for the life of a settler.

Mandela I can handle. The Berlin Wall is just about credible but Scotland playing San Marino in the European Nations Cup? Haud the ba'! Even I know that San Marino is half the size of Drumchapel. We might as well play the Faroes! Then there was all that stuff about Glasgow being the City of Culture. Next thing they'll be building a concert hall at the top of Buchanan Street. Let me tell you, boy. Ah'm no' that easily fooled.

So what is going on? What exactly is this conspiracy? I thought at first that there might have been a bloodless coup by the Monster Raving Loony Party or perhaps the Black Death had made a reappearance; but now I've got it sussed. I'm fairly certain we've been visited by a team of extra-terrestrial zoologists and most of you have been carted off to a stellar Calderpark. Clever audio and video tapes have been left running to gull us rejects. Mind control by satellite. Pretty plausible, eh?

There's only one person on the island I can speak to on this delicate matter. Tommy is the nearest we have to a backwoodsman in this treeless land. In his caravan, surrounded by a shield of concrete blocks to stop it blowing over the banks, Tommy watches

the telly with his cats, and he knows things. That unusually warm Saturday afternoon I found him, as usual, with his ear to his battered portable radio. 'Listen to this. A roo of games off, one after another. It disnae mak' sense in weather like this.' Nor did it. On this balmy spring day someone out there had got the tapes mixed up. But how could I start to explain this, even to a boiler-suited shaman like Tommy? Was I on my own? Perhaps not. I wandered to the shore for a blether with the seals. They don't say much, except when the wind is in the north. But when they talk, by God, they make a lot of sense. Thought control, talking seals, Robinson Crusoe – cabin fever? Whit me? Nae chance!

These flights of fancy aside, it really is strange to wander the muddy tracks and deserted beaches in midwinter and fail to meet a single visitor. We become accustomed to their smiling faces, characteristic backpacker trudge and their silly bunnets. (I'm a fine one to talk cries the island in unison!) For better or worse Papa Westray now seems a less real place without our guests.

Mind you, some of them can be a bit too adventurous. Instead of taking the easy option and pitching their tents on the open ground beside the Clover Bowl (our school playing-field), a few head for the east shore and the long grasses above the banks. One expedition didn't bargain on a nocturnal visit from a cheerful but unsteady dweller by the shoreline who stumbled over the guy ropes in the dark and fell headlong into the canvas, bringing down the entire shooting match.

When I begin to miss their innocent, cheering and sometimes cheeky comments about the island, I head for the guest-house and have a swatch at the visitors' book. Here is a wee selection from the summer of 1989:

> A place where people matter (B. and T.S., Sheffield); deceptive weather (P.T., Australia); seals stole my lunch (A.M., Birkenhead); afternoon sleeps a must (C.H., Australia); lovely but too cold (K.J., West Germany); remain unchanged (P.B., USA); wonderful, but too much barbed wire (J.M., Edinburgh); we'll be back! (M.B., Derby); seduced by island, mugged by cat! (A.K., Devon); [and a cheeky entry from a close neighbour] lack of sun (D.L., Westray).

SHINE ON HARVEST MOON

Beyond the security of our porch light where the cats gather to miaow over the evening's sortie, most of Papa Westray is inky black. However, our little kingdom is not so much in the dark as it used to be. You see, in the past few years we've acquired – amidst, it has to be said, a wee bit controversy – a line of streetlights, eight to be exact, spaced down the hill on the main drag between the shop and the school gate.

My favourite view of Orkney is a giant satellite photograph of our archipelago in the Tankerness House museum in Kirkwall, taken obviously on the clearest and brightest of days. But I've often wondered how Orkney would look at night from that self-same satellite. Clusters of light, I suppose, around Kirkwall and Stromness, a flare perhaps marking the Flotta oil terminal, luminous dots around villages like Finstown and Pierowall on Westray. I know for sure how Papay must look from one hundred miles up – a line of eight sodium specks running west to east across the centre of the island.

But the installation of the eighth – and last – streetlamp did cause a bit of a stushie. The debate featured in my column in *The Washington Post*:

> Any day now (that, in Papay chronology, could be tomorrow or anytime before the end of the century) an eighth lamp-post will be erected a bit east of the school, designed to cast some light on Willie and Robina's retirement cottage at Daybreak. When the lights were originally installed there seemed to be a general mood of quiet self-congratulation among the islanders. It was a source of pride that the community council had successfully pushed for this improvement while other larger islands such as Hoy are still seeking streetlights.

However, the community council meeting which eventually voted that extra lamp for Daybreak showed just how dramatically attitudes can alter in the space of a year or two. The council minutes tell it all. When the business came round to the letter from Willie and Robina 'most members were of the opinion that there were already too many streetlights, those between the shop and school being quite unnecessary and unsightly'. A motion to reject the proposal was put.

An amendment recommending the go-ahead for the lamp followed. This is roughly where things start to get complicated in a tight-knit little place like Papa Westray. Jim Rendall, the chairman and originally a staunch advocate of the streetlights, declared his interest and abstained (Willie is his brother) and Alex Davidson felt obliged to do the same (Robina is his sister). At the end of the day the light was approved on the casting vote of the vice-chairman, Ian Cursiter of Charleston.

Why this sudden coolness towards nocturnal illuminations? We can but speculate. The advantages of streetlights in cities and towns are not so obvious hereabouts. We have no crime to speak of, therefore no need to deter burglars, prowlers or peeping toms. The lights are indeed ugly and, it must be said, decidedly out of place. Even the seemingly unchallenged benefit of safer roads is not so clear-cut as you might imagine. Drivers find it disconcerting moving from the amber sodium glow into impenetrable darkness and vice-versa. The sudden contrasts at each end of the illuminated stretch may actually be dangerous. The general view, as ever unspoken, seems to be that the lights have done nothing for the island. On a more practical level, it would seem that Willie and Robina's light got the thumbs up simply because it would have seemed churlish to refuse the request when the other lights were already in place.

But all of this has much more than local significance. Whether you know it or not we are currently in the midst of Dark Sky 2000, a 10-year campaign by astronomers worldwide to combat light pollution – their goal: to reclaim the night from the skyglow of a million communities which is shutting off their view of the universe. I know what they mean. Perhaps this is a bit airy-fairy or nebulous to be spoken of in this tough, agricultural community but the lights of Papa Westray have, quite frankly, clouded our window on creation.

Shooting stars, the northern lights (sun glinting off the shields of Odin's handmaidens, didn't you know?), multi-coloured gas clouds, the arc of the Milky Way, the spectacularly coloured moons and, of course, UFOs . . . we have them all. A visiting doctor and his wife once saw what they thought was a meteorite perform a remarkable U-turn as it approached the earth and shoot off into oblivion. Nowadays folk in the centre of the island see these miracles with clarity only when there is a power failure.

Total blackouts, however, can bring with them their own confusion. Witness the incident during the Second World War when Papay was at the centre of a spy scare. Four or five of the island men used to mount the night-time watch on the North Hill for enemy aircraft or shipping movements. On one occasion, while using a flashlight to find his way south over the rough ground and home, Donald Mackay, Tommy o' Maybo's father, was spotted by an RAF reconnaissance aircraft. At the same time a youngster was out on the links at the south end of the island after rabbits. He also had a flashlight and from the air the pilot was convinced that the lights were those of enemy agents signalling to each other. The strange lights on Papay were reported and intelligence officers despatched to the island. Much close questioning took place before they were convinced that Papa Westray was not a hotbed of espionage.

GHOSTS ON THE MESSIGATE

Suddenly, it's spring and for the wind-weary residents of School Place, shattered by six months of darkness and six weeks of gales, bodies locked at an angle of 60 degrees from constantly bending into the westerlies, it's the equivalent of a cease fire. There are never any formal negotiations but one sweet morning silence creeps in under the doors. How do we mark that first memorable day of reawakening? Here's my experience.

Having reflected, perhaps too briefly on this mystical change, I begin to climb to my attic for yet another morning on the word machine, a ritual well established in the dark months just past. But almost-forgotten sunlight is splashing through the porch windows, chasing the gloom from even the darkest corner. From his den beneath the stairs the dog looks balefully at me through the steps. He knows and I know that this special day should be celebrated. We ought to be out and about. St Tredwell beckons.

So, it's on with coat and boots, binoculars stowed in the pocket and away we go down past Bina's neat white-harled cottage with its regiment of sparrows chirping from the chimney head. These wee guys sense the charge of energy in the air. At the Old Pier, amid the salty scents of the seaweed shore, waves gurgle and slurp musically beneath the weathered and slippery stone steps, running under and between the great sandstone blocks, through dark, secret places, emerging to chatter of a gentle summer to come, days of sparkling sunshine and black guillemots bobbing on the swell. The creel boats, still high and dry in the sheds, will soon be back in their element.

Onwards down Bill's track – still studded with clay-brown puddles – towards the leaning gable of the Mill. Cotton-wool clouds bump gently across the sky where occasional patches of blue begin to show themselves. It's the sort of radiant day when singing aloud snatches of the 23rd Psalm or a favourite football anthem comes as naturally as falling off a dyke. In pastures green he leadeth me, down past the planticruies, the oystercatchers screeching an accompaniment.

The dog, up to some serious sniffing among the dockens by the ditch, lifts his head for a moment as a lark soars skywards and hovers, spilling his song – a sure signal of summer a-coming. At Hookin' on the abandoned south-east shore, beneath an increasingly warm sun, I pick my way carefully among the tumbled stones inspecting the damage to this isolated croft on its narrow neck of land between the sea and St Tredwell's Loch. Winter storms have bitten great chunks out the seaward bank and I ponder the likelihood that we must eventually witness the ocean bursting into the loch and changing the landscape for ever.

Across the still boggy meadows in the direction of the chapel we proceed, the dog shimmying between the tufts, veering off from time to time, threatening to pursue some fleet-footed rabbit but thinking better of it and trotting back to my side. In summer this passage was a great adventure, when cattle grazed close by. Sam was an enormous attraction for the beasts and a swift crossing, avoiding a stampede, was recommended. Spring, before thick grasses cloak the masonry, is the best time to trek round to the chapel. A female skeleton was discovered below the floor of the modest chapel last century – perhaps this was St Tredwell herself.

I clamber over the walls and through the passageways to my favourite spot inside one of the roofless beehive cells atop the mound. This is another of Papa Westray's secret, timeless corners, where the twentieth century slips away and it's easy to imagine you hear the murmured prayers of the medieval pilgrims as they trudge down the Messigate. Hands behind my head, I lie back and feel the remarkable vibes which ooze up from this site. Except for one puffy cloud drifting west to east across my hideaway, the sky has cleared. Sam snaps lazily at a passing bug. Around the rim of my sheltered bowl the breeze ruffles the grasses. They whisper a message for those simple-hearted or uncomplicated enough to hear. Somewhere along the line, as we've drifted away from the natural world, we've lost the ability to listen to the wind.

Out there, beyond my hidey-hole, there will be a few creatures bemoaning this gift of a day. We'll pay for this. It'll be a poor winter, you'll hear them churlishly declare. Clouds to come. Of course. But, meantime, let's enjoy what we have. The grey days are gone. Let the rekindling of the spirit commence. Let's ask the lark for another cascading chorus.

SHADES OF THE BELLYSHAKER

Sic' a stir must have been familiar on Papa Westray when the longships of the noble *Dagfinn Bellyshaker* and gentle *Thorfinn Skullsplitter* reached the sheltered havens of Orkney, brimful of booty. In more recent times only the return of the victorious Papay team from the North Isles Sports or the escape of a big brown bear from the loft at Holland (sole survivor, it's said, of a shipwreck at Vestness) have stirred the blood to the same extent.

Initially, most folk tried to tackle their day-to-day business on the land, at the shop or pier, as if life was progressing along its familiar, if slightly rusty track. In truth, it was a thin veneer of normality; excitement was in the air, you could taste it on the breeze. The fact was that Jimmie Macgregor had arrived and even the legendary bear hunt began to pale into insignificance. Anyone who stepped ashore at Moclett during that autumn week expecting sleepy hollow would have been stunned to see the veil of inactivity raised, temporarily, for the all-seeing eye. Springburn lad, folk singer, broadcaster, student of the wild corners of Scotland, Jimmie descended from the afternoon *Islander* flight from Kirkwall to open a peculiar chapter in Papay's 5,000-year chronicle.

Within hours, dressed in his familiar 'tramping through the heather' toggery, he set off to explore our byways. We're kind of short on highways, as you've already discovered, the only road of any consequence leading nowhere or, more accurately, towards a cliff edge. What brought the Beeb to Papay? *On the Outer Edge* was the title chosen for the four-part series on Scotland's island fringe. Programme planners, looking for good scenery and diverse communities opted for St Kilda, Foula in Shetland, Rhum and Papa Westray. Now, St Kilda has its stark emptiness, Foula its record-breaking cliffs and Rhum its famous deer. What about Papay?

Jimmie spoke to all the island personalities, allowed himself to be rescued by the coastguard helicopter, did all the walks and fielded the inevitable: 'And where's Robin Hall noo?' They also

Golden winter sunrise looking south to Eday

TOP LEFT: *Ruined toonship at Via set against the backdrop of the Holm*

LEFT: *Boris explores a German helmet at School Place*

ABOVE: *Retired farmer Tommy Mackay beneath a rainbow at Maybo'*

RIGHT: *Ancient kirk of St Boniface – the first Christmas service after renovation*

Old fishing-boat on the shore below Nouster

ABOVE: Lobster fisherman/farmer John David Hume of Sooth-hoose

BELOW: Sunset over the Bay of Moclett and the New Pier

Breakers on the east shore at Savil Less

Working at the silage above the North Wick

Darkness at noon – midwinter half-light on Papa Westray looking south down the spine of the island from the north hill

Searching for 'spoots' at Surhoose Taing

Huge breakers dwarf the crofts at Hundland and Bewing

Maggie Harcus in her kitchen at Midhoose

Schoolboys Sam, Barry and Gary prepare their Christmas decorations

needed lobstermen. Where else could they go? Three months at the job and suddenly I'm a Nordic Hemingway, right down to the bait-stained Thunder Anchor cap.

When I got round eventually to writing up this odd adventure for *The Herald* I found a need to bare my soul:

> I may be breaking my contract, endangering my Equity card and the series may be cancelled as a result, but I have a confession to make. I'm a cheat. As my creeling companion, Jim, and I took the *Valkyr* through her piscatorial paces in the South Wick with camera and sound men perched in the bow, we hauled up a creel. Lo and behold, a good-sized lobster hove into view. He looked bloody marvellous. Up he came, a shiny, blue-black monster, two pounds of primitive nipping, kicking crustacean, glaring at the lens through his little bulb eyes. Great television. Cries of 'That's a beauty!' and 'Hold him there a sec!'. Ah, but there's the rub. That lobster was in the creel when we first hauled earlier in the day – a bit of creative stage management. Could we let those nice TV people slip away without a shot of a bona fide Papay lob? No harm meant, you understand. All in the cause of realism. God, it feels better getting that off my chest.

But one star from the sooth never makes a Papay summer. We expect much, much more. That year he came in the shape of country-and-western crooner Keith Manifold. The guest-house dining-room was well filled for his one-night stand. As ever, tea had been taken and Keith had just conquered that vocal Everest 'She Taught Me to Yodel' when little golden-haired Gary from Sooth-hoose decided enough was enough. 'Mammy, when's yon man gonnie stop shouting? It hurts thee ears!' He then took off on a high-speed weaving circuit of the tables.

A seasoned campaigner like Keith (you don't finish second to Lena Zavaroni on *Opportunity Knocks* without learning to be philosophical) had seen it all before and smiled patiently at the wee man. Unfased, he was on familiar ground here in the wild north. Almost Heaven, Papa Westray, in fact. Even the veiled threat of a power cut as the wind battered the guest-house skylights and bulbs blinked, failed to force him out of his stride. 'I'll finish this, electricity or no electricity,' he promised (or threatened) as he sipped his pint of lager which, perched on his amplifier, had just miraculously survived a bouncy, foot-thumping number about big

16-wheel trucks rolling by under Georgia skies (or was it Louisiana?).

One of our young men, let's call him Pecos Pete after his CB 'handle', could be quite overcome by these country and western soirées or even by a Western on the telly. It took only a couple of choruses of 'Home on the Range' or a glimpse of Audie Murphy to have him cussin' and a-shootin' off his pistols down Kweenvie Geos. He was missing a horse but drove in his high-heeled boots and leather jacket as if he had a pressing appointment at the OK Corral. At high noon staff in the shop would cower as the sound of spinning rubber on gravel announced his arrival. The door was flung wide and in sidled Pete (yes, yes, you're way ahead of me) and with a Papay drawl announced: 'The Milky Bars are on me!' Unlikely, I know, but I swear this story is true. On my last redeye I swear it. Now that's durned sacred!

A BRIDGE TOO MANY?

I don't suppose such tales help lessen media interest in remote islands but sometimes things can get out of hand. On one occasion I had to come to the conclusion that the Old Thunderer was simply breaking wind. It was the only logical explanation for a tale in *The Times* of London which suggested that the guid folk of Papa Westray (one of those quaint, out-of-the-way Scottish islands, don't you know) were sick to the teeth with isolation. Seems we were unanimous in our desire for a causeway linking us to our big neighbour Westray – a one-and-a-half-mile lifeline to a secure future. Apparently, we were prepared to sacrifice our island status for the sake of becoming part of some Greater Orkney. In the Papay idiom the only response was: 'Whit a load o' bruck!'

Sure, the causeway has been talked about for close on 30 years but, for the moment, the generally held view seems to be that it would bring more problems than it would solve. As we strive to broaden the island's economic base, the last thing we need are the uncertainties such a link would bring. For the second time in less than a decade Orkney Islands Council had discussed what one councillor was moved to describe as this 'visionary' causeway project. The plan, however, was thrown out; perhaps not surprisingly because it was to cost £18 million, around £250,000 for each man, woman and child on the island.

There are certainly 'causewayites' on this island and in Kirkwall whose voices may be more significant than their numbers but the bulk of folk with an interest in Papa Westray have serious concerns about the possible effects on the community of this chimera of a causeway. There is, of course, an interesting precedent in Orkney. The islands of Burray and South Ronaldsay were united with mainland Orkney during the Second World War by the Churchill Barriers after a German submarine slipped into Scapa Flow and sank the *Royal Oak*. And in the Western Isles, Vatersay has, and Scalpay is about to, benefit from expensive connections to larger islands.

The most recent OIC study declared that a causeway across the Papay Sound would be the most efficient and, eventually, the most economic link between the two islands; there is little dispute about that. In addition, the Westray doctor would not have to face the hazardous sea crossing and Papay children attending the secondary school in Westray would have a more settled education and face less dramatic winter crossings. It's also possible that the causeway could be harnessed to provide tidal power. But what about the debit side? And what could we lose?

Island status: perhaps a rather vague concept for some people but it is our remoteness, our insularity, where access is just that little more difficult, that gives the island its special character and brings hundreds of 'veesitors' to our green acres each year.

Medical care: in hard economic times what logic would there be in basing an island nurse on Papay, as we have today, with the Westray surgery a short car journey away?

Post Office: economics again would suggest that our Post Office, dealing with only 25 homes on a far-flung peninsula, must be an extravagant luxury.

School: with a large primary school on Westray what need would there be for a one-teacher school with five or six pupils on the peninsula of Papay?

Air services: it's certain that the world famous short hop between Papay and Westray (less than two minutes with the correct wind) would cease, and there is no guarantee, although Papay has the better airstrip, that pressure from Westray might not keep their airfield open at our expense.

Tourism: would our guest-house and new bed-and-breakfast establishments benefit? This is debatable. I'm convinced that the type of visitor would change. Day-trippers taking the roll-on, roll-off to Westray with their car and 'doing' the Papay peninsula in an afternoon would become the norm.

So there we are. Strike island appeal, nursing and postal services, school and airstrip. In total, strike a way of life. There may yet come a day when Papay welcomes a causeway. But for the time being we'll struggle on, thank you very much.

Actually, while you folk in the southlands are either gnashing your teeth or being consumed by indifference over the recent reorganisation of local authorities in Scotland, I have to tell you that the government of the clapshot republic of Papa Westray is in good hands. No, haud on a mo'. That's just a wee Ealing-type fantasy of mine – our four-mile island, a sea-girt Rubovia; a pocket-size independent nation on the fringe of Europe.

The reality of how we run our affairs out here is actually much more interesting and quietly impressive. Although we're in the care of Orkney Islands Council, out there somewhere across the briny, the truth is that, thanks to the enlightened view of the role of community councils fixed upon the OIC, the islanders of Papa Westray, through their seven-member council, have more say in their own future than perhaps any group of 70 people in the land.

Papa Westray and Westray, our big straggly neighbour across the way, share an Orkney Islands councillor in the industrious Stephen Hagan. Inevitably, pressure from the much more populous larger isle means that Stephen is restricted in the amount of time he can devote to arguing Papay's corner in the council chambers of Kirkwall. This is where the community council comes into its own. The success story of the 'peedie cooncils', particularly on the islands and especially on Papay, is down to several factors. Certainly here on Papa Westray, unlike our counterparts in the south, the community council is not a pressure group which simply responds to developing situations by kickin' at the council door. Here they make a positive input and take initiatives in a variety of projects crucial to the good government of the island.

A large part of their success is attributed to the fact that the small island councils have very clearly defined geographical edges, cradling distinct cultural and historical backgrounds and close family ties. In the cities, I'm told, it's possible to find community council boundaries which run halfway down a suburban street. Hardly a formula for successful lobbying. Then again, unlike other parts of Scotland, Orkney Islands Council has looked at existing legislation and encouraged the island councils to seek their own roles.

Fruits of this philosophy are not difficult to trace on Papay. In the past decade the council has pushed through a pioneering grant-aided water scheme which now sees well over half the homes linked to a mains system; they joined in the lobby for restoration of the old kirk of St Boniface and have members on the project trust; they regularly test public opinion on the crucial lifeline air and ferry links with Kirkwall, and have gone to the town to argue their case. The list is long and impressive. Less high-profile work such as restoring tracks to isolated farms, caring for the kirkyard, providing passing places, litter bins and tourist information boards and brochures, goes on. Small fare, perhaps, in a Scottish or even an Orcadian context but it keeps the lifeblood of local enterprise flowing on Papay.

Like every council they do encounter seemingly insoluble problems. For ten years they've tried to get some sort of safety fence outside the school. Everything from sleeping policemen to kissing gates have been suggested, but there has been frustration at every turn. However, their track record suggests that a result will eventually be forthcoming.

Two of the younger members of the community council – Alistair Hourston of Cott and Ian Cursiter from Charleston – are proud of what has been achieved, but they visualise the council's role as becoming even more central to the life of the island. Alistair suggests: 'I now see the council taking on the role of ensuring that there will be a future for Papay, making certain that this is a place where people will want to stay. The survival of the island could be our remit, if you like.' Ian echoes the statement: 'I would never have gone on to the community council if I'd thought it was just going to be a talking shop. I've always thought we provide a voice for the community and that we've a big part to play.'

Rainy afternoons, I've found, are ideal times to contemplate the make-up of Papa Westray's first post-independence Cabinet. There's likely to be a job for almost every citizen (now that's democracy) and most portfolios take care of themselves – piermaster Jim Davidson (transport); nurse Fiona (health); far-travelled Jocelyn of Micklegarth (foreign affairs); ex-sojer Rab o' Windywalls (defence); Christine the teacher (education); lobsterman/farmer John David Hume of Soothhoose (agriculture and fisheries); Alistair of Cott, Peter Pan of the games arena (sport); and Bill o' the Links, not one to suffer fools gladly, head of the diplomatic service. We're maybe a wee bit stuck for a Prime Minister but, then again, so is the United Kingdom.

Obviously, the world at large takes quite an interest in how we run our island affairs. Jim the postie, representing the Papay

Community Co-operative, was in New Zealand a few years back imparting his knowledge of community co-operatives to an international conference at Christchurch. The Maori groups in particular seemed interested to learn what had been achieved on a small island on the other side of the world.

Jim did have to admit that everyday facilities which most people now take for granted, like using a cash machine, are denied to us here on the outer islands. Bankers fly out once a month from Kirkwall and set up shop in the front rooms at Links or Backaskaill. In fact, Anne Rendall from Holland made a career in finance and is one of the flying bankers. Over the years she has attracted a lot of attention from feature writers because of this unusual aspect of her job.

During a visit from a journalist called Craig Foreman who was researching banking in Scotland's remoter corners for the *Wall Street Journal*, we recalled that in the years before the advent of the inter-island air service, the National Commercial Bank of Scotland used a boat – the famous *Otter Bank* – to service Orkney's north isles, including Papay.

Looking back to the nineteenth century, we come across the remarkable situation where money was almost unknown on Papa Westray. If the crofters needed anything over and above what they were able to produce for themselves, they approached the laird and, as we've already seen, he was paid in services such as wall-building, gathering kelp, etc.

John D. Mackay tells us that cloth was woven on the island by the local weaver who would keep part of the fleece as payment, medicines were doled out by the minister free of charge, furniture and boats could be constructed out of driftwood or timber from shipwrecks, and although the laird normally acted as coal merchant he would take grain in exchange. Tobacco, and possibly brandy, were among the items obtained by barter with foreign vessels which called by. The need for tea, flour and sugar hardly ever arose, these commodities not playing a part in the diet until relatively recent times.

The folk of Papa Westray had, in fact, gone one better than the South Seas islanders with their shell coinage – they did without money altogether. Echoes of this barter system are found even in the 1990s when a day at the baling might entitle you to a bucket of partans or the repair of a sticky clutch.

Only towards the end of last century when the first island shop, owned by James Miller, opened down at Backaskaill where the Post Office is today, did money begin to circulate. This caused something of a social revolution as, for the first time, people were able to buy little luxuries. The replacement of home-brew by tea as the island's main beverage can be traced to this period and whisky became available at 2/6d a bottle for weddings. 'Sunday best' suits and dresses also began to make an appearance. By coincidence this improvement in the lot of the ordinary people occurred at the same time as the dramatic and final dip in the Traill fortunes, and the Crofters Commission was in the process of bringing some justice to the outer islands.

While we're talking about money, I must tell you the sad tale of Yves Venisse. Ever since the summer of 1994 I've been unable to wander around St Boniface kirk without my eyes straying to that wee donation box in the dark corner and recalling the French canoeist who was lost on his way to Fair Isle. His tragic drowning clouded a memorable midsummer weekend of celebration on the island.

On the Sunday morning when people began to emerge, as rabbits from their burrows, after the ceilidh in Holland's grain loft, the boys from the coastguard were already out along the shore. Overnight a general alert had been called throughout the north isles when Yves disappeared after leaving North Ronaldsay on the Saturday afternoon. 'Fair Isle in sight, au revoir,' he wrote in the visitors' book.

On Papay, as plans were finalised over breakfast for the three-mile pilgrimage round St Tredwell's Loch to mark the restoration of St Boniface kirk, the talk drifted to the missing canoeist from the hamlet of Dampierre on the outskirts of Versailles. He had camped for a couple of days on the banks of Moclett, hauling his canoe up on to the machair above the surf.

By dinner-time that Sunday we learned that he had drowned, found beside his upturned canoe by a rescue helicopter. We may never know exactly what misfortune overtook him out there in the solitude of the Fair Isle Channel. During his brief stopover on Papay he spoke to only a few islanders but Morag, who was cooking the evening meals at the guest-house, got more opportunity than most for a blether. The canoeist, as well as enjoying the fare at Beltane House, used the public phone to speak to his family so many miles away. Morag learned of his previous canoeing adventures including a trip to the dangerous waters off Greenland, of his wife who had died of cancer the previous year, of his children and his love of canoeing and the open seas.

However, Yves also spoke with genuine affection of the

uncomplicated – and honest – way of life enjoyed here on our island; of how he could happily leave his tent secure in the knowledge that it would remain safe until his return. More poignantly, he spoke of the collection box left unguarded in the old kirk by the Atlantic shore. 'Anywhere else, it would be taken,' he told Morag with a quiet sense of wonder.

As Yves set out on his last journey the Papa Westray festivities were just getting under way. Visitors had been arriving by boat and plane, the sun was breaking through and a brisk so' westerly chased the revellers down to the playing-field. The afternoon games were, in Papay terms, a spectacularly hectic affair, with scores of folk milling around. All a bit much for a would-be hermit like myself.

The most interesting aspect of the event, apart from nurse Fiona's popular burger bar, was surely the total and mysterious domination by RSPB personnel of the traditional Orcadian Tossing the Welly contest. In retrospect, if anyone is in a position to assess the flight potential of everything from an albatross to a rubber boot, it must surely be the 'birdie' folk.

On to the evening where Emma Kirkby and Anthony Rooley (last stop Sydney Opera House, next stop Tel Aviv) lent a bit o' culture to the festivities with a homely concert in St Boniface kirk, tightly packed with visitors and islanders and the splendid new roof and gallery looking good for 1,000 years. Birdsong, rather appropriately, was their chosen theme and their Baroque and Renaissance melodies were echoed by an enthusiastic blackbird perched on a lichen-covered gravestone out in the kirkyard.

A mural depicting one of St Boniface's storm-tossed sea voyages, created by the four boys from the primary school, hung beside the performers. Less than 24 hours later, when the sad news reached us, we were reminded how much the sea still dominates life hereabouts. Even an experienced and well-equipped traveller like Yves was facing up to unimaginably powerful and unforgiving forces out there.

Next venue was the grain loft at Holland where, after a belt tightener, the music of the Orkney Strathspey and Reel Society had the feet tapping and the old polished loft floor bouncing beneath the tread of the dancers. Into the wee sma' hours the loft was a maelstrom of whirling bodies as old Papay favourites like 'The Nine Pins' were given laldie and the home-brew did the rounds. I've seen one cynical London writer describe a Papay dance as resembling a quiet day in an old folk's home at the North Pole. He must have left early. Sure they take a bit of time to get going, but once they do . . . Wow!

As our overnight guest at School Place we had band member Sandy Dennison, far-famed VAT officer for Orkney. The fact that this very civil servant is also a very skilled fiddler is something surely to ponder.

Amid the celebration, there was time to reflect on the amazing fund-raising effort which had brought the kirk back from the brink. As Mary Spowart, minister for Papay and Westray until 1991 pointed out, the restoration had created something very special for the future. The plan is to offer the kirk on an ecumenical basis to islanders and visitors alike.

So many memories of that weekend. For me at least, however, that undefended offering box in the corner beneath the gallery, containing a few coins from his pouch, will remain forever a memorial to an adventurer who, albeit at the end of his life, discovered with surprise and delight, auld, almost forgotten, values on our green isle.

A SCENT OF SOMETHING

Gravity? Don't talk to me about gravity. When you try to rise from your pit it holds you fast between the warm sheets and when you need this strange force to get the septic tank flowing smoothly, it's posted missing. At such times of crisis I cry for the 'sludgie' men. Perhaps you've already got the drift, a scent of what's in store. It's not for those of a nervous disposition but it's an issue that needs airing, ventilating even.

You city dwellers who press a button, pull a lever or perhaps still haul on a chain, can have little idea of what it's like to have waste products still lurking in the vicinity long after city sewage is processed and off for a trip doon the water. Ecologically sound is our sewage system here on Papay. We're a shining example to the rest of humanity – each croft having its own tank and soakaway, material being gradually reabsorbed into mother nature's welcoming arms. At least that's the theory. However, problems arise.

For example, in exceptionally wet weather when the ground is saturated or when a foreign body – for example, a rat – perishes in there, our antiquated tank just can't cope. The soakaway effect disappears and the water begins to back up the pipes. The toilet bowl fills ominously when flushed and strange, unearthly noises

issue from the plug holes. After a few days of this and an avalanche of not-so-subtle hints from the family, I reach for the welly boots and it's in at the deep end. Well, not quite literally. Our septic tank, now beginning to show its age, is covered by an old green door which, on reflection, seems very appropriate, even symbolic, for such an earth-friendly process.

However, behind, or should I say below, the green door lies the problem. The tank is full to an unreasonable level. Both inlet and outlet pipes lurk somewhere beneath the surface. I plan to spare you the details of appearance, smell and mutability of the material down there, suffice to say it's nasty. Surprisingly perhaps, the biggest problem in getting these tanks to work properly is the soapy water from the washing machine which, I'm told, hinders the process of decomposition. Big slugs in the vicinity are a good sign. Actually, a Papa Westray tradition suggests that a chicken carcass, deposited in the tank, helps the process along nicely.

Anyway, enough delay. It's time to get rodding. I screw together two or three plastic poles and working by feel trace the outlet pipe. A couple of good thrusts and with luck the blockage will have cleared.

But what of the 'sludgie' men? In civilised country districts sewage tankers will appear regularly to drain rural septic tanks. Until quite recently this never happened on Orkney's outlying islands. Once every three years or so, like visitors from the other end of the galaxy, these cosmic dynarod men now appear off the steamer with their big orange tanker. The truck couldn't get into our garden so the 'sooker' snaked over the garden wall from the school playground. The boys set about their task in a wholesome, matter-of-fact sort of way. The older of the two (let's call him Ivor) stood back and ran a seasoned eye over the murky tank and the job ahead. 'Hand me a spoon, Tam,' he said, gravely turning to his young companion who was peering over the dyke; he sounded like a surgeon demanding a scalpel from the theatre assistant.

The sewage operative's right-hand man reappeared carrying a long wooden pole with a crosspiece at one end. The gaffer proceeded to stir the tank while chatting about the weather, then like a cordon bleu chef he tested the consistency and declared himself satisfied. 'That should do it,' he announced to the world in general, passing the spoon back over the wall.

Sludge would now pass through the six-inch 'sooker' and into the tanker without any unforeseen hitches. As the septic tank slowly emptied, a new world appeared out of the cloudy depths. Underwater objects of which I had been only dimly aware in my prodding with the rods began to surface. Shattered sections of flagstone which had once formed the cover to the tank, a chimney pot and several roof tiles. 'It wid work a lot better wi' that lot oot,' says Ivor. His drift was clear. I was to climb down there and remove them.

While I laboured, the 'sludgie' men opened their sandwiches (cheese and pickle as it happens) and got themselves comfortable atop the dyke. Descending into the depths, the occasional shout of encouragement reached me over the lip of the chasm as I struggled to manhandle pieces of sandstone up to garden level. And that was that. The tank soon filled again and for a while worked a treat. Then at night I began to hear the tell-tale gurgling from the bath outlet. Time to venture again where the nose of man should never be asked to probe. Voyage to the bottom of the septic tank. Ah, the joys of the country croft.

Chapter Eight

The Runaway Wheel and Other Stories

DON'T FORGET THE BALER TWINE

Each spadeful of earth and rubble brought increasing excitement amongst the diggers. The prospect of a momentous find seemed close at hand. It must have been a bit like this as those Victorian pioneers broke into the tombs of the pharaohs in a dusty valley so far from the rain-soaked earth of Papa Westray. We burrowed as moles into the mound – a little hillock like so many on this island which, over the years, have yielded archaeological treasures. Anything lumpish hereabouts is worth exploring. The mound was of easy access, in fact, it was in the back garden. Downwind of the septic tank, a few yards from the compost heap, it was an overgrown jungle of nettles and dockens in summer but a bare, clearly artificial little mound in winter. Legends about it were few but sufficient to justify the dig.

Finally, as the rain began to drip down our necks, the mysterious knoll gave up its secret. There was no mistaking the artifact, its shape and style betrayed its antique origins; it was a symbol of a culture long forgotten, of a time when life was more simple and straightforward. We stood back. There was no doubt; it was an Austin A40. Strange in a society of trade-ins and big business scrappies to have the grave of a car in your vegetable plot.

Not so on Papay. Here the car almost always ends its days on the island, finally pegging out, eaten by the salt air and twice round the clock, halfway up the Sandy Road or on the mudbath track that the east shore road becomes in winter. They were laid to rest with their comrades on the farm track or by the shore, useful only as a source for cannibalised parts. With no MOT necessary the cars run until they literally fall apart. No journey is undertaken in one of the many bangers without a roll of baler twine in the back seat to tie down the bonnet, tie up an exhaust pipe or prevent the battery from wandering around the engine compartment.

With scarcely four miles of metalled road to negotiate, road hazards are that wee bit different. Britain and Europe have been at odds for ages over the merits of driving on the right- or left-hand side of the road. With our Norse-Scottish heritage we've achieved the obvious compromise. We drive up the middle! Learning the clearance distances between you and Holland's John Deere tractors, the Co-op minibus and our flying senior citizens, as well as the turning arc on the pier, are fundamentals in the Papay handbook of driving skills.

Walking has ceased to be a popular mode of getting about on Papay and local people can still be seen gazing with a degree of disbelief and wonder at the ruddy-cheeked hostellers striding out for the North Hill.

Despite the absence of cut-price filling stations (we have one solitary pump at the shop and the most expensive gallon in the galaxy) and the high level of car ownership (1.19 vehicles per household according to the most recently available figures) traffic is generally light. Often you can drive the length of the island, possibly even getting into top gear, without meeting another car. Even at the mighty crossroads, the Papay version of Spaghetti Junction, among the corbie-stepped buildings of Holland farm, it requires a conscious effort to remember to glance over your shoulder and check the north road. Inevitably it will be deserted.

The only occasion when there is any traffic to speak of is when the north isles steamer appears in the distance. The Viking trumpet gets word around and the island shakes itself, somewhat reluctantly, into action, ready to meet the world. Half-an-hour later as the ferry sweeps into the Bay of Moclett, with food supplies, hostellers or the kids back from school in Kirkwall for the weekend, the little pier is jammed with floats, tractors, vans and cars. A similar scene is enacted when a distant drone from the direction of the misty hills of Rousay signals the imminent arrival of the twice-daily Loganair flight from Kirkwall.

A startling versatility is required from each vehicle, whether it's the hatchback transporting a calf to the pier or the school estate-car which used to ferry the children one day and might double as a hearse the next.

Disposing of this fleet has been one of the biggest environmental headaches faced by the island in the second half of this century. It has been a relatively recent dilemma because, until the late 1940s, there were perhaps only half-a-dozen cars on Papay. For centuries the horse and ox, attached to the plough or cart, provided Papay's pulling power. Although there are only a handful of horses on the island now, you find rusty horseshoes everywhere. We have a jangling collection hanging in the shed, surely guaranteeing us good fortune. A legacy of those horse-dominated days, apart from the archival photographs, can be seen at the impressive mill tramp at Holland farm. Actually, it's surprising that Orcadians could get horses to work for them at all. Apparently, a favourite Orcadian trick to determine the temperament of a horse was to pull its tail! Dangerous work.

Acceptance of the motor car as the coming form of transport took many years. The islanders, faced with these grinding and banging monsters, shared the view of the *Catcher in the Rye* character who decided that cars didn't interest him. 'I'd rather have a goddam horse. A horse is at least human, for God's sake!' The first vehicle, a Morris Cowley van, was brought to the island, so the legend states, in 1922 by one Geordie Rendall, the postie. Motorcycle units from the army had been sent here during the First World War but Geordie made the breakthrough.

He apparently looked at his van for several days before deciding that the awesome task of setting this mechanical demon in motion should be given to someone with a bit of know-how. Enter Tom Drever of Skennist, a veteran of the Great War who had served as a lorry driver on the Western Front where in the thick of the action his co-driver had been killed during one fierce bombardment. With a fascinated audience peering out from behind a dyke (today, ironically, you'll get shouted advice about how to handle horses from the same position), Tom got under way and, perhaps still imagining himself at the wheel of a heavy truck, took off on a meandering path down the road, making sweeping turns of the wheel he had mastered in the mud of Northern France. Onlookers grinned when it was suggested that Tom was taking such a weaving course because he thought he was still under artillery fire.

Thus Geordie finally took to the road. One islander recalls that his gas headlamps were rendered useless by the brisk Orkney breezes and so Geordie, a baccy-chewin' individualist, would hang a box lantern out of the vehicle on dark, wintry afternoons.

The school run was part of the taxi service he later operated and among the stories passed down is the saga of the forever troublesome offside rear wheel. Seemingly, it parted company from the taxi on the steep brae down to North Via with alarming regularity. To the delight of the bairns in the back it would overtake the vehicle before bouncing over the banks and on to the beach. The children would wait for the familiar scratching of the head as Geordie declared: 'Noo, whaur did that kam fae?'

Today there are many scores of cars on the island. Numbers lie rusting around the farm buildings, where they occasionally find a new calling as hen houses, potato stores or greenhouses; most

eventually sink into the soil. One thing is certain, archaeologists of the twenty-first century will find little trace of them if the observable rate of decay is anything to go by. The mounds will hold many disappointments.

In the past more civic-minded citizens, rather than leave them to disintegrate, might offer the wrecks up to the sea. Speared on a tractor's fork they would be sent crashing from the craigs into a geo where the grinding motion of the sea in one winter would leave scarcely anything recognisable. Breakwaters were built from a selection of wrecked saloons, a good subject for the visiting photographer but no solution either. The scrapman, who was really only after heavy engine blocks, came with the same regularity as Halley's Comet and left the place in a bigger mess than he found it.

Now, in the enlightened 1990s, the hulks are gathered together every few years and a boat makes a special run to Papay from Kirkwall to take them to the crusher on the mainland. However, one interesting question lingers. Do our 'veesitors' really regard the decaying lumps of metal as objects of disfigurement? One group of German high-school students went home, their backpacks lined with a collection of door handles, number and name-plates and windscreen wipers from our array of wrecks. The Papay car crisis had been a holiday bonus for them. One farm, North Rendall, has a magnificent but ageing traction engine as a gatepost and a bewildering collection of hulks which once included parts of a light aircraft which was written off when it failed to clear the airport dyke. Imagine Alex and Alice's delight when a tourist inquired earnestly: 'Is this the agricultural museum?'

MEDITATIONS ON A MIDNIGHT FLIGHT

Taking refuge behind the low wall, I eventually spied the plane emerging from the darkness to make a reconnaissance run over the airstrip before banking for a second approach. The luminous hands of my watch stood at midnight. The aircraft, its three powerful headlights puncturing the night sky, had appeared fast and low from the south, out of a great canopy of stars, searching for the marker flares which identified its target.

The cutting wind dropped a little and I stepped out on to the track, raised my binoculars and watched the air ambulance sweep in over the dyke on the top road and vanish from sight, gently touching down on the grass runway which dips toward the west

shore. At that moment, perhaps inevitably, it came to mind that up there in that same night sky, thousands of miles from Papa Westray in the Gulf, there were other night flyers whose goal was not a mission of mercy but something akin to mass destruction. A strange life, eh?

David had been complaining of a pain in his side in the mid-afternoon. Fiona, our island nurse, took a look at him after tea; appendicitis was suspected. Within a couple of hours the doctor had arrived from Westray by boat, confirmed the diagnosis and summoned the air ambulance. I suppose there must have been upwards of 20 people involved in the exercise, all abandoning their Saturday night to help our David to hospital.

At Kirkwall an ambulance crew and a nurse (who flew out with the plane), firemen, air traffic control and engineers were called in. At this end John Henry from Newbiggin' brought his versatile estate car to School Place to serve as an ambulance. Up at the airstrip Bobby and David set out a line of paraffin marker lights and, as a reference point for the pilot, an arc light was illuminated on the roof of the tiny terminal building. We were blessed with a night of brilliant clarity, so sharp, in fact, that the runway at Kirkwall had to be de-iced before the *Islander* could get airborne.

Fog is the only threat to Orkney's air ambulance service which has been operating since 1967. In all that time only three out of many hundreds of flights have been grounded because of visibility, the Kirkwall lifeboat doing the necessary in these crises. To Papa Westray went the distinction all those years ago of the very first air ambulance flight when an island woman with a diabetic condition was flown to Kirkwall. David followed in historic flightpaths.

The turnaround at the airstrip was speedily completed. David was stretchered aboard, his mum close by. Soon the plane was airborne again and swiftly vanishing into the starry backdrop. David had his operation a few hours later and made a speedy recovery.

Now, I would never suggest that our islanders take this remarkable rescue service for granted but over the years they have been accustomed to a medical facility which is unique in Britain, perhaps in Europe. Some would argue that it is no less than Papa Westray deserves since for centuries the islanders were left to fend for themselves without formal medical care. Bill Irvine from Links told me how his great-grandfather, a sort of medicine man, came off the North Hill with a satchel full of herbs and roots to make marvellous potions. Ironically, the old man was carried off by the infamous 1919 European flu outbreak which claimed a number of lives on the island.

DANCIN' ON THE NEEPS

Before qualified doctors ventured out to the remoter isles last century, the people of Papa Westray, sometimes with a little amateur dabbling from the meenister, dealt with all their afflictions using a combination of folk remedies and common sense, seasoned with a dash of superstition. The old 'howdie' or midwife commanded respect around the farmsteads. In addition to her duties in the delivery-room, she was said to have been what we might now call the island genealogist, with the power of veto over proposed marriages which might have involved too close a blood link. More than most she would have had knowledge of the folk cures – and, indeed, some remarkable remedies were to be found.

Disorders of the digestive system could be cured by taking crushed cuttlefish and milk; *helix normalis*, a snail found only among the ruins of St Tredwell's Chapel, helped alleviate rickets when boiled up in a hot drink; salt water, as we've seen, was a famous cure-all; a pellet of black twist-tobacco eased the pain of toothache; and a poultice made from champit neeps and fresh cow sharn worked wonders with earache. Really! Give it a try.

Our Katy's chilblains had been giving her so much discomfort that, having tried all the orthodox remedies, we decided to have a go at one of these famous Papay cures. This consisted of steeping the feet in tattie bree and then bandaging them with turnip peelings next to the skin. Drastic, but it was worth a try. It is certainly much more civilised and less anti-social than the last technique we tried which involved stuffing Katy's socks with peeled slices of garlic. Her chilblains did not improve with this procedure but we were able to declare School Place a vampire-free zone!

My own favourite tale relating to these old techniques mentions the odd practice of placing a dish of earth from the kirkyard in the room of an ailing person. Apparently, a Sanday man who had settled on Papay was distressed to find his second wife had fallen ill. Strangely, he concluded that only earth from his first wife's grave in Sanday would restore her. With a full gale blowing he set off across the North Sound in a small boat. Disaster was predicted. However, he reached Sanday and returned with a cargo of precious earth, placed it in a wheelbarrow along with his wife and then wheeled her seven times round the house. The bizarre remedy brought a speedy recovery, so the story goes.

On a more serious level, the twin scourges of typhoid and typhus regularly visited the island. Dirty wells, particularly during summer droughts, led to typhoid. Typhus, a louse-borne disease, was usually introduced to the island via the second-hand clothes which were sent home by sailors. We've seen how malnutrition was often a precursor to tuberculosis, and smallpox and cholera were much feared (could these imported illnesses help to explain the Papay caginess about outsiders?).

Leprosy has been absent from Scotland for so many years that it's easy to forget what devastation it once caused and the fact that our hero-king, Robert Bruce, died from the disease. Yet in this remote location I have come across two echoes, reminders of how widespread this disfiguring illness once was. At the old kirk of St Boniface there is a leper squint, a narrow slit window in the north wall, which was used in medieval times to allow lepers, standing outside the building, to take part in the mass. A mile away in the centre of the island is a field called 'Vanglee' where, according to tradition, a house once stood on a grassy knoll. It was burned to the ground when the tenants contracted leprosy. Interestingly, the last recorded case of leprosy in the British Isles was noted in 1798 on Papa Stour in Shetland.

In the 1800s the doctor from Westray would be rowed across

the Roost by a crew from Papa Westray, in emergencies. Latterly, he used the boat *Aileen* which figured in the famous *Badger* rescue and was named after the daughter of one of the visiting doctors. In the 1890s, the people of our island began to agitate for their own GP. A procession of recent medical graduates, mainly young women, came for brief stints but difficulties over finance and obtaining permission from the estate to build a house meant that it was the mid-1920s before a settled Papay doctor materialised.

Emergencies continued, of course, even after the arrival of a doctor. Imagine an urgent appendix case, like our David's, between the wars. The patient would be trundled in an open cart, perhaps in midwinter, down the bumpy length of the island to the Bay of Moclett. A dinghy would be waiting to take them through the heaving surf to a waiting trawler where they would be hoisted unceremoniously aboard to begin the three-hour haul to Kirkwall.

In the late 1970s medical economics demanded the withdrawal of the doctor. Our population was too small to sustain our own practitioner and since then we have had a resident nurse. The islanders put up a brave, but ultimately unsuccessful, campaign to retain their GP, the older folk no doubt recalling the struggle to secure one in the first place.

Nowadays Dr Shirley Haunschmidt journeys over by boat once a week from Westray for a surgery and, as per the demands of the islanders, is on call to travel to Papay when needed, night or day, fair weather or foul. And waiting in the wings is the air ambulance. It's kind of comforting to realise that despite the powerful militaristic images of the past few years, aircraft, with all their amazing gadgetry, can be agents of salvation as well as devastation.

But not all aircraft are welcome hereabouts. On and off over the years the subject of military low flying has cropped up in the media with reports of near misses, terrified cattle, disruption of examinations and terrified old folk. This is unusually important for Papay because it is common enough to see jets skimming along the horizon or low across the island on their training exercises. Orkney, because of its geography and low population density, matches the Highland glens as an important tactical area. However, with flights by Loganair now reaching out twice daily to Papay, this potential clutter of commercial and military aircraft is a cause for concern. A sensible option which has already been suggested by MP Jim Wallace would be for Orkney to be given the same exclusion status as the Isle of Man.

Everyone who travels on the inter-island service between

Kirkwall and the north isles has stories to tell of Christine, Amanda and the counter staff in Kirkwall who seem to know everyone in the islands by their first name, of bumpy flights, eccentric passengers, aborted landings and unexpected deviations to look at the seals or the sea caves.

My own favourite tale is of an American art teacher (and amateur conjuror) who joined a flight which was buffeted alarmingly all the way out over the isles. Seeing the anxious faces of his fellow passengers, this gent, to the delight and relief of everyone, started pulling long strands of coloured paper theatrically from his mouth. The plane was in hysterics and the tension evaporated.

It is not unknown for passengers to help give the plane a push start and you just know this is 'seat of the pants' flying when, after a hairy landing, the pilot turns round, wipes his brow and whispers – 'Hell, that was close!'. Now, don't you wish you had that sort of passenger involvement on a jumbo jet?

Skills exhibited by these pilots remain a daily wonder. During an atrocious spell of weather in the winter of 1990–91 I recorded one such incident:

> Winds built up all day from the nor' west and by the time Katy and I staggered down the field, more a bog now, with a bale of hay for the horses, it was blowing a gale, an icy wind with an edge which threatened to cut you in half. Away towards Eday in the gathering gloom we saw the bright wing lights of the afternoon flight. Heading into the teeth of the gale, the plane took an age to reach us. Eventually, it was directly above, seeming to hover over the loch for an age, engines revving. Slowly it edged in over Holland and vanished beyond the crow-step gables. Now that's flying!

The future of the inter-island service in Orkney has regularly been a source of anxiety but currently our islanders – thanks to a generous subsidy from Orkney Islands Council – can make the 50-mile round trip to and from Kirkwall for less than it would cost to take a taxi across the centre of Glasgow.

Even the big bad world of business wheeling-dealing and takeovers does reach out and touch us now and again. We were reminded of that one afternoon when the plane swung in over the North Wick in preparation for landing, dressed in the executive grey and red of British Airways Express who had taken over the service. Gone was the familiar red, white and black livery.

Islanders of Papa Westray have a quiet, unspoken pride in their air service (pioneer of Highland aviation Captain A.A. Fresson first landed on the Sooth Toon near Holland farm in the 1930s) and I suspect that despite administrative changes the plane will always be known simply as 'The Loganair' just as the ferries, no matter how sophisticated they become, will always be the 'steamers'.

SALAD DAYS AND SAD RETURNS

Equally important to the island is the regular boat link to Westray which is provided by genial Tommy Rendall. All three of our children have travelled to school by this service over the years and we have some fond memories of these adventures. I remember in particular one occasion when David's face was tripping him as he trudged up the concrete steps from the *Amarinth*, lying at last in the shelter of the New Pier.

Angry seas surged around the steel piles as he leaned into the wind and made for the Land Rover. Clambering into the front passenger seat, he pushed a well-travelled plastic ice-cream tub across the bench seat towards me. Pointing disconsolately at the tub, he sighed as only a twelve-year-old can sigh: '*That* was supposed to be the salad for tonight's tea.' A quick shuftie inside confirmed a strange metamorphosis. What had started off an hour or so ago in Mrs Ploughman's home economics class as a stylish display of sliced, boiled eggs, cress and tomatoes on a bed of lettuce was now something the dog might think twice about for breakfast.

Every day, weather permitting, the school boat, which also provides a regular through-the-day service in the summer months, has taken my children to the secondary school on Westray. Each day with changing winds and tides, presents different problems for Tommy, but he takes it all in an unruffled, matter-of-fact way.

On the day of the rearranged salad, waves had been breaking over the boat from stem to stern as she headed for the shelter of Moclett on her return trip. David's grip on the tub just hadn't been firm enough and he could only watch open-mouthed as his masterpiece skited the length of the cabin. Two careers, one as Scotland's goalie and the other as a chef of renown, vanished on the back of that breaker.

Schooling for my children has been a world away from my own formative years in Clydebank and the damned predictability of

Elgin Street primary school and the local high school where only a ship launch, burst pipe, exams or sports day ever interfered with the rigid routine. Lindsey, David and Katy have learned to be philosophical about the way the elements rule their education. If at first light the torn fertiliser bag on the fence outside our kitchen window was standing out straight then it was a sure sign that Tommy would be staying in the sheltered anchorage at Westray's Gill Pier and that the children were destined to spend their day over the dyke at the Papa Westray school working on exercises set by telephone or in later years on the whiteboards and the fax machine.

Midway through his standard grade prelims David found himself stranded on Papay, a victim of the rapidly deteriorating weather. It must have been cold enough out in the Sound for the fish to be pulling on their mittens, and there was no way Tommy could make the crossing. Hurried, last-minute arrangements were then made to fly David over on the scheduled morning hop between Papa Westray and Westray while the French exam was held up to await his arrival. Westray's only black taxi met him at the airstrip and whisked him down to the classroom in Pierowall. Oh yes, it was worth the effort. He got a good grade in the eventual examination.

Often, when they did negotiate the sea crossing, winter storms kept them marooned in Westray for days and they found lodgings with Mr Sangster, the head teacher. They became well used to carrying an extra set of clothing, plenty to read and spare pocket money. School dances could also present problems. What parent in the south would rest easy if he thought his 14-year-old daughter, setting off for a Friday night disco, would not reappear until the following Tuesday? In these stormy islands it happens.

HIDE THE CATALOGUES

When such weather does set in I've noticed another strange, unnamed malady which overtakes the islanders, especially in the first dismal weeks of the year. Sufferers can be observed in the Co-op shop gazing sad-eyed at the last forlorn box of Christmas crackers or the rapidly fading pot plants imaginatively purchased to widen the seasonal choice of gifts. At home, the victims contemplate the mail order catalogues and shake their heads in despair. Let's call this complaint SDS (shopping deprivation syndrome), the compelling need to buy something different, to purchase some pointless luxury unavailable in our northern

fastness. On an island of one shop, dedicated to providing simple, practical fare, this compulsion is no fanciful illusion. No, it's very real. I know. I am a victim.

For the womenfolk the only cure seems to be a day in the Kirkwall shops, or even an adventure to the teeming commercial centres of Aberdeen or Inverness. My own particular strain of the disease centres on these self-same catalogues which seem to flood the outer isles during the winter months. Obviously the marketing folk believe we're ripe for the picking on these short, grey days . . . and they're spot on. Once, I almost settled on an ioniser which, I was promised, would waft fresh mountain breezes through my home, when I recalled that the Atlantic breezes had recently wafted our coal shed door off its hinges.

Then my gaze came to rest on an alarm clock designed like a tennis ball which stops complaining when you lob it at the wall. Marvellous, and so practical. No home should be without one – but we have at least four alarm clocks and the animals in and around School Place are famous for their dawn chorus. Could I justify this extravagance?

This shopping syndrome – which I'm convinced involves not only the need to buy but the desire to sniff the distinctive aroma of shoe shops, wander through colourful clothes stores and handle crisp, new publications in the bookshops – is a relatively recent problem for Papay . . . a disease of the twentieth century, you might say. For centuries the islanders' expectations were far more modest. Until fairly recently, as we've found, the island enjoyed an enforced self-sufficiency in most things. Life was hard and the luxuries few, perhaps non-existent in our terms. Oil came from the whales and seals, as did the skins; food from cattle, sheep, pigs and hens; fuel and fertiliser from manure, seaweed, driftwood and peat. Papay would have had its own cobbler, miller, tailor and blacksmith.

Recently it has been suggested that in Neolithic communities there may even have been an individual whose sole employment consisted of wandering the pastures and turning over cowpats with a primitive spade so that they dried to perfection in the sun before being collected for burning. Sharnspinner of Papay – now there's a job I could warm to!

By the butter-yellow flickering light of cruisie lamps last century little necessities would be produced during the long winter; the men making baskets, the famous straw-backed Orkney chairs, tubs, buckets and model ships while the women would be occupied principally with knitting and spinning.

Direct contact with the outside world was almost unheard of for the farmworker until the occasional letters began to return from a relative at some Canadian frontier trading-post or Australian goldmine. Before that even the coffee houses and shops of Aberdeen, Edinburgh and London might as well have been on the moon. In the 1700s a journey as far as Edinburgh was considered such a serious matter that the Papay traveller would always ensure that a will had been completed and affairs set in order before saying his or her farewells.

This business about Orkney being only a relatively recent Scottish acquisition and the Scottish mainland being a vaguely alien place is a lot more deep-seated than you might think. The story is told of an island farmer who, during the Second World War, boasted that he had three sons serving overseas – one in Canada, one in Africa, and one in Aberdeen. Of course, the Orcadians are Scots, but they also hold more ancient allegiances. It was fascinating and instructive to read a little paragraph in the winter of 1990–91 which described a Papa Westray social night at Beltane House where 'John Henry Rendall of Newbiggin' showed slides of a touring holiday he had spent in *Scotland* last summer'. Clearly, the Pentland Firth is more than just a stormy piece of water.

In the eighteenth and nineteenth centuries the landlords of the big estates of Orkney, including our Holland Traills, had sloops and smacks which plied the dangerous waters around Orkney. On Papa Westray the most famous of these was probably the *Mary Traill*, which was stored in what is now the roofless shed by the Old Pier. The boats were used to bring basic provisions to the island but also to keep the laird's wine cellar well stocked. Occasionally, the men of Papay might venture as far as Kirkwall in their 20-foot skiffs on some specific errand, but these journeys were fraught with dangers and difficulties.

The arrival of the steamships in the mid-1800s signalled a new era for the north isles. The people, previously living in a state something akin to feudal serfdom, were catapulted out of the Middle Ages. Their expectations of life and their demands as consumers began to grow. Up to this period the only regular service had been from a fast-sailing cutter which had taken mails to and from Kirkwall twice weekly, but with the arrival of the first *Orcadia* the outside world was suddenly much, much closer. Through the isles folk quickly became accustomed to the new-fangled boats bringing all sorts of surprises from the south.

On Papa Westray a pier was constructed on the east shore

between the farms of Skennist and Nouster. Being tidal, however, the original *Orcadia* and her successors, *Sigurd* and *Thorfinn*, were able to make the Papay pier only once a week. On other occasions they would stand off the south or west shore and little boats would row out to collect mail, supplies and even animals. This difficult manoeuvre was carried out hundreds of times and only once did the cargo shift in the small boat and the crewmen had to jump for their lives as their boat capsized. They clung to ropes slung over the side of the steamer and clambered to safety.

Later shop boats, which called in at Papa Westray, became a feature of inter-island trade during the last century. In their book, *Days of the Steam Earls*, Alastair and Anne Cormack tell how these boats were equipped with grocery, drapery and feedstuff departments and were welcomed by the islanders because they brought a much wider range of goods than any island trader would risk stocking. By this time money was changing hands, of course, but barter was still common. Often, say the Cormacks, the shop boats returned to Kirkwall from the north isles with 1,500 dozen eggs and a thousand lobsters.

In common with many remote locations in the past 50 years, transport improvements have brought dramatic change to Papay. In 1970 a new pier was built at the south end, enabling the second *Orcadia* to make Papay a more regular port of call. Around the same time Loganair launched its island-hopping air service.

But it hasn't all been smooth sailing. When, in the early 1990s, Orkney Islands Council found to their embarrassment that there wasn't enough cash for the foreseeable future to complete the much-vaunted north isles roll-on, roll-off service, who lost out? It was Papa Westray, wasn't it? The community, on record as being 'saddened, aggrieved and dismayed' by this betrayal, went, uncharacteristically, on the offensive. Feelings ran high enough to prompt the islanders to stage a peaceful, placard-waving demonstration at the opening of the Westray terminal at Rapness. Reassurances were given by councillors and officials that a hard ramp would materialise eventually. You will still search in vain for our roll-on, roll-off terminal but for the moment we have regular calls from the *Sigurd* and *Thorfinn*, and we have the aforementioned air subsidies. It may yet come down to a choice between the air service and a much improved ferry service. There are strong lobbies for both modes of transport on the island but the roll-on, roll-off experience reminded us that it is often hard going when you're at the end of the line.

All the island's necessities, including cars, still have to be laboriously winched on and off the steamers at the New Pier and there can be further complications. It's clear when the councillors began to backtrack they took absolutely no account of the Papay Thursday Club's annual outing to Kirkwall. On one memorable occasion a less mobile member of the club, on returning from the day trip, had to be spectacularly swung ashore in a wheelchair which was securely strapped into a cattle float. Boy, were the tourists on the boat astonished! Such theatre had not been anticipated in the distant isles.

But back to the mail order catalogues. I've lost interest in that 'bash it against the wall' tennis ball clock. Silly idea. I've spotted something much more practical – a magnificent American-style burglar alarm system which illuminates a 50-square-yard patch in the front yard and produces a deafening high-pitched scream as intruders strike. Morag reminds me that there hasn't been a housebreaking on Papay for at least 5,000 years. A mere technicality, surely. Shopping Deprivation Syndrome – they surely don't mean me!

SECRET OF THE BLACK BOX

From the Aladdin's cave of the north isles steamer many delights are lifted ashore to help enrich life on the island, not least my occasional drinks order. Medicinal, of course. But out on to the windswept pier at Moclett emerge cars and cucumbers, cakes and cattlecrushes. My own special joy, however, particularly in the winter months (September to April if you're an optimist), is to spy a little waterproof black box among the parcels, fence staves and fertiliser bags as they swing landward.

Evenings of relaxation and/or research are signalled by the appearance of the box. It is an Orkney institution, the famous library box, a unique service which over the years has made the outer isles probably the best-read remote community, certainly in Britain, perhaps in the world. The mobile library now travels to islands linked in with the new roll-on, roll-off ferry service. For Papa Westray, without the full advantage of the ferries, it's certain that the island's bookworms will still be looking for their black boxes off the boat for some time yet.

Folk in the know say Orcadians have always been good readers, devouring any book they could lay hands on. The box service began in 1954 but the Orkney Library, currently planning a new home in Kirkwall, was established by William Baikie in 1683 and claims to be the oldest in Scotland. It's kind of sad to think that (hard ramps permitting) someday we'll be deprived of the pleasure of loosening the security strap and delving into the cornucopia of delights. Choosing books from the shelf just won't be the same.

When the box is returned the reader has the option of filling in a form indicating their subject or author preference. Personally, I've always found it much more fun to leave the choice to the anonymous librarian. If it's been a busy day at Laing Street you're likely to be confronted by a bewildering cocktail of Shakespeare, Mills and Boon, and the *Guinness Book of Records*. There is no truth in the suggestion that the librarian is blindfolded while making their choice but the keynote on these hectic days does seem to be variety. On more thoughtful days the library will provide you with such an entertaining selection of goodies that the six-week loan period just isn't long enough to work your way through the dozen or so volumes.

Beware, however, of expressing too specific an interest. For months afterwards the diligent staff will consult your card and try to provide you with all there is to be had on your specialised topic, whether it be wild flowers of the Andes or snails and slugs as household pets. The world is surely becoming a much more organised place, what with databases, desk-top computers, satellite dishes and the like. But if everything is predictable and quantifiable does that not remove the random factor, the fun from living? Yes, when it happens, I'll weep a little for the demise of the black box and its cargo of unexpected delights.

Our own community library in the school, also topped-up with books from Kirkwall, opened recently. It is being well patronised and maintains the tradition of avid reading on the island. Keeping in touch with the outside world, whether by reading or writing, by phone or fax is, as we've seen, important.

However, there's something quite distinctive about the two dozen or so front doors of the farmsteads and cottages scattered around our island home. We don't have letter boxes, not a single one. It would be unthinkable for Jim the postie to drop off the mail without calling in for a quick blether about the latest on the roll-on, roll-off, the unseasonable weather or the hot news from the Co-op.

Jim's arrival at School Place, once announced by a traditional wolf-like howl from Sam the Alsatian, was for long enough the signal for a mad scramble by the kids to sift the letters in search of airmail envelopes. You see, a rash of letter writing had broken out among the Hewitson children. Pen pals were the current fad, arranged through a Finnish computer agency after the kids spotted an ad in one of the Caribbean newspapers to which I contributed. Cosmopolitan, eh?

During these days we awaited the arrival of plane or steamer, eager to read the latest despatches from Conrado in San Jose de Campos, Brazil; Brendan in Port Fairy, Australia; Matt in Maine; Chrystelle in France; Majken in Denmark and the splendidly named Alf Kjetl Walgerno from across the water in Norway. Photographs, musical birthday cards, football stickers and magazine clippings of rock idols began to wing their way from all over the world to our front door.

Scribes tell us that the art of letter writing has been lost, pushed out of vogue by the omnipresent telephone. But for just a little while, in this out-of-the-way stronghold, we defied the telephonic tide. Here, albeit temporarily, the pen remained mightier than the spoken word. The sudden burst of scribbling, combined with a remarkable nineteenth-century letter which had passed through my hands, set me thinking about just how important the written word must have been to remote islands like Papa Westray in the days before newspapers, radio, television and, of course, the phone.

When the sad job of clearing out Daybreak after the death of old Jess Miller had been completed, an intriguing letter dated 7 June 1864 came to light. Penned by John Baikie to his brother-in-law and nephew on Papay, it came literally from the wild frontier. The letter was datelined Fort Victoria, Vancouver Island, on Canada's west coast. John bemoans the death of his sister and warns his nephew Peter against coming to Vancouver Island because of false reports of fortunes that were to be made and complains that the Hudson's Bay Company will give the 'heathenest Indian a situation sooner than to civilised men, or say, white people'.

Can you imagine the excitement the arrival of such an epistle would have provoked on reaching Papa Westray, like a radio signal from a distant galaxy? And the epic journey it had undergone to reach its destination? With a bit of basic research it was possible to reconstruct the likely path of the letter. I reported in my *Herald* column:

> Perhaps it was brought back in the pouch of a returning Orcadian; possibly it travelled with the mails. After crossing the ocean it may well have come north with the steamer from

Leith to Kirkwall. According to the Post Office services to
the outer isles tended to be intermittent. Our letter probably
travelled out with one of the sailing packets to Westray, an
open boat bringing it on the last leg to Papay.

Older folk on the island remember how, even in the early years of
this century, with the arrival of such a letter, all worked stopped
until there was a formal reading. Our Post Office opened in 1879
but in the days before mail deliveries on the island, letters were
propped up for collection between the sweetie jars in the little dark
shop at Backaskaill . . . a highly original system of *poste restante*.
Right up until the 1940s, a huge quantity of correspondence moved
in and out of Papa Westray, both local and international.

Currently the island's champion letter and card writer must be
Tommy o' Maybo' who, over the years, has acquired pen pals all
over the globe, many of them politely ambushed as they wander the
east shore. One afternoon I recall meeting Tommy as he guided his
old tractor into the Post Office road. He touched his cap in the
customary friendly greeting. Tommy had every reason to be happy
that day. The carrier bag on his gear change was crammed with
Christmas cards, ready for despatch. Tommy pressed on. After all,
it wouldn't do to miss the last plane. Post early for Christmas is the
traditional appeal from the postal service and Tommy takes them
at their word. It was almost October!

Not so long ago, when Papay's population was numbered in
hundreds, there were two postmen, one for each end of the island.
On one famous occasion the Christmas mail consisted of 30 bags.
Nowadays, with our much smaller settlement that would mean a
bag of mail – at least – for every family.

On the topic of epic journeys, it was fitting somehow that Norah
Babanou's final homecoming should have been a bit of an
adventure. It turned out she was that kind of lady. Increasingly it
had become apparent that the effect of a series of minor strokes
meant that she would be unable to take care of herself down at
Fulmars, her tidy cottage looking out across the Sound to the hills
of Westray. She left Papay for a nursing home on Sanday. Then the
news came, only a week after her departure, that she had died,
slipping away quietly in the night.

Word went round the island that the funeral had been arranged
for the Saturday morning at St Ann's with the burial thereafter
down at the kirkyard. All were welcome, as ever. But here on the
outer edge nothing can be taken for granted, even in death. All

week a nor' westerly had been building, huge waves crashing into the geos and clouds of spray drenching the narrow waist of the island and making window cleaning on the north side of School Place pointless.

On the morning of the funeral the *Islander* took a severe buffeting as she poked her nose into the Bay of Moclett. It was too risky to try for the New Pier and she turned off for Westray. We waited for news here, while over on Westray, Edwin Groat agreed to take his lobster boat across the Sound. She had a much better chance of squeezing into the pier between gusts. So Norah (and the Co-op milk) came home safely on a little boat called *Wings of the Morning*. Despite the anxiety, Norah would not, after all, be late for her own funeral.

Mary Spowart, the silver-haired minister, crossed over also on the *Wings* and Peter Miller, one of Norah's neighbours and closer friends on Papay, used his works van to serve as a hearse for the last few miles. After a simple, straightforward service, tractors, vans and cars followed Peter's van west, bumping down the rough track to St Boniface. At that time the church was almost roofless and it wore a battered and forlorn look that stormy morning; moss-covered gravestones hugging close to the kirk walls, as if for shelter.

Funerals always serve to remind us of our own mortality but on an island where we cling precariously to a living without the many distractions of city dwelling, such a loss is felt more acutely. Every individual here is seen to matter for the welfare of the community, our personal futures being bound so closely together. Surely such a sense of 'belonging' is one of the most significant losses in the teeming anonymity of the cities. So, as we quietly mourned Norah, we also pondered the fragility of our lives and future prosperity.

Down in the sheltered corner of the graveyard, Norah was laid to rest beside her husband, Ronnie, who died in 1984. For the couple who had played an invaluable part in the early development work of the Royal Commonwealth Society for the Blind in West Africa, India and Malaya, before 'finding' Papay, a plan for eternity was fulfilled.

It was a functional funeral with little ornamentation, as they always are on Papay. Animals have to be fed, ditches dug and boats met. At some unspoken command the boys went round the corner of the kirk to retrieve spades and wellington boots. They set to work, shovelling the rich, dark earth of Papay back into the grave. Gently, Bill o' the Links used his spade to smooth the mound and Jim o' Backaskaill arranged the little cluster of wreaths. The knots of mourners then drifted away to the chores of the day. We learned later that Norah had left her house to the RSPB and a generous legacy to help with the restoration of St Boniface. No one was surprised.

Very few of the short, dark days of winter had passed before news came that Ian and Marina from Charleston were bringing home their new baby boy, Sam, from Aberdeen and that Neil of Holland was to wed his English sweetheart, Jocelyn, and they were to settle on the island. Up at Sheepheight Jim Davidson managed to breathe new life into an ailing lamb by leaving it for half-an-hour in his mum's oven. Yes, the big wheel keeps on turning.

Chapter Nine

The Thrice-Laid Egg

THE MERRY DANCERS AND E.T.

Creation can be mighty and mischevious at the same time out here on the Atlantic edge, whether it's the northerly gale which demolished our garden hut (it had become known to the kids as the floppity shed because of its ability to bend with the breeze) or the island's unnerving catalogue of mysterious appearances and disappearances.

In addition, the natural world seems capable of some subtle, surprising effects. Passing the shed beside the farmstead of Links, Bill emerged cussin' over the loss of a batch of home-brew which was destined for an upcoming island shindig. 'The thunder got to it,' he sighed. A couple of nights previously we did have a whopper of a storm so who's to say he's wrong. Apart from his famous home-brew, which is equally tasty sipped from a dainty china cup or straight over the neck from the legendary yellow plastic bucket, Bill has, over the years, perfected other specialities including tea wine and a Drambuie which creates a heady – but very temporary – sense of well-being.

Thunderstruck home-brew is the least of Papay's miracles. There are island wives who, on a calm night with a big moon, I'm told, will leave their sheets out on the green to bleach in the cleansing moonlight. Something a bit more sensational here than yer biological whiteners! It seems possible to get your sheets a variety of colours hereabouts if there is any value to this procedure because more than once since we've settled in the outer isles we've seen a classic blood-red moon. Less romantically this amazing sight is probably caused by airborne pollution from the steel and chemical plants of Central Europe carried by south-easterly winds.

Willie Groat of Kimbland remembers seeing a blue moon between the wars which is thought to have been the result of a vast atmospheric smokescreen thrown up by a forest fire in North America, while in Papay folklore a yellow moon is often a precursor of rain.

Last century sheets left out on the bleaching greens of Papay fell victim to another strange natural phenomenon – drifting ash from the eruption of Mount Hekla in Iceland which is said to have penetrated as far south as the Mediterranean. Stories from Orkney connected with this eruption tell of girls returning from church, their white dresses covered with volcanic dust.

Reward for keeping your eye on the heavens – night and day – on Papa Westray can be substantial but watch the deep ditches. Rainbows regularly arch across the island, framed by the black backdrop of the rainclouds; double or triple rainbows of vivid hue are reported and just occasionally the solar corona, the vast geometric pattern of light rays and false suns (sun dogs), is seen spreading across the sky. All of these I've witnessed myself. Sunrises are often special. In the School Place diaries in the winter of 1990–91 I recorded one such morning:

> Magnificent – the only description for this morning's sunrise. Such an event is guaranteed perhaps only two or three times each winter in these latitudes. From an orangy-red patch on the eastern horizon the great globe rose surprisingly rapidly through the morning mist, shrouding our neighbouring island of Sanday, away out over the North Sound. The binoculars showed our star shimmering around its rim and, through the protective screen of mist, dark blotches, presumably sunspots, could clearly be seen in the north-west quadrant . . . Stunning!

Just as magnificent and awe-inspiring are the Merry Dancers, the Northern Lights or the Aurora Borealis. If you're lucky enough to witness a display while you're on Papa Westray it's a memory which you'll cherish for the rest of your life. I've heard it said that some sensitive islanders even feel a gentle electrostatic swishing and crackling at ground level on such magical nights. At their best the Dancers are bands of light which sweep at high speed across the heavens, swinging back and forward almost like the beam of some gigantic searchlight. Scientists tell us they are caused by particles from the sun colliding with the earth's magnetic field and can be monochrome or multi-coloured. But these technical details tell less than half the story. They are a sight to take your breath away.

During the first winter here I joined the family outdoors to witness this, one of nature's greatest miracles. The entire sky was lit up by a pulsating reddish hue, even the sea out towards the Holm seemed to have taken on a fiery tinge. Once I read of the Northern Lights described by Dunbar-born naturalist John Muir as 'the folds in God's robes', but words are not enough; this is one natural phenomenon which really has to be seen to be believed.

And while we're scooting about the heavens how about the possibility that aliens are keeping an eye on Papay? Unlikely perhaps, but in the spring of 1991 a luminous blue globe about the size of the moon was seen hovering above the North Hill beyond Bewing, low on the horizon. It was there for an hour or two and was seen by at least three reliable, and more importantly, sober, citizens. The rather mundane explanation offered by the more level-headed members of the community was that it was most likely a runaway weather balloon, its trailing tether having snagged, temporarily, in a rocky geo. But you never know.

WORLD BEYOND THE WINDOW

Although the natural world here on Papa Westray is capable of being splendidly – and sometimes spectacularly – creative there is no such guarantee for a humble wordsmith like myself, even surrounded by such glories. I've often wondered in what sort of proportions William Wordsworth had his vacant and his pensive moods.

Truth to tell, mine are mainly vacant. When the muse has flown up the lum and the white, untenanted paper stares mockingly at me from the word machine, my eyes are drawn to the world beyond the attic window. I treasure the land, sea and skyscapes which unfold out there. No host of golden daffodils dancing in the breeze on Papa Westray, just dockens beaten flat by the westerlies. But there is magic here, nonetheless.

An inspiration, a distraction, a comfort; from my lookout the view of Papay is all of these things. Compared with my previous work stations the panorama is literally an eye-opener. Over the years I've laboured at my writing in a dusty cellar, at a tree-shrouded bay window, in a cramped hall cupboard, in the back of a Land Rover in the mountains of Greece and Bosnia, and in an assortment of newsrooms where the outlook was mostly uninspiring, including a grandstand view of Glasgow's Ramshorn kirkyard.

In North Berwick, faced with a blank garden wall, I conjured up a fantasy Narnia-style gateway which Morag painted on the whitewash. In unproductive moments I could escape through this portal and soar with the winged horse around gilt turrets, above green meadows and tumbling waterfalls. Just me and Pegasus. Neat, eh? But back to Papay. On any ordinary working day what can I see from my eyrie at School Place? What moves across this timeworn landscape? At first glance you would have to say not a lot.

Close at hand, over the dyke in John Bill's field, the scene is deceptively peaceful. Lapwings dip and dive, and the breeze from the so' west ripples the unkempt grass, the carpet of daisies and clusters of dandelions. Our cats pad across this territory from time to time, playing on the rusted skeleton of an ancient harrow by the surgery wall. The scene is immediately animated by the arrival of Clarissa, our black pig, who scampers into view, spins on her wee, dumpy legs and shoots out of sight in pursuit of Verdi, the smallest of our cats.

Beyond the former doctor's house at the end of our track the land slopes gently to St Tredwell's Loch. Wisps of white on this normally opaque sheet of freshwater hint that the wind is rising over Tirlo. Gulls squabble above the ruined chapel and cattle wade in the shallows. On the far side of the loch, low hills shelter the derelict farms of Cuppin' and Blossom, and just beyond lies the desolate Bay of Burland. Along a path nearby pilgrims walked to the chapel. Their route marked now only by a field name: Messigate. Tramping three times round the loch, or perhaps even crawling – a fair hike even in the upright position – followed by a quick dicht in the waters was guaranteed to work wonders for eye complaints. This was based on the legend of the beautiful St Tredwell who plucked out her eyes and sent them on a twig to a randy Pictish chieftain to cool his ardour.

This corner of Papay is seldom visited now, even by the islanders. It has a distinctly abandoned feel, undisturbed acres stretching south to Hazedale, Jim and Phemie's farm above the craigs. Today, however, a solitary figure traverses the scene. Who can that be striding up over the Knowe o' Burland? A backpacker retracing the pilgrims' steps? Alex out after a runaway heifer? Binocular time, methinks.

Spy glasses are to be found in every house on the island. Whether you're keeping an eye on the old ewe in the bottom field or watching the creel boats returning from Weelie's Taing, binoculars are as much a part of the equipment for life on Papay as a calm souch, a pair of sturdy boots and a ferry timetable. Even from a mile away, there's no doubting it, the gait is unmistakable. It's Willie Gray o' Hundland who, despite having left his three score years and ten well behind, covers more miles in a week than most islanders half his age. (Sadly, the empty corners of Papay are even emptier now. Willie died in April 1995.)

Looking south again across the loch, the angled mast and twin red-and-black funnels of the *Earl Thorfinn* appear beyond the sand dunes at Moclett. She's manoeuvring towards the New Pier after the voyage from Kirkwall. In the distance other islands lie, hugging the horizon. Nearest, the gentle green slopes of Westray, dotted with farmhouses, conspicuously fertile. Beyond, the backdrop is provided by the barren, brown peat hills of Rousay. There's rain on the way. Those far-off hills are capped by cloud. Sweeping to the east the long outline of Eday comes into focus, from the quaintly named London airport north to the massive sandstone headlands. East again lies Sanday, parts of the island so low that the houses seem to float on a shimmering sea. One islander confessed that as a kiddie he had only seen the sauce bottle image of the Houses of Parliament and was convinced that was what he was viewing across the North Sound, Westminster over the water.

Finally the hum of the typewriter calls me back to the job in hand. I know this is the turning point. I write now or give up the day as a lost cause. One word is typed, another cries out for attention. Soon the sentence takes shape. Heads down, we're on our way. Outside, my window world, unwatched for a moment, continues its eternal dance. Given a couple of hours of sustained, if modest, creativity and I'll be out there birlin' with the best of them. Yes, there is much to be said for a room with a view.

COUNTING OUR BLASTED BLESSINGS

In this blustery realm where apologies for trees hide behind houses for shelter and strangers are told of the hen which laid the same egg three times, we know a good gale when it materialises. Over the centuries Orkney has left aside the rather formal and decidedly un-Scottish Beaufort scale for something much more interesting when measuring the ferocity of the winds which scud in from the Atlantic. In this place we have substituted something perhaps unique in the science of statistics – the Orkney hennie hoose. The record achieved on this odd register came on 15 January 1952 when 7,000 poultry houses took off for Norway. 'We had salt on our lips that day,' recalled an island farmer and older folk still remember the banshee scream of that wind.

The folklorist of the east shore, Bill o' the Links, points to a piece of wood from the hen house at Daybreak which is still embedded in his stone dyke from that wild night. 'I've never been fit to pull it oot,' Bill admits. A testimony to the strength of that gale or the gullibility of a Glasgow journo. Take yer pick. Certainly old photographs of Papay pre-1952 show a landscape studded with hennie hooses while today, there is not one to be seen.

Another occasion when the Hen House Scale was pushed towards its upper limit was 7 February 1969. On that day the biggest gust ever recorded at a low-level site in Britain was noted – 137 mph at Kirkwall. Flying hen houses were scarcer that day, but only because the bottom had fallen out of the egg market.

It might surprise and slightly annoy Orcadians, I suspect, to discover that Orkney lags well behind Shetland and the Western Isles in the number of windy days annually. It's a matter of local pride. However, with its gently rolling landscape behind the western cliffs, the gales can throw themselves at us with unchecked rage and Orkney can, indeed, often feel like the windiest place on God's earth. In any normal British context our winds are formidable. Here on Papa Westray it is not uncommon to see the orange windsock at the airstrip standing out horizontally for days on end when the weather is coming in from the Atlantic.

And folk from south are constantly underestimating the strength of our Orkney breezes. I remember one summer our trainee minister, our missionary, was the personable Margaret Pearson from Milngavie on Glasgow's outskirts. On her first day on Papay she produced an umbrella (a wise old sage suggested that it may have been the first to be unfurled on the island this century). Against what was hardly a severe blouster, she struggled to negotiate the climb from the church to the manse. 'I felt if the wind got much stronger, the islanders would be asking why Mary Poppins had joined the ministry,' admitted Margaret, stowing the strange device away for use in calmer climes.

As one gets older, I believe, attitudes to the mighty forces of nature change from enjoyment to anxiety. Childish defiance, in my case, as I lay snugly listening to the monster battering at the chimney head, has turned to a gnawing apprehension of the elemental forces. Did I shut the goat shed door? Will Jenny be blown halfway to Fair Isle? Can goats swim anyway? What about the shrubs we planted by the school wall? Will they survive? And what about the horses? That TV aerial, secured by baler twine and elastic bands, looked none too safe last time I looked roofwards; and what about those loose slates behind the nor' west gable? All this is surely a sign of losing the innocent confidence of youth.

I started pondering the wind and the way if affects our lives here on reading a copy of *The Island Sun*, a sort of Caribbean version of *The Orcadian*. My journalistic endeavours and my modest reflections on life take me into some odd corners of our wonderful world, one of them being Road Town on the Island of Turtle Doves (Tortola) in the British Virgin Islands. The little nation of 11,000 people (scarcely half the population of Orkney) had only just begun to pick itself up from the devastation wrought by Hurricane Hugo which packed winds of 145 mph. As the extent of the damage became apparent my thoughts were with Vernon, Giorgio and Delseita at the *Sun*. BVI is a group of islands east of Puerto Rico, 16 of which are inhabited. Hurricanes are regular and unwanted visitors here, death often blowing in on the storm. In 1819, 94 people were killed and in 1929, another 25 lives were lost.

Here we build low and sturdy with hefty Orkney slabs. I imagine in centuries past the islanders would have raised their houses as the Amish sect in America raise their barns – through a communal effort. And all hands were needed in this backbreaking work. However, once erected, the unyielding sandstone walls, often three feet thick, deny entrance to even the fiercest of blasts. But the BVI are without the benefit of such formidable raw materials and houses – containing people and not hens – are blown away. Almost miraculously when you consider the dozens of fatalities on Montserrat and Guadelope, no fatalities were reported on the occasion of the visit of Hurricane Hugo to the BVI, although roofs were ripped off and yachts thrown into the main street.

In an article listing the lessons to be learned from Hugo, the *Sun* writer stresses that the most important precaution must be to see that your house is properly tied down! Perhaps then we will set aside our Hen House Scale after all. It is too flippant. And perhaps we should be thankful to God that we don't have to spend our days in a hurricane zone. On the practical side, I'm already looking for some enterprising Orcadian with a freighter to spare who will find a ready market for our old red and grey sandstone among the palm trees of the Caribbean.

Living with the drone of the gale as a constant companion for long days or even weeks in the depth of winter takes a bit of getting accustomed to. The roof above David's attic bedroom creaks and cracks ominously with each blast as if threatening to lift off. Windows in the west porch bend in the ferocious, horizontal showers of hail. And we quickly learn that it can be a great mistake to underestimate the power of the wind. Extracted at random from the winter diaries of 1992–93:

> Stubbornly, in the midst of a power cut and the worst storm of the winter so far, Morag decided to put a kettle of water on the gas stove round at the school. She only got as far as the end of the track before being lifted off her feet and blown across the carpark. She escaped with bloody knees and a bump to her ankle but it could have been much worse. She crawled home. You treat the forces of nature lightly hereabouts at your peril.

Amazingly, that same day, the steamer made the pier but Lindsey, returning to the Grammar School hostel, had to leap aboard as it was felt unsafe to raise the gangplank. Katy and David had been stranded on Westray for the previous few days but eventually reappeared off a fishing-boat which had been hired for an emergency run over to Papay with mail and food supplies. I remember that particular winter how our coal stock dwindled rapidly and our pile of driftwood in the yard was put to good use.

A few weeks later, with snow and hail sweeping in from the west, we decided to venture on foot to the Post Office. Big mistake! Rounding the windy corner at Holland we were met head-on by the storm and Katy, at the head of the pack, ended up on her back. Alas, she had been clutching the bag of letters which spilled open, the despatches spiralling 30 to 40 feet in the air before heading off for Scandinavia. We retrieved a few of the heavier letters from the snowdrifts by the dyke but a batch of airmail letters got off the ground much quicker than anticipated and were never seen again.

Another memorable winter was 1990 when the remnants of Hurricane Isidore reached Orkney with winds gusting up to 90 mph. In all we were 30 hours without power or the 'hydro', as it is popularly known up here. Before the arrival of mains electricity,

via submarine cable from Westray, all the farmsteads had a backyard generator, the night-time hum of the equipment being a distinctive island sound up until the 1980s. Our family congregated by candlelight in the kitchen; real frontier spirit, including some competitive games of Cluedo, was in evidence. On emerging I couldn't get over the way in which the wind had burned black most of the plants in the back garden. The kirk, the new school and School Place enclose our backyard but obviously create a powerful vortex when the wind is strong out of the west. It looked for all the world as if someone had been at work with a flamethrower.

Later that same winter more low-pressure areas (giant's thumbprints, I once saw them elegantly styled) came racing in from the Atlantic. With the weather centre warning of 100 mph blasts, the noise on the west-facing wing of the house was horrendous. A group of fishing-boats (we later learned they were Dutch) took shelter in the lee of Papay and it was nice to see a row of bobbing lights on that wild night, out there on the briny where it is normally as dark as the Earl of Hell's parlour.

Listening to the news days later we learned of the loss of a Morayshire fishing-boat north of Papay in the Fair Isle Channel. Her crew of six drowned. Next evening was unimaginably calm; such a strange, almost tranquil night followed the storm which claimed the Longhope lifeboat and her crew in 1969.

Other, unexpected, hazards can be experienced during these storms. Morag was on the phone to Grace at Tredwell ordering some plasterboard when a bolt of lightning sent a burst of static through the telephone wires. Morag got a jolt which sent the phone spinning from her hand in a shower of sparks. Grace, hearing the crack and the scream, thought Morag was a goner but was reassured by a burst of foul and abusive language which came down the line from School Place.

While we're on the topic of communication, I was stunned to learn in 1991 that my Viking trumpet theory might be much nearer the mark than I'd ever imagined. The Orkney Science Festival found its way out to Papay in the form of a lecture in the school from an Inverness gent who worked with British Telecom. His novel theory was that the Picts used to signal to each other – pass on the parish news – using giant hunting horns, blasting out their messages from the top of the brochs which, of course, pepper the Papa Westray and Orcadian landscape.

The scale of notes, he conjectured, was based on the ancient Ogham alphabet and was, in fact, a kind of morse code. Sounds bizarre, but we really shouldn't judge such theories by the standards of our own time. Wouldn't the Picts have found the idea of the telephone a bit hard to handle?

TESTBED FOR GLOBAL WARMING

You'll have to indulge me for a moment or two while I enjoy a moan, or more accurately a wee attack of paranoia, but I'm convinced that the last few splendid summers up here have lulled us into a false sense of well-being. If you are to believe some of the predictions, then we're in for more summers of tropical splendour with palm trees swaying on the tattielands. Frankly, I'm sceptical. Too often I've seen May and June drop us here on Papay into a summer of grey mediocrity while the rest of the nation sweltered. A more informed view suggests that, as global warming takes hold, we can look for strong winds and heavy rain; violent extremes in weather patterns are forecast. I'm with the cynics.

And I'll take it a stage further and suggest that these balmy Orkney summers just experienced are part of some sinister softening-up process. Nature has begun her experiments for this new climatic era and she's chosen our dear, green islands as her testbed. Some might suggest that I'm bitter and twisted over the usual pattern hereabouts when the sunshine stops short at the Pentland Firth. Some truth in that. Over the years there has been a real problem trying to explain this anomaly to visitors. Long since islanders have learned to shrug and accept the inevitable.

Often, while you lot in the south are baking under cloudless skies with temperatures in the eighties, water being rationed and polar bears suffering heatstroke, for God's sake, Orkney sits beneath a fringe of cloud held in place by the very high-pressure area that is giving you so much fun. Admittedly, we've come to expect less than Mediterranean conditions here on Papa Westray. It's been maybe 5,000 years since tourists could be guaranteed a summer sun tan. We have what could loosely be described as a maritime climate, one in which the sea plays a major role, threatening from time to time to swallow us up. In winter our climate can mean gales and rain. In summer, alas, it can also mean rain and gales.

So much so, in fact, the people of Papa Westray can scarcely conceive a place with more 'weet and gutter' than our beautiful sinking island. I remember a visit to the guest-house by a Venetian couple. The merchant of Venice and his lady asked me to explain an earnest but puzzling inquiry made of them by an islander during their afternoon walk: 'Dis yer hoose no' get awfy damp?' A reasonable question from a resident of one watery world to another, I suggested.

What is so galling for everyone here, particularly the tourist people, is that we seem to be so near the sunshine action – yet so far. A few miles away across the Firth the temperatures soar and we can only watch as you settle back for an extended warm spell. It's all very well for people here to shake their heads sympathetically at

TV pictures of dried-up reservoirs and water-wagons in Hammersmith and tell each other about skin cancer and how they just couldn't cope with such heat. I don't want that heat either, just a few extra degrees, please.

In some way we have clearly angered the forces of nature and Orkney has been selected for this great global warming experiment. At the back of my mind I can't help wondering if my decision one spring afternoon to stop and talk with the minister on the way to creels, brought this misfortune. I found out later that this is taboo.

Dealing with our own disappointment is one thing but, as I've already hinted, trying to appease visitors is quite another matter. They are, by and large, very understanding and kind about the whole business. 'Gee, don't worry,' said the nice lady from Cincinnati, the rain dripping from the end of her nose. 'We didn't come here for the weather, we can get that back home.'

My futile attempts at a cover-up were explained in a despatch to *The Inverness Courier* in 1990:

> I think about mid-July my dismay gives way to paranoia as I struggle to explain away the overcast conditions as if I was personally responsible. You see, if you start talking about elemental forces at work to hard-headed holidaymakers from Ohio they look at you very oddly. Each morning I see it as my calling to rearrange the recently arrived newspapers in the Co-op shop so that any banner headlines suggesting that 'Scotland Sizzles' or 'Britain Boils' were discreetly tucked away.

When my own relatives begin to arrive I truly lose the place. My forlorn hope is that they might never find out what they're missing in the sun-soaked south. My only means of preventing great weeping, wailing and gnashing of teeth at School Place is to ensure that the TV weather bulletins and radio forecasts are unavailable. But feigning power cuts, loose wires and arranging for walks to coincide with the six o'clock news can only be effective for so long. Incoming mail had to be censored for signs of too much enthusiasm over the weather and all phone calls 'fae sooth' intercepted. It's all a bit of a strain. I finally threw in the towel one year when my nephew, Robert, asked his mum: 'Does the sun never shine here?' Perhaps I'll never convince Robert that we do actually have some quite stunningly beautiful days. Honest. However, being a realist, I must remember to have the leaks in the porch roof repaired before summer comes.

OH, FOR A SIXPENNY WIND

Halfway to Hether Blether the tilting gable of the Old Mill appeared through the gloom. A familiar stretch of rocky coastline ran northwards. Had we remained in the swirling fog for longer would we have been transported to the mystical vanishing island where seafarers are taken by the seal folk in Orkney lore? Ah, who knows? But it surely felt for those long minutes that we had been displaced somewhere in time and space, ever so close to Hether Blether where intuition and the old magic push back reason; there among the fogbanks. I felt my grip on the gunwale relax and tension eased from my muscles.

Beautiful and sultry the evening had been when we set out in the *Valkyr*. The target for our fishing expedition was a rather cheerless, exposed piece east of the island known locally as 'The Shooders'. The sun was on our backs as we headed through spray for the unmarked spot out in the swell of the North Sound. When the metal gate aligned itself with the gable of Holland farm and the cliffs at Fowl Craig provided a backdrop for the tail of the Holm we knew we'd arrived. The old fishing marks never let you down.

Those smart Westray folk used to say that when the Papay men were out at the cuithes they would note the prolific fishing sites with a white-chalked cross on the outside timbers of their boats. But that's daft, of course, the sea water would soon wash it off.

The hand lines were laid out on the bottom of the boat and we prepared for action. Many fathoms below us, according to the nautical charts, lurked the twin pinnacles of rock which gave the location its name. At the turn of the tides the place can often be alive with cuithes. Forbidding The Shooders may be, but you're seldom alone out there in the quest for fish. Porpoises play in the distance; a bull seal pops his head up through the swell for a moment as he takes a breather and then gets deep down to business again; a hundred yards off to the east a pack of black-backed gulls plunder a shoal of sand eels; and a few feet from the boat a dozen young fulmars, rocking gently on the tide, casually tear apart a jellyfish as they await the feast of fish scraps which never comes.

That particular evening we hadn't been fishing for many minutes when a haze appeared around the sun. It grew colder and darker by the moment and with some urgency the outboard was summoned back to life. Before we had gone any distance on the 20-minute haul to the Old Pier, visibility was down to maybe 50 yards, then 25 yards, the horizons with their precious landmarks vanished as the grey swirl closed in. The greatest fear of the seawise fisherman is to lose sight of land. It's so easy to become disorientated despite a close watch on the movement of the waves. Doubt your judgement just once and you're done for.

Bessie Miller, the old witch of Stromness, sold favourable winds, sealed in glass jars, to mariners for a modest sixpence during the days of sail. Many seamen refused to leave the port until they made their purchase. That evening out there on The Shooders I'd have settled for a cut-price wind of any sort to disperse that fog.

Oddly, we had been talking earlier in the day about the strange superstitions of sailors. On board the *Valkyr* the number which is one greater than 12 and one less than 14 (some say 12a) is never spoken. Meeting a minister on the way to the fishing, as we've seen, is always an ill omen. Quoting from the Bible can carry a great risk at sea, except, of course, during a funeral. Most significantly of all, whistling is taboo on board ship. Even this century, it's said seamen have been disciplined for breaking this law and threatening the ship with ill winds.

So as we purred warily through the murk and I broke into a nervous whistle designed to ease the gloomy silence, the skipper gave me an indulgent smile. You see, apparently the only occasion when mariners are permitted to whistle at sea is when a vessel is becalmed or lost in fog, when summoning up a stiff breeze would be a bonus.

Eventually, the Old Mill ghosted into view; we were further round the Bay of Burland than Jim had anticipated but we were safe – and the whistling had to stop. As a result of this little scare, however, the old compass salvaged from a wreck generations ago was refilled with the only alcohol available (vodka as it happened) and was stowed in the bow, just a little reassurance now that Bessie is out of business.

That episode brought memories flooding back of an odd adventure years ago when I travelled north to Papay with friend and former colleague Iain Gray to complete the blockbuster novel which we had promised ourselves we must finish. Arriving in Kirkwall we found October fog had settled over the islands, grounding the inter-island air service. We had almost resigned ourselves to the heady delights of a weekend in Kirkwall when some folk from the north isles, stranded also and keen to get home, persuaded us to share the hire of a boat as far as Eday from where a fishing-boat would take us across to Westray and eventually, God willing, we would find our way out to the end of the line, Papa Westray – in all a journey of some 40 miles.

This escapade was described in a *Glasgow Herald* article some weeks later:

> The fog was as thick as ever as we crossed Eday by car and clambered out over the rocks to join the fishing-boat for Westray. We were, to say the least, an unusual party. Two reporters who wouldn't have known if the next stop was Westray or Baffin Island and three ladies: the wife of the local Baptist minister, a young woman suffering from MS and Molly Henderson, wife of Bob, then the manager of Papay's Co-op. Oh yes, I almost forgot the budgie. Safely stowed in a shoe box, the lid pierced with holes.

The bottom line is that we got lost. Somewhere in the Sound of Faray, or was it the Rapness Sound? You could hardly have blamed the skipper who stood with furrowed brow at the helm, staring out into the pea-souper, no doubt wishing he'd stayed at home with his feet up in front of the fire. You can have sailed these waters for 50 years and learned all there is to learn about tidal races, skerries, weather conditions and shortcuts. You can be regarded as a knowledgeable sort whose advice about the temper of the sea is worth having . . . but fog is a great leveller.

Talking about the experience afterwards, Iain and I couldn't agree exactly when it was we realised that all was not as it should be, when it dawned on us that we were in a bit of trouble. Was it when the skipper stood on the wheelhouse roof and asked for silence so he could pinpoint the waves breaking on the skerry so close to the boat you felt you could reach out and touch the seaweed? Or was it when the ladies gathered in the wheelhouse and began, unnervingly, to sing hymns? I could swear that 'Abide With Me' was on the repertoire but fogging of the imagination can also play strange tricks. Or was it when Iain was handed the budgie in the box? He looked overawed by this feathered burden of responsibility but was, perhaps, cheered at the prospect that it might be a case of 'women and budgies first'.

Anyway, over an hour late we finally made landfall at Rapness on Westray with much relief and self-congratulation that we hadn't been swallowed by the Atlantic. Iain set off a few weeks later on a trip to Brazil which took him into the heart of the rain forest. He

swears to this day that the journey to Papay was of epic scale
compared to that jaunt up the mighty Amazon.

Even with your feet on solid ground, when the fog lingers
around the north isles for days, a strange weight seems to bear
down on you. On my morning walks with the dog the Holm can be
scarcely more than a blur on the horizon, yet somehow appearing
much, much closer than normal. The bleating of sheep on our
desert island and the eerie, echoing conversation of the seals out on

the taings carry across the South Wick. Imagination and disorientation can play odd games in these persistently foggy conditions. It's as if everything beyond the hazy limit of vision, solid landmarks which you know have been there since the Orcadian clock started to tick, have slipped quietly away . . . and you're alone in grey emptiness where sea and sky are indistinguishable.

ONE PSYCHIC AURA, SLIGHTLY DAMAGED

Maybe the world is too much with Papa Westray of late – a condom dispenser in the Co-op toilet and helicopter inspection of the hydro lines, too much talk of ferry timetables, coastal erosion and the price of beans in the shops. Perhaps all these mundane, workaday matters have damaged the island's psychic aura. It's been ages since I last experienced a hallucination, visual or otherwise. Perhaps we are no longer quite far enough removed from everyday cares to act as a channel for information from the otherworld.

In years past I would have expected at least one annual sighting of the old chap from the New Houses, even though he's probably been dead since Victoria was a girl. One of my early morning chores in the late spring and early autumn when the bairns were at school was to escort our goats, Jenny and Rebecca, from the byre at School Place up the road to the glebe, the field surrounding the now eerie and unoccupied manse.

I recall it was a totally still October morning, so rare in the north isles. The loch away to my left was glassy, the road deserted; the island slumbered still. A couple of hundred yards ahead, emerging from behind Beltane House, formerly a row of farm cottages and now the island's Co-op, was a man dressed in working clothes, from what I could make out, his trousers were tied at the ankles and he was wearing a bunnet that looked several sizes too big for him.

He strode uphill towards the big farm of Holland but at this point Jenny spotted a delectable docken in Mr Gray's garden wall at Bilbo' and dived into the ditch – two goats and their custodian tied in a knot among the thick grasses. Having untangled ourselves, I glanced up the hill. The odd figure had vanished. He wasn't a tourist, I'm sure. He wasn't a local. I've seen, or at least think I've seen him a couple of times since, the stranger disappearing when my gaze drifts for a second.

But Papay, as you might expect, has other mystical experiences on offer. The place just feels different; something, I suppose, to do with the remarkable continuity of human settlement. A few years ago while walking along the tideline of the North Wick in search of a beautiful grey heron who had been flapping over the skerries for a week, I was amazed, on focusing the old binoculars, to discover that away across the North Sound the Braeswick district of Sanday had been transformed. It was a clammy day with a heat haze on the horizon but Sanday had been, at least in part, magically altered. Instead of the open, bare landscape I saw a patchwork of shimmering fields and tree-lined lanes. Even the roads didn't seem to march across the landscape as they invariably do in Orkney but meandered in a way I remember the country lanes of Devon.

As I trudged south only gradually did the island reconstitute itself into the familiar pattern of tracks and houses. Had this been a window to elsewhere, a mirage, a trick of refracted light, or maybe a glimpse of elsewhen? Who can say? Hereabouts it's said that during the Second World War the Norwegian coast, some 300 miles away, was visible on the horizon. Such odd experiences are not uncommon on Orkney.

Several additional examples, which you might like to put down to island fever or overactive imagination, come to mind. The mysterious shadow in the west window at Nouster; the feeling that something small and mischievous is watching from behind the tumbled dykes around North Via; the sound of footsteps behind me on the silvery, empty sands of the North Wick; the creepy, otherworldly sensation that almost everyone feels down at the St Boniface settlement site on the west shore. Here I've heard singing – no, more like chanting, clear but soft as though coming from a distance in space and time. Incoming waves rushing among the rock cavities? Perhaps.

Mysterious disappearances are as numerous hereabouts as appearances. The vanishing of single socks, leaving partners abandoned and forlorn at the back of the drawer, is a common enough phenomenon – it happens in the most well-ordered households. But when a stream of objects as diverse as the gear knob from our old Sunbeam and the Mitchell Beazley *Book of Birds* start to adopt the cloak of invisibility, then some sort of explanation is needed.

Perhaps School Place is not the tidiest house on Papa Westray but we've made an effort of late; we've even abandoned the parlour game of guessing the number of objects on the kitchen table (it occasionally took us well into three figures), for weeks I puzzled over the disappearances but as often happens, while watching the grass on the back green grow, the answer came to me in a rush. School Place is perhaps the location of a hole in the universe – a rip in the space-time continuum, a pathway to other worlds and dimensions through which my bits and pieces are emigrating; to what purpose I can't even begin to guess. What use, for example, could a tenth dimension being have for a scratchy tape of Tamla-Motown's greatest hits?

And yet the scenario is not as unlikely as at first glance. Papa Westray could, indeed, be the location for such a bizarre, relativistic gateway. You see, for centuries the folklore of this far-flung place has spoken of strange, outlandish events – appearances and disappearances, mysterious lights and sounds, presumably occurring in this tear in the fabric of our four-dimensional world.

The opportunity to study one aspect of this strange scenario came when I joined in the investigation of the odd flashing lights which were coming from the tumbledown outhouses near the shore at Backaskaill. For months folk had been seeing eerie blue flashes from the roofless drystane building, the interior of which is a clutter of collapsed joists and shattered roofing flagstones. Showers of rain seemed to trigger the activity. People were getting edgy and there was a reluctance to venture into the building. Spiritual visitations were mentioned.

Although the site has no record of hauntings it was almost certainly the site of a Viking longhouse (there's a burnt mound or cooking depot close by) and who knows what funny business might have transpired at those pagan parties 1,000 years ago. I delved into my little library and came up with a theory. Nothing fanciful but it seemed to fit the facts. Will o' the wisp, iridescent marsh gas had been spotted on the island before, mainly on the marsh below Tommy's caravan at Maybo'. But the Loch o' Saivey lies a few yards to the north of Backaskaill. Perhaps an old drain ran from the outbuildings into the marsh and the pressure of rising water during heavy rain was forcing gas up into the ruined building where somehow it was being ignited. Our postmaster general Jim promised to call me in next time the mystery light put in an appearance.

The call came, but by the time I'd got the old wheels trundled down to the west shore the puzzle had been solved. David o' Whitehowe and Jim had bravely ventured into the shed as the most spectacular manifestation to date was under way. Relief was tinged with a sense of anti-climax, I think, when they discovered that some redundant electrical wiring was exposed to the weather and was cracking and flashing when the rain got to it. A simple, straightforward explanation – this time at least.

However, the Backaskaill phenomenon set me on the trail of another eerie aspect of island folklore which seems to have relevance to my disappearing nicknacks. This little isle, perhaps more than most in the magical Western and Northern Isles of Scotland, is the haunt of tribes of thieving, mischievous, even vicious, supernatural beings.

The late John D. Mackay, teacher and folklorist, was very familiar with the tracks and shores of his home island. Sifting through the oral legends he was able to identify three clans of little people on Papay – the hillyans, the peights and geyros.

The North Hill is the island's bleak, uninhabited northern third, a barren moor fringed by sandstone cliffs, the haunt of wild birds. The only shelter is among the hollows and miniature valleys such as the Dale o' Caman, the Sink o' the Moul and between Berry Hill and the Old Face o' Bewin'. This seems to be the home ground of the occult and sometimes sinister hill tribes of Papay.

From time to time, if the folk tales are to be believed, they ventured down past Hyndgreenie and in among the farmsteads. They were fascinated by humankind. In the nineteenth century islanders resisted a plan by the laird to plough out the North Hill by breaking their ploughshares deliberately on rocky outcrops – partly because the hill had common grazing for centuries and partly because they were afraid of offending the hillyans. These are small, grey people, about half the size of a normal man. They are thought to disappear before dawn and the safest time to visit the North Hill is just after sun-up. At other times you run the risk of being stolen away to their fairy kingdom beneath the hill.

A superstitious islander called George Foulis wanted to wall in part of the hill as a cattle park but, because of the legend, he would only work in the three or four hours after first light. He took elaborate precautions to avoid falling into the clutches of the hillyans; one ritual involved working half-dressed. No one now can recall which half!

Troublesome though the hillyans can be they are nothing compared with the fearsome, child-eating geyro. He always selected the darkest of nights for his visits. Right up until the First World War, 'Geyro Night' took place at the end of January or the first week in February. Dressed as girls, young men swung seaweed tangles round their heads and would attack any youngster foolish enough to be abroad. This tradition seems to have been mirrored in the Faroe Islands.

The third North Hill tribe were the peights, a kind of ghost or fairy people and perhaps a race memory of the Pictish folk who occupied the stone towers of Papa Westray before the coming of the Vikings and the Christian missionaries. Peights were less rowdy but had the disconcerting habit of watching the islanders at work. We must also have our share of fin folk who are found in the lore of all Orkney isles and perhaps we even housed relatives of the gang of trolls who were said to have been seen on Hoy as recently as the Second World War. That famous collector of remarkable and unexplained phenomena, Charles Fort, once suggested that there are lands and strange people waiting out there to be discovered. I wonder. Certainly at the Papay dances there's often a wee chap in a flat cap who sits at the back of the hall smiling fixedly. All folk will say is that he is 'fae north by'. Now, the only feature north of Papay is the Arctic. Maybe he's off the Hill? Perhaps he knows where my gear knob has materialised?

Chapter Ten

A Procession of Pasts

A HARD DAY'S NIGHT

Just after midnight the kirk door swings wide, a shaft of pale electric light illuminates the west end of Bill's sodden tattie patch and out spill the watchnight worshippers to gather in little knots on the road. In a wee frenzy of goodwill, hand-pumping, back-slapping and hearty good wishes, folk gird themselves for another epic round of merrymaking out here on the wild frontier. Papa Westray's New Year is up and running. Despite all the difficulties faced by the island, Hogmanay, as ever, offers the hope of fresh opportunities and new starts.

A bell rings from the cramped confines of the church entrance. As the first-footers move off towards the farm at Links, their first port of call on what is always a long night, the rhythmic tone of that solitary bell goes before them, sounding out over the puddled fields only to be snatched away by the Atlantic gusts. The brass bell, rescued from the stricken *Bellavista* up at the north end, ushers us into the adventure of a New Year. Our celebrations tonight in the smaller islands of Orkney are mirrored, I'm sure, in a thousand communities around the fringes of Scotland.

In the cities and towns much of the real significance of New Year may have been forgotten, it may simply be a fine excuse for another stress-relieving boozy weekend. But here on the edge it is still enjoyed as a novelty, a rare opportunity for self-indulgence and for the hope it brings of better times ahead. Maybe this year some sense will be made of the ferry subsidies, we'll get a bit better organised to meet the demands of tourists, another new family with something positive to offer could decide to settle, perhaps the mart prices will pick up, and maybe this dark winter will bring just a little less rain to the island. Maybe.

MEMORIES OF HOGMANAY

For the islanders New Year was always a more important time than Christmas which, up until recent years, we treated as a normal working day. The significance of Christmas as a holiday only increased this century with the presence of service personnel from the south coming to the islands during two world wars and the steady trickle of settlers since.

Of course, until the modern era, 1 January was still not celebrated on Papa Westray as New Year's Day. In the Northern Isles, the reckoning was by the Julian calendar, which put Auld Ne'erday on 13 January. The last outpost of this tradition is said to be the island of Foula, west of Shetland. I must, however, admit to having seen some of our old boys lickin' their lips and hinting at a certain mysterious drouthiness around the 12th or 13th of the first month. Old, enjoyable habits die hard.

First-footing in its present form – and the grand tour in particular – can probably be traced to the night of 1 January 1952 when a watchnight service was introduced at the kirk by Ian Young, the schoolteacher and lay-preacher. Maggie Harcus o' Midhoose, a tidy croft by the east shore, remembers that first service: 'Mrs Young – a houseproud kind o' buddy – had invited everyone round to the schoolhouse for a cup of tea after the service. It was such a terrible night o' rain and everybody was trailin' mud into the hoose. Well, we set off first-footin' and hours later, not far from dawn, we passed the schoolhouse again and found the lights still on.' Mrs Young, who hadn't expected such an avalanche of visitors, was still cleaning up after the muddy feet which had decorated her parlour. However, she had set the first-footing ball rolling, and it rolls still.

The pattern of first-footing in the late twentieth century is now well established. Beginning at the Links, the revellers – possibly including one or two visitors from the world outside – enjoy a glass of Bill's invigorating brew and move up the road, house by house, to Holland, where Annie Jean will have a restoring pot of soup simmering. By 3 a.m. the team will have reached Charleston or Windywalls, or Peter the builder's at Tredwell where Grace will be persuaded to get out the squeezebox and let rip. The south end celebrations begin.

At some houses it can seem as if the whole island is crowded in the front room. At School Place a year or two back I counted 40 merrymakers from grandpas to tiny tots, packed in like sardines, seeking a blast of heat from the stove or a glass of something reviving. These are the crazy, surreal hours when even the most sober (sorry, upright!) citizen can be persuaded to attempt 500 pull-ups on the byre beams at Holland, the most retiring resident might offer excerpts from Handel's *Messiah* on the clicking spoons and our most cerebral islander happily batters himself on the head with a tin tray while yodelling like a demented thing. Ah, sweet memories!

First light approaches, and if the timetable has been roughly adhered to the company will have drifted along the north road by car or on foot and will be installed at Bewing (now sadly empty with the departure of the Fletts for the bright lights of Kirkwall) or the Caravan, the last outposts below the North Hill. Usually only those of the strongest constitution stay the course this far. Alcoholic concoctions by now can be pure dynamite, and later, ditches and byres will be checked for tired and emotional stragglers.

Finally, as the sun lifts through salmon-pink clouds out over Sanday, it will be time for some shut-eye; glorious, almost-forgotten sleep. Yet, within a few hours these survivors will emerge, bleary-eyed, like rabbits from their burrows, to join the New Year's Day visiting. As indicated before, it's always a hard day's night. In a small place like Papay the sense of community remains important the year round. Cementing ties here is neither artificial nor short-term; they will matter during the coming months. It's also a chance for the youngsters to relate stories of life in the 'toon', to seek reassurance from old heads, to voice hopes and fears, to question authority, and to enjoy a jar or three among well-kent faces. For the older folk it is also a time of reminiscing.

Old Johnny, from the farm of North Rendall, now in his eighties, remembers how, in the 1920s, fishing trawlers often came into the Westray Roads around Hogmanay to shelter and would sound their hooters in unison. An echo here of my own childhood in Clydebank. 'I've seen 20 or more anchored out there at the New Year. It was quite a sight. Today they seem to make straight for their home port,' says Johnny.

Willie Groat o' Kimbland, who has a family tradition of service with the coastguard, recalls New Year 1937 when one of those boats – a Belgian trawler called the *Marie Louise*, with a crew of 13 – ran aground at the Point o' Vestness, just as families were finishing their tea. 'The rockets and rescue equipment had to be hauled in a cart by hand down to the shore. When we got there the crew had taken to the lifeboat. We stood by, awaiting developments, but fortunately the trawler, from Ostend I think she was, was refloated on the high tide.'

Food and drink, as you might expect, played a vital part in the New Year celebrations. Old Johnny again: 'Every festive season a cow was butched up at Holland and the meat sold off for a few pennies. It was a rare thing in those days to get a joint of meat and the menfolk would bring home the spoils in a sack over their shoulder. Do ye know, I can still taste that meat to this day. It was extra special.'

The Groat family of Quoys, a farm now occupied by our teacher, Christine Hopkins, were famous for their monstrous consumption of festive season duff which was boiled up in pillowcases in one of the outhouses. Hot, cold or even fried, this Christmas-style pud remains an island delicacy to this day.

Alcohol was not forgotten. Hogmanay was the only time of year that you were likely to see any of these hard-working folk the worse for drink. Whisky and porter, a dark-brown bitter ale, were in evidence but the classic Papay home-brew always stole the show with its variable flavour, bouquet, colour and consistency (from nectar to dishwater) but highly predictable potent effect. Although home-brew remains popular among the crofts, much of the festive season drink is imported on the steamer.

It could be that Papa Westray is just about the safest place on earth to drink more than your fill, providing you keep away from the craigs! No muggers, no speeding traffic, and no hard pavements coming up to smack you in the face. But there are dangers not normally encountered in the city. Johnny from North Rendall explains: 'I remember one New Year when we called in at a house where they'd had a water diviner out and were digging for a well.

'They ended up wi' a hole 12 feet deep and because it had been a terrible weet Hogmanay the hole was full of water, right up to the brim. Having taken spirits the boys were thirsty and got down on their knees for a drink. But the face was so muddy and slippy one of them went right in head first. After a real struggle we managed to pull him out. It could have been a tragedy; what wi' a fill o' drink and the muddy slope, he would never have pulled himsel' out.'

But what of the traditions of New Year? Even in this out of the way spot it is certain that many have been lost for ever. It is known, however, that in centuries past New Year was not merely a day of leisure and pleasure, it was a day of preparation, a day to begin work of all sorts. Men would fish, if only for an hour, a wee bit sewing might be started, and the byres tidied. Such honest endeavour, it was hoped, would set the tone for the year ahead and receive the Lord's blessing. Then there was the obligatory visit to family and neighbours (often the same thing in this closely woven community) where, crowded round the ingle, the islanders might sing hymns or swap stories. Music always seems to have had a role to play.

Tommy o' Maybo' has a story of last century which sums up the quiet magic of the Papay New Years. 'My great-grandfather, who died in 1914, was a great fiddler. In those days there were no organised dances. My father told me that one calm, frosty Hogmanay night a lot o' young folk came round the house. There was a green just where my caravan stands today and my great-grandfather took a lamp outside, hung it from the shaft o' a cairt, lifted up his fiddle and played. The young ones danced oot there under the stars.

'Such nights are rare noo,' Tommy adds ruefully. 'Most often we seem to be up tae wir knees in gutter.' Another case of distance lending enchantment?

The New Year's night which seems most firmly fixed in the minds of the older folk was the first after the Second World War. Celebrations during the war years had naturally been rather restrained with numbers of the younger folk off to the services. But at New Year 1946 Robbie o' Nouster and his wife celebrated their silver wedding and a dance was organised in the tiny barn across the yard. For the first Hogmanay since the outbreak of hostilities rockets illuminated the night sky and people remember stepping out at midnight with the weight of war finally lifted from their shoulders.

HAVING A BA'

In several ways New Year has been marked as a watershed, a time of special celebration in Orkney. Perhaps the most well-known North Isles pursuit at this time of year is the famous Kirkwall Ba', when a vast throng of men representing different areas of the town – the Uppies and the Doonies – compete in a mad scramble to move a ball by fair means or foul to a predetermined spot, the harbour or crossroads, for victory.

Here on Papay, down at the now-empty farm of Ness where the sandy soil is never saturated, even in the wettest of winters, the menfolk would take part in their version of the Ba'. This rough-and-tumble football match, with a specially made leather-and-cork-stuffed ball is said by some wags to have originated with the dainty Viking habit of kicking the severed head of the opposition commander around the park. Nowadays it's more politically correct to think it developed from a thirst for sporting achievement, but I prefer the old story.

Teams represented the north and south ends of the island and the main object of the contest seemed to be to get your toe to the ball and kick it as far and as high as possible. Bruised shins were the order of the day and, apparently, if the ball was sodden, it could deliver a knock-out blow when caught full in the face. However, as with so many aspects of life on Papay, the Second World War was a watershed for the Ba' and it returned on Papay only briefly in the late 1940s before being abandoned once and for all as the population began to dwindle. There is also a feeling that modern youth doesn't have the stamina of their predecessors, who thought nothing of charging around the Links o' Ness for three or four hours then burning up the floor that same night at the New Year dance.

New Year in these north isles is a broth of many things – renewed friendships, music and mirth, tables groaning under home bakes, warm fires, a surfeit of heady liquors, a cocktail of sadness and gladness. Long may such far-flung communities celebrate New Year as something out of the ordinary, something significant and magical still, because in a very profound way they are celebrating their own continued existence.

ARCADIA AMONG THE SKERRIES

Although visitors to Orkney may find the abandoned, desert islands with their roofless crofts, rusting farm equipment and tumbledown jetties atmospheric, I find them infinitely sad. The wind cries out for the generations who brought life to the hearth, the fields and the shore. These empty places are a sad legacy of communities and townships who failed to cope with the pressures of the twentieth century when the just expectations of young folk for a less severe lifestyle could often only be met across the water, as we've seen. As this century draws to a close two factors have combined to begin to turn this situation on its head. The first is tourism and the second, the influx of settlers from south – the not so quiet invasion.

Gone are the days on Papa Westray when horse and oxen teams worked every available field, the fleet of fishing skiffs went out in strength, when kelp was big business and babies were baptised with regularity. While farming in particular still holds sway, the tourist trade now touches most families on the island.

At this crossroads for the island several schools of thought meet. There are people on Papay who are convinced we should go flat out to exploit the boom while it lasts, others argue that with increased leisure time tourism is certain to grow steadily and look for phased development to protect our special social and physical environment and there are others who simply get on with the work around the farm and wonder what all the fuss is about. However, for such a small island the debate is significant. Learning from mistakes made elsewhere, it should be possible because of the convenience of scale to strike a balance between these two extremes, conservation and development.

The other intriguing element in this modern-day 'Orkneyinga Saga' is the arrival of the growing numbers of incomers, white settlers, ferryloupers or just 'thae folk fae sooth'. Compromise will be necessary in this sector, too, if Orkney and its component islands are to benefit from this infusion of fresh blood and new ideas.

For a thousand years these islands have accepted settlers from far afield and the happy integration of the latest batch, as we approach the century's conclusion, is vital if Orkney is to flourish.

On this occasion the islands are being asked to absorb a very diverse bunch from an outside society where values are being transformed. They consist of the disenchanted, the disaffected, the neurotic, those who seek solitude or beauty, those who wish to work in a community where their role is immediately discernible and not lost in an urban scramble, those who seek to be part of a strictly defined society where they can bring up their children in a safer and cleaner environment, a few who will patronisingly try to impose their theories of life on a sensitive and intelligent people, those who wish to be big fish in a small pond, clients of the DSS, those who can no longer cope with urban life and simple misfits like myself.

Blind animosity and whispered prejudice will, however, have to be put to one side if this partnership is to be achieved . . . if Orkney is not to be split into two societies. An understanding of the ground rules which must apply in this coming together is essential.

New arrivals must prepare themselves psychologically for a lifestyle which, although less pressurised, remains complex, where tolerance and, above all, patience are essential. In Orkney, *mañana* is often even further off than in Latin lands. Being prepared for all eventualities (power cuts, cancelled ferries, etc.) and never expecting too much are also useful disciplines. Your Sunday papers will never arrive on Sunday and if you need the dentist or the optician then it's a flight into Kirkwall. Unwritten rules include mucking in when required and being prepared to pass the time of day with the neighbours. The key for new arrivals is to follow these traditions. Start trying to change them and you might as well start looking for a new home.

But this is not one-way traffic. Islanders must exhibit understanding. Many still find it odd that people should tear themselves away from the relatively affluent south. People with influence in the community must take a lead in ensuring that if newcomers offer their talents openly and without precondition, seeking to serve rather than direct, then they must be made welcome. It must also be made certain that local people, particularly young adults, are not disadvantaged in the housing and jobs markets.

Islanders must guard against resentment and irrational hostility prompted by strange accents, attitudes and ideas and, while it's natural for remote and embattled communities to want to weigh up new arrivals, surely the incomers shouldn't have to plant three generations in the kirkyard before they're really 'at home'. For the small island communities there just isn't time left for such caution.

It's a humbling experience to stand on the rock shelves below St Boniface and scan the jumble of buildings and scattered masonry exposed in the bank by the summer dig. These stones, a procession of pasts, which stand witness to triumph and tragedy, joy and despair, are a poignant reminder of the remarkable continuity of human endeavour on this little dot of an island clinging to the Atlantic edge.

Maybe it takes a footloose pilgrim like myself, who pays social calls on sandstone slabs and who, through my own inadequacies, stands just a little apart from the action, to report on the important chapter currently being written in the annals of Papay. Are we building Arcadia among the holms and skerries of Orkney? Is Papa Westray's golden age just around the corner? Will it even be a good try or are we destined to be swept away beneath the flowing tides of social and physical change? Even in this land of elastic time I may not be around long enough to have these questions answered but the stones, unmoved by transient human ambition, will note the outcome. As ever.

Meanwhile the greatest expression of hope for this amazing place is contained in the final line of every exciting and longrunning serial . . . TO BE CONTINUED.

Glossary

backie	the great blackbacked gull
banks	the top of the beach
caddie lamb	an orphaned lamb
clapshot	potato and turnip mash
corbie-stepped	crow-stepped
craigs	cliffs
creeling	lobster fishing
cuithes	coalfish
doondie	a saith or a coalfish in its third or fourth year, or a big thin cod; nickname for residents of Papa Westray
geo	sea-cut cleft
glaur and gutter	mud and filth
kindlin'	wood scraps used for starting a fire
machair	grassland next to the sea
naust	stone-line boat shelters
neeps	turnips
North Isles	the outer north isles of Orkney
partans	edible crabs
pickieternos	Arctic terns
scarfie	a cormorant
selkie	a seal
sharn	farmyard excrement
shoogly	shaky
singlin'	thinning
smoothmoothers/ toonies/ ferryloupers/ white settlers	newcomers
taing	tidal reef
tysties	black guillemots
twitchers	fanatical birdwatchers
ware or tangles	seaweed
velvets	velvet crabs